Computerizing Your Small Business

Bryan Pfaffenberger

Computerizing Your Small Business

Copyright © 1992 by Que® Corporation.

All rights reserved. Printed in the United States of America. No part of this book may be used or reproduced in any form or by any means, or stored in a database or retrieval system, without prior written permission of the publisher except in the case of brief quotations embodied in critical articles and reviews. Making copies of any part of this book for any purpose other than your own personal use is a violation of United States copyright laws. For information, address Que Corporation, 11711 N. College Ave., Carmel, IN 46032.

Library of Congress Catalog No.: 90-64398

ISBN: 0-88022-691-9

This book is sold *as is*, without warranty of any kind, either express or implied, respecting the contents of this book, including but not limited to implied warranties for the book's quality, performance, merchantability, or fitness for any particular purpose. Neither Que Corporation nor its dealers or distributors shall be liable to the purchaser or any other person or entity with respect to any liability, loss, or damage caused or alleged to be caused directly or indirectly by this book.

94 93 92 91   4 3 2

Interpretation of the printing code: the rightmost double-digit number is the year of the book's printing; the rightmost single-digit number, the number of the book's printing. For example, a printing code of 91-1 shows that the first printing of the book occurred in 1991.

Screen reproductions in this book were created with Collage Plus, from Inner Media, Inc.

Publisher: Lloyd J. Short

Associate Publisher: Karen A. Bluestein

Product Development Manager: Mary Bednarek

Managing Editor: Paul Boger

Book Designer: Scott Cook

Production Team: Scott Boucher, Sandy Grieshop, Denny Hager, Betty Kish, Phil Kitchel, Anne Owen, Cindy L. Phipps, Joe Ramon, Louise Shinault

To this country's sole proprietors and small business owners, whose spirit of enterprise provides the lifeblood of our economy.

Product Director
Shelley O'Hara

Production Editor
Fran Blauw

Editors
Jo Anna Arnott
Kelly Dobbs
Cindy Morrow

Technical Editor
Brian Underdahl

Composed in Garamond and Macmillan
by Que Corporation

Bryan Pfaffenberger

Bryan Pfaffenberger, Ph.D., is the author of more than 25 books on personal computing, including *Que's Computer Users' Dictionary*, Harper/Collin's *Microcomputer Concepts and Applications*, Osborne/McGraw-Hill's *Using Timeslips III*, Que's *Using Microsoft Word 5.5*, and Que's *Harvard Graphics Quick Reference*. Nationally recognized for his ability to convey computer concepts and skills clearly, he currently teaches technical writing and computer applications in the University of Virginia's School of Engineering and Applied Science. With his 20 years of teaching experience, Pfaffenberger is the ideal author to convey the concepts and strategies of small business computing to readers struggling to meet the challenges of computerization.

TRADEMARK ACKNOWLEDGMENTS

Que Corporation has made every effort to supply trademark information about company names, products, and services mentioned in this book. Trademarks indicated below were derived from various sources. Que Corporation cannot attest to the accuracy of this information.

1-2-3, Lotus, and Freelance Plus are registered trademarks of Lotus Development Corporation.

Adobe Illustrator is a trademark and PostScript is a registered trademark of Adobe Systems Incorporated.

ANSI is a registered trademark of American National Standards Institute.

Apple Computer, Inc., ImageWriter, LaserWriter, MacDraw, and Macintosh are registered trademarks of Apple Computer, Inc.

CompuServe is a registered trademark of CompuServe, Inc.

dBASE II, dBASE III and dBASE IV are registered trademarks of Ashton-Tate Corporation.

Harvard Graphics and PFS: First Publisher are trademarks of Software Publishing Corporation.

Helvetica is a registered trademark of Allied Corporation.

Hewlett-Packard and LaserJet are registered trademarks of Hewlett-Packard Company.

IBM is a registered trademark of International Business Machines Corporation.

Microsoft, Microsoft Excel, Microsoft Windows, Microsoft Works, and Microsoft Word are registered trademarks of Microsoft Corporation.

PageMaker is a registered trademark of Aldus Corporation.

PC Tools is a trademark of Central Point Software.

Q&A is a registered trademark of Symantec Corporation.

R:BASE is a registered trademark of Microrim, Inc.

Rolodex is a registered trademark of Rolodex Corporation.

Ventura Publisher is a registered trademark of Ventura Software Publishing Corporation.

WordPerfect is a registered trademark of WordPerfect Corporation.

ACKNOWLEDGMENTS

An estimated 13.7 million personal computers are now found in America's home offices, small businesses, and larger firms—and all too many of these computers aren't being used, largely because sole proprietors and small business people just don't understand how this technology can be fruitfully applied to their businesses. Lacking the expert advice and guidance that larger firms offer, these users need a book that surveys a wide range of small business computer applications and shows graphically and vividly just how these applications can benefit a small business. *Computerizing Your Small Business* is the first book that addresses this need in simple, clear language. Whether you're a small proprietor working out of a home office or an owner of a well-established small business with several employees, you'll find that this book contains a treasure trove of strategies, tips, cautions, scenarios, and examples for successful small-business computing.

Writing this book was unusually challenging, given its novel approach and breadth of coverage, and I am fortunate to have had the assistance of an unusually talented editorial and production team. I would like to thank Lloyd Short for his confidence that I could pull off a project of this breadth successfully. This book's technical editor, Brian Underdahl, subjected all that follows to his deep grasp of personal computing applications and hardware, and made many very useful suggestions. At Que, a world-class editorial team, led by Fran Blauw (and including Jo Anna Arnott, Kelly Dobbs, and Cindy Morrow), did their usual, impressive job. Very special thanks are due to this book's developmental editor, Shelly O'Hara, who worked with me with good cheer as we together developed a workable plan for the book. I would also like to thank the many small business people who so graciously allowed me to interview them about their small business computing successes and failures.

Many of this book's chapters include scenarios which tell the story of how a computing application was successfully applied in the small business context. Although these scenarios are inspired by real-world examples, the names and business settings are fictional, and are not intended to suggest a resemblance to any actual person or business. In addition, this book mentions many application programs, generally because they are among the leading programs in their categories or because they offer special benefits for small business computing. However, my mention of a specific product should not be considered an endorsement against other programs that aren't mentioned: this book doesn't attempt to survey comprehensively the thousands of programs available for small business computing, and there are many fine programs that do not receive coverage in this book.

I would like to reserve my warmest thanks for my wife, Suzanne, and my children, Michael and Julia, who put up with my long hours at the keyboard, and even more extreme acts, such as erasing Michael's copy of Captain Comic (a neat shareware game) so that I could install on my crowded hard disk all the programs this book surveys.

CONTENTS AT A GLANCE

TABLE OF CONTENTS ▼

I   The New Tools for Small Business Success

II   Getting Organized

III Communicating With Clients and Customers

IV Keeping Business Records

V Selecting and Using Your System

Introduction

Throughout the 1970s, businesses large and small were stuck with much the same technology offices and businesses used in the 19th century. In the 1970s, white-collar worker productivity grew by only 4 percent, at the same time that office labor costs were rising by an estimated 8 to 10 percent per year. With white-collar salaries making up as much as 75 percent of the labor costs of many firms, managers were naturally interested in office automation. After all, factory automation had earlier produced the productivity gains that made the United States a major world economic power. Couldn't technology do the same for offices?

Despite a decade-long buying spree, U.S. firms have discovered that PC technology doesn't necessarily lead to huge productivity payoffs, and in their experience lies many important lessons for small businesses. You can't just stick a personal computer on someone's desk and expect automatic productivity gains—quite the opposite, in fact. A poorly-conceived computerization strategy can bring about huge productivity losses, and more than a few businesses have gone down the tubes after installing computer systems that introduced inefficiencies, blunted a business's competitive edge, frustrated or threatened their employees, and turned away customers.

Even so, it's clear that some businesses have managed to harness computer technology very effectively. To cite a straightforward example, a company set up a product development team whose members were working in three states. Just to cut down the time spent in sending documents back and forth, the company equipped all the members with PCs and an electronic mail (E-mail) account. The team estimated that transferring documents via E-mail enabled them to get their product plan finished in 10 months instead of the projected 12 months, so the company got the product out two months early. The company received two months of additional profits (to the tune of $110,000) thanks to a $10,000 investment in PCs and E-mail.

So what's the lesson here? Simple. There are three basic steps to an effective computerization strategy:

1. Understand the unique capabilities of personal computer technology and learn to see them as a repertoire of resources that can bring big payoffs in specific areas.

    You'll need a pretty good idea of what PCs can do, including an awareness of the full range of PC applications. And that means understanding more than the basics of word processing, electronic spreadsheets, and database management. In the E-mail example, somebody realized that point-to-point electronic mail—a simple E-mail technique in which people can exchange files directly via the telephone system—offered a simple, low-cost solution to the team's communication problems.

    To grasp the full dimensions of the promise of PCs for your business, you'll need to understand the application potential of PCs in many other areas, such as inventory control, point-of-sale terminals, form letters, mailing lists, desktop publishing, business form design, and many more.

2. Focus on a specific, high-payoff task—one that's critical to your business' mission.

    Right now, you probably have only a vague idea of what such tasks may be—and if so, that's because you don't really grasp the full range of what PCs can do in a business setting. As you learn more about the full range of PC applications in business and the specific capabilities of today's treasure-house of application software, you start getting ideas about the areas where PC technology can pay off big for your business. When you apply PC technology to critical application areas, there's a potential for huge payoffs.

3. View computerization as an opportunity to simplify, streamline, and improve the way you do business.

Sad experiences with big-business computerization add up to a single, clear conclusion: if your business is a mess, you get an automated mess when you automate. Computerization isn't just a way of inserting technology into an existing way of doing business; it's an opportunity to improve the way you do business. Even further, the biggest payoffs from computerization really aren't attributable to the technology at all, but rather to the changes the technology made possible in the way people work (and what they're doing while they're working). In the E-mail example, the team members didn't just wait around for slow-mail documents to arrive; they did something else.

But the E-mail strategy enabled them to concentrate on the tasks that made the business the most money.

If this three-step plan sounds like a simple recipe for success, think again, because it isn't. As for Step 1, personal computer technology is still very new, and many people don't really grasp its true nature and capabilities.

If you don't really understand the range of a PC's capabilities, it's close to impossible to pull off Step 2, drawing a connection between the PC's capabilities and specific areas of opportunity in your business. What's more, you'll need an equally lucid grasp of your own business, and how computerization can change it, before you can pull off Step 3.

Frankly, computerizing a business is conceptually an extremely challenging process, and even the experts have a tough time pulling it off successfully. If you've had the experience of buying a PC and some ill-chosen software, only to have it sit around unused, you'll appreciate this point very well.

TIP

It's difficult to computerize a small business effectively, but it's not impossible. And bear in mind that you have one tremendous advantage: nobody knows your business like you do. You've acquired that knowledge through long experience, and more than likely, nobody else could share that knowledge unless he or she were to spend a good chunk of time trying to run your business, as you have. What you need is a book that can show you vividly what PCs can do in specific business situations; chances are you'll see almost immediately how you can computerize your small business in a highly effective way.

How Can This Book Help You?

An effective computerization strategy selects specific capabilities of PC technology, targets specific, high-payoff areas of your business, and improves the way you do business. Because you know your business so well, you have a tremendous advantage in the second and third areas. This book seeks to give you the same advantage in the first area: knowledge of the full range of potential personal computer applications in the business setting.

The chief objective of this book is to provide detailed scenarios in which specific PC capabilities are applied to specific high-payoff areas. In place of the vague generalities you'll find in other books on this topic, this book is loaded with specific information about the potential benefits and payoffs of a huge variety of business application programs, ranging from the usual Big Three application programs (word processing, electronic spreadsheets, and database management) to the much-less-frequently discussed realm of special-purpose and vertical-market software, including mail list managers, desktop publishing software, business form designers, financial analysis packages, checkwriting programs, "do-it-yourself" accounting packages, and many more. You'll find that this book is a treasure trove of potentially useful applications for your business.

You'll also find ample guidance on virtually every additional aspect of computerizing your small business, including hardware selection, system maintenance, system security, and much more.

Who Should Read This Book?

As this introduction makes clear, this book draws on the experience of larger firms, but it's intended specifically for small business people and sole proprietors who are interested in applying personal computer technology to their businesses. According to the Department of Commerce, a small business is defined as a firm that employs fewer than 100 employees; by this definition, there are approximately five million small businesses in the United States alone, and another 11 million sole proprietorships.

But this book is mainly targeted at the smaller independently owned retail, service, and professional operations—the sole proprietorships and firms with just a few employees, for whom personal computer technology has finally become sufficiently inexpensive that they can consider a first-time computerization effort. More specifically still, here's a profile of the reader-ship that this book assumes:

- *You're not exactly an expert on PCs and PC applications.* Perhaps you're a complete beginner, never having touched a PC before. Maybe you've learned one or two applications, such as WordPerfect and Lotus 1-2-3, but you know you don't understand the full range of potential PC applications in business, much less how you can make the connection between this potential and critical application areas of your business.

- *You don't have the luxury of turning to a computer support de-partment or an expensive, outside consultant to help you.* Here's where small businesses are at a big disadvantage, and sometimes it can seem as if the whole world is trying to get its hands into your pockets. Here's what you're facing: advertising you don't understand, products you're not sure you need, consultants who charge big bucks for puny payoffs, and programmers who promise customized dBASE systems but don't seem to have the faintest idea of what makes your business tick.

- *You're interested in efficiency, but it's not your only objective.* You're in business for several reasons—to make money, of course, but much more. You're interested in serving your customers, in adding a rich and attractive resource to your community, and in delivering the highest quality product or service you possibly can. You want to know how PC technology can help you with every facet of your business, not just the bottom-line picture.

- *You can't afford to waste money on a system that won't work.* That's why you're so cautious. A bigger firm can swallow a horrendous purchasing error, but you can't.

- *You're looking for bargains, but you're afraid the low-end products won't meet your needs.* If it's going to cost you $20,000 to computerize, you'll wait a few years, thank you. But if you can buy a $99 checkwriting program and a $1,299 computer, it's another matter. You've read all those ads for low-end programs such as Microsoft Works, Quicken, Pacioli 2000, and all the rest. Will they work for you?

If you find yourself in two, three, or more of the points in this profile, welcome aboard. This book is for you.

Is a PC the Best Solution?

This book is about the do-it-yourself application of personal computer technology to small businesses and sole proprietorships, but other technical (and nontechnical options) are available.

If you're looking for a point-of-sale system that offers inventory control with bar-code readers, for example, you may be better off purchasing a turn-key minicomputer system rather than trying to work up such a system using PC technology. But it won't be cheap!

If your firm has dozens of employees, you may need more computational horsepower than one stand-alone PC can provide. Many small firms are implementing local area networks (LANs) successfully. In a LAN, several PCs—or as many as several dozen—are connected to a central machine, in which software and data are stored. This software and information is accessible to all the machines on the network. In many cases, the software is identical or nearly identical to the programs discussed in this book, but setting up a LAN isn't an ideal task for novice do-it-yourselfers.

If you're looking for computer assistance with professional engineering, industrial design, or architectural work, you'll probably be better off with a professional workstation, such as a Sun or NeXT.

And maybe you don't need a computer at all: The biggest payoffs from PC technology don't come from the machines as much as they come from changing the way you do business. Maybe you can make an enormously effective change without buying the computer.

Many of the applications in this book require your willingness to switch hats and take on the role of writer, graphic designer, financial analyst, or accountant. You must consider very carefully whether you're willing to spread yourself a little thinner than you're already spread. If not, it may make much more sense to take your problem to an outside service bureau, such as an accounting firm that may be willing to handle all your payroll needs for a few hundred dollars per year.

If you're not sure whether PC technology is the best bet for you, read on. You'll have a much clearer idea of what you're getting into, and whether it's right for you, after reading this book.

What Is This Book's Bias— Macintosh or IBM?

Neither.

This book's bias can be very simply stated: it's toward software. From everything that has already been said about what makes or breaks a business computerization strategy, it should be evident that detail is everything. Suppose, for example, that you decide you need to find the mailing list program that enables you to eliminate duplicates and print bar codes on envelopes. Everything else recedes in importance because without these two features, you can't solve your business's problem.

If this program (and the other ones you need) only run on a Macintosh, you buy a Mac. If the program runs on a PC under DOS, you buy a PC and run it under DOS. If the program runs on a PC under Windows, you buy a PC and run it under Windows.

You may notice that most of the applications discussed in this book are IBM PC programs, but bear in mind that many of these same programs (such as Quicken, Timeslips, and Microsoft Works) are available for the Macintosh. Why the favored treatment of IBM products? More business programs are available for the PC than for the Macintosh, and for this reason alone, a high proportion of this book's readers will decide to purchase IBM PC systems as part of their computerization strategy. But there's nothing wrong with the Macintosh for business applications, and as time goes on, more and more high-quality business applications will become available for the Macintosh environment. If you're interested in desktop publishing and other graphics-intensive applications, the Macintosh may well have an edge in your purchasing decisions.

Should You Hire a Consultant?

You would be wise to have a professional computer consultant look over your plans before you leap, but here's a way you can save lots of money. Remember the first time you went to an accountant to do your taxes? If you went in with a shoe box full of disorganized receipts and no records, he'd say, "This is going to cost you plenty." But if you went in with beautifully organized records and a draft of your returns, he'd say, "This is really useful. Thanks to your preparation, I can do this job for a very modest fee."

The same applies to computer consultants. Using this book, you can get pretty far down the road toward a well-conceived computerization strategy. When you've developed such a strategy, take it to as many people as you can, including consultants and especially colleagues in your line of work. Show it to them, and ask for comments and analysis. Have you targeted the right areas? What's the experience of other firms that have tried this? What's your competition doing? How about the software choice? Have you overlooked other programs that may do a better job?

How Is This Book Organized?

This book is divided into five parts, as described here.

Part I: The New Tools for Small Business Success

Start here if you're new to personal computing. You'll find an expanded discussion of the points this introduction raises (Chapter 1, "Three Steps to Effective Computerization"), as well as an introduction to the world of personal computer software resources (Chapter 2, "Software Resources for Small Business").

Part II: Getting Organized

Part II of Computerizing Your Small Business begins this book's detailed survey of leading small-business applications of personal computers. You'll begin with four important chapters on using personal computer technology to get organized and gain control of your day-to-day business affairs.

Here's a brief guide to what is covered in Part II. You learn how to get control of your appointments, contacts, and projects (Chapter 3, "Managing Time"). You learn how to get control over one of your most valuable business resources—your customers' names and addresses (Chapter 4, "Developing a Mailing List"). You learn how to get control over the facts and information that are unique to your business (Chapter 5, "Managing Information"), and you learn how to get control over the numbers you've got to deal with on a day-to-day basis (Chapter 6, "Crunching Numbers").

Part III: Communicating with Clients and Customers

In Part III, you learn the many ways that personal computer technology can benefit you as you communicate with your clients, colleagues, and customers. In Chapter 7, "Tackling Routine Business Correspondence," you learn high-productivity approaches to one of the most tedious of daily tasks, writing business letters. In Chapter 8, "Writing Reports and Proposals," you learn 10 ways you can use little-known features of a word processing program to help you compose effective reports and proposals quickly. In Chapter 9, "Getting into Desktop Publishing," you learn how desktop publishing technology, including fonts and graphics, can help you stay in better touch with your customers and present an appealing image of your business. In Chapter 10, "Designing and Using Business Forms," you learn how you can save money and time by designing your own custom computer forms, right on your computer's display. Chapter 11, "Selling Your Ideas with Presentation Graphics," shows you how to use your personal computer to help you create professional-looking slides and transparencies for those crucial presentations you give to prospective clients. And in Chapter 12, "Going Online," you learn about the new world of electronic communication—and whether it holds any promise for you and your business.

Part IV: Keeping Business Records

In Part IV, you explore what is involved in performing your own computer-based billing and accounting. Chapter 13, "Billing for Time and Expenses," explores software resources for time billing. Chapter 14, "Keeping the Books," explores a range of involvements in desktop accounting, beginning with the simple step of using a checkwriting program to the more complex matter of running a desktop accounting package.

Part V: Selecting and Using Your System

In Part V, you learn how to narrow your software choices to the ones that are strategic for your business, as well as how to select and install a system that's optimal for your software choices. Chapter 15, "Identifying Your Primary Application Area," guides you to the selection of your most important application—the one that stands to make a genuine difference in your business. Chapter 16, "Designing Your System," guides you through the hardware selection process, while Chapter 17, "Buying and Installing Your System," provides assistance with the difficult matter of purchasing your system and getting it running right. In Chapter 18, "Maintaining Your System," you learn indispensable procedures for maintaining your system and backing up your work.

A glossary of computer terms is included at the end of this book. If you come across a term that you are unfamiliar with while reading this book, refer to the glossary. For a complete listing and fuller description of terms, see *Que's Computer User's Dictionary*, 2nd Edition.

A Word from the Author

My parents ran a retail art supply business for 33 years. For those three decades their store was not only a profitable business that put their two sons through college, but also a pivotal community resource for local amateur and professional artists. More than a few artists who picked up their first paint brush in my parents' store went on to earn national and even international reputations for their work. But in the early 1980s, my parents realized that just to keep up with the competition, they had to computerize or get out of the business. My father recalls talking to computer consultants and salespeople, and getting the distinct impression that they were speaking in a long-dead, classical language, and what's worse, they were quoting figures that equalled half the firm's annual sales. There just wasn't anywhere else to turn, so they sold the business and retired. In retrospect, I know that I started researching this book from the day I heard the full story about why they closed their business.

Happily, small businesses have an impressive new range of allies as they face the challenge of computerization: incredibly powerful desktop computers that sell for $1,500 or less, outstanding business application programs that sell for as little as $59, and a new range of resources, such as Que's outstanding line of personal computer books, to help them. It's a bit late to help my parents' business, but I'll be very gratified if this book becomes a significant new ally for small businesses facing the prospect of computerization.

Part I

The New Tools for Small Business Success

Includes

Three Steps to Effective Computerization

Software Resources for Small Business

Three Steps to Effective Computerization

T oday's personal computers are such capable and appealing devices that you may think you can get big gains just by buying one and keeping it around. But that isn't so. In the introduction, you learned that you must take three steps before you can profit from computerization:

- Understand the unique capabilities of personal computer technology and learn to see computers as a storehouse of resources that can bring big payoffs in specific areas.

- Focus on a sharply-defined, high-payoff task—one that's critical to your business's mission.

- View computerization as an opportunity to simplify, streamline, and improve the way you do business.

This chapter explores each of these three steps in detail. If you are a beginner in personal computing, this is an obvious place to start. But even if you're experienced with computers, you should read this chapter. It offers a perspective on business computing that is fresh and exciting.

Understanding What Computers Really Do

What *do* computers do? If you ask a computer science expert, you may be told something like, "Computers process information." But this definition really isn't very helpful. Strictly speaking, computers are machines that run programs. In the main, computers run the programs that have been successful in the market. It follows, then, that a computer can help you— *if* a program is available that genuinely addresses your business's needs.

Which programs have proven to be successful in the market? All the successful personal computer applications—word processing, electronic spreadsheets, database management, desktop publishing, and telecommunications—are little more than electronic versions of letters, reports, accountants' pads, index cards, artists' layout tables, and memos. And what's more, people are using computers, not just to represent such documents on-screen, but to print ever-mounting numbers of computer-generated paper documents, such as letters, essays, memos, reports, charts, newsletters, fliers, bills, price lists, and more.

The success of such programs astounded the experts, who confidently predicted at the beginning of the computer era that computers would eliminate paper documents. In the 1950s and early 1960s, computer pundits predicted a "paperless society," in which computers would replace all those inefficient, old-fashioned checks, invoices, letters, reports, forms, file folders, and cards. While these authorities talked, businesses bought systems that enabled them to deal with paper documents more efficiently and to print them in ever-increasing quantities. All the basic software functions—word processing, electronic spreadsheets, database management, graphics, and telecommunications—not only represent paper documents, but they also print them—and the result is a stunning explosion of paper usage.

So what do these facts mean to you? For the most part, the best place to look when you are contemplating computerization is your "out" box, correspondence, and trash can. What kind of paper-based documents are you producing? Which ones are gobbling up huge amounts of your time? Could you improve your business by using the computer to create documents you can't afford to produce now?

TIP

Even though most people are using computers to crank out more paper-based documents than ever before, you should remain alert to applications that make paper printouts unnecessary, such as electronic mail, computer-generated slide transparencies for presentations, and online database research. Many computer experts still believe that the greatest productivity gains with computers lie in the future, when people finally break the paper habits. For now, though, most of your applications will involve pushing paper more effectively, efficiently, and cheaply.

Understanding the Benefits of Computerizing

Businesses use computers to help simulate, automate, and enhance the operations people once performed on paper. To realize the benefits of computers in your small business, you should concentrate on the tasks that are slowing you down and costing you money. This chapter helps you to identify these tasks. For now, you learn how—and why—computers can help you extend your paper-pushing prowess.

Computerizing can help you do the following:

- Automate tasks

- Acquire new skills

- Make your work more efficient

- Reduce errors

- Produce more attractive output

Automating Tasks

One of the first computers, a gear-driven calculator, was invented by an eighteenth-century philosopher and mathematician named Blaise Pascal, who worked in his father's accounting practice. After spending some years adding up columns of figures, he concluded that it was beneath human dignity to perform such operations day in and day out, and so he invented a four-function calculator.

If you have ever spent any time alphabetizing a customer mailing list or trying to find a customer's invoice in a huge stack of bills, you surely agree with Pascal's point of view. And for a small business, avoiding tedious hand labor isn't just a way of avoiding unpleasant tasks: it's crucial to your success. You make money by concentrating on the tasks with high profit margins—and you can be sure that summing and alphabetizing aren't among those tasks.

Task automation can save you time. The best application programs provide task automation with a minimum of user input, keyboard fussing, and command memorization. Look for programs that minimize the need to perform such tasks as summing up numbers, alphabetizing lists, sorting in numerical order, and making identical copies.

As an example, consider the Toolbar in Microsoft Excel 3.0 for Windows (see fig. 1.1). Microsoft Excel 3.0 for Windows is a spreadsheet program—a program that enables you to enter and manipulate numbers and data. Important spreadsheet tasks, such as summing up a column of numbers, are available merely by selecting the numbers you want to sum and choosing a pushbutton.

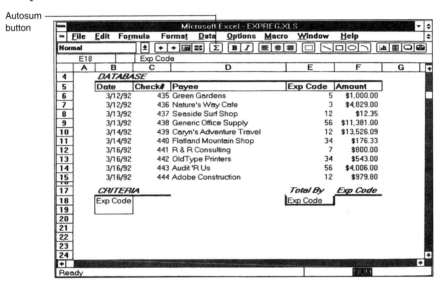

Fig. 1.1. *The Menu bar containing pushbuttons for frequently accessed tasks (Microsoft Excel).*

Excel typifies the best that task automation has to offer: the capability of making tedious operations (such as finding information or alphabetizing addresses) available and virtually instantaneous.

Acquiring New Skills

The second major benefit of computerizing lies in the capacity of computers to spread skills throughout society that were formerly possessed by only trained, experienced specialists. Consider the task of using a typewriter to type a document with centered headings and properly-positioned footnotes. You had better get ready for some arithmetic! How many spaces do you backspace? How much space should you leave for the footnotes? It takes a professional typist to type a document with beautifully-positioned footnotes. But just about any full-featured word processing program can perform the necessary computations automatically—you just insert the note, and the program takes care of the rest.

This benefit makes available to ordinary people the skills and competence of professionals and experts. In so doing, the computer saves you the money you otherwise would pay to hire experts.

In a spreadsheet program, for example, you can choose from many built-in formulas for performing complex financial analyses—the kind of analyses (such as computing the net present value of an investment) that you would learn if you were to study finance at a business school. In a desktop publishing program, you can use many layout techniques that would otherwise require years of experience with layout boards, razor knives, and sharp blue pencils.

A personal computer can help you acquire some of the skills of an accomplished professional typist, layout artist, financial analyst, graphic designer, or professional business writer. But *you* still bear the responsibility of making sure that the skills meet the highest professional standards. Not all programs can ensure that such standards are met. In figure 1.2, for example, a popular program automatically scales the minimum and maximum values of a graph, but the program doesn't always set the minimum value to zero. Frequently, the effect of setting the y-axis with a value greater than zero is to exaggerate the rate of change that the graph displays. In figure 1.2, Buncombe Corporation's stock seems to be zooming up at a rapid rate. But figure 1.3, with the y-axis set to zero, tells the real story.

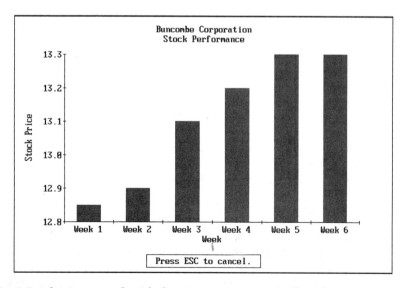

Fig. 1.2. *A business graph with the y-axis set automatically.*

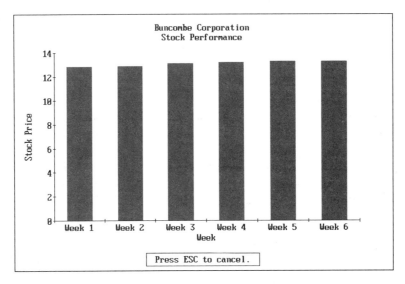

Fig. 1.3. A business graph with the y-axis scaled manually with a minimum value of zero.

Making Your Work More Efficient

If you have ever worked with tools around the house or a shop, you know that power tools—drills, pneumatic hammers, power sanders, power saws, and all the rest—dramatically improve your efficiency in carpentry work. Using power tools, you can frame a basement in a fraction of the time it would take with hand tools.

Personal computers provide power tools for your tasks. You can reorganize a filing system with hundreds of documents just by dragging *icons*—pictorial images of computer resources, such as programs and data files—around on-screen. You can archive thousands of client records and print hundreds of bills just by choosing a command from a menu. You can search a 100-page technical report for spelling errors just by choosing a spell-checking command; your only role is to confirm the corrections.

Power tools are useful, but buying and using a computer system does not guarantee that you will do a better job of running your business with a computer than you did before. A power saw doesn't guarantee a good carpentry job; if you start with a bad plan, you get bad results. A poorly designed PC system used as a point-of-sale terminal at a computer store illustrates this point. The system requires the sales clerk to ask every customer for his or her name, work address, home address, telephone number, and future purchasing plans before it is possible to compute the sales tax and total. Obtaining this information from computer purchasers makes sense, but it only serves to irritate customers who drop in just to buy a magazine or some other, small purchase. After undergoing several minutes of interrogation just to pay cash for a box of disks, some customers will decide to go elsewhere.

Avoiding Errors

Many programs come with features that can help you avoid embarrassing or costly errors, such as spelling mistakes, calculation errors, and incorrect data entry. Just bear in mind that these features aren't foolproof.

Producing More Attractive Output

Like it or not, your competition is probably using computers already—and these scoundrels are producing very attractive, well-designed price lists, brochures, letters, and fliers. Worse, the public is increasingly accustomed to professional-looking output. Your typed letters (complete with clumsily whited-out mistakes) and mimeographed price lists may be sending the wrong message about your firm.

Identifying Which Tasks To Computerize

To get a better idea of where you can use computers in your business, gather all the business-related paper documents you use (or would use, if you had the time and skill), and make a list of them. Rank these documents in order of importance to your business. In particular, circle the documents that are critical: documents that are fundamental to the central objectives of your business.

You will do more analysis of your needs throughout Part I and Part II of this book, but for now, following is a brief survey of the task areas that are most likely to produce gains, should you decide to computerize these areas. Keep in mind the tasks you want to computerize and check off any of the following that seem to apply:

- *The task is routine, but it takes a lot of time.* You should spend as much of your work time as possible doing the things that make the most money for you. If you're spending lots of time doing paper-shuffling tasks that fall far below your level of professional competence, you should consider taking advantage of the computer's capacity to automate certain routine tasks (such as checking spelling, alphabetizing mailing lists, and keeping track of who hasn't paid their bills).

- *The task requires skills you don't possess, so you become dependent on the assistance of professionals.* In many cases, it makes perfectly good sense to farm out certain tasks to professionals. It may be wise, for example, to spend $500 per year to let a professional accountant handle your payroll—especially if you have no knowledge of accounting and no interest in working with figures daily. Just how much computer-based skill you're willing to acquire depends on your needs, interests, and motivation. But if you find yourself paying good money for services you believe you could easily perform for yourself with a personal computer, it makes sense to try the computer approach. But be sure to get professional advice, not only to choose the right product, but also to implement the application in line with professional standards.

- *Your present methods don't enable you to adapt rapidly enough to changing circumstances.* Restaurants that depend on printed menus can't respond quickly to variations in the availability of fresh foods, the cook's favorite new dish, and the changing demands of customers. That's why many restaurants use a computer and a printer to print a daily or weekly menu.

- *Performing the task is too tedious or outright impossible with your current methods.* If you're using a simple, paper-based accounting system, can you figure out quickly whose bill is more than 30 days late? More than 60 days late? More than 90 days late? How long does it usually take your clients to pay their bills? A major advantage of computerizing your firm's books is that rich new sources of information become available to you—information that you otherwise would have to compile manually.

- *You're performing the task adequately using your current methods, but if your business starts booming, the methods will become inadequate and could swallow up too much of your time and resources.* Suppose that you run a small mail-order business along with your retail operation, and for a payment of only $5, your customers can receive their shipments overnight via Federal Express. You type each Federal Express airbill manually. At first, there were 5 orders a day, and then 10. Now there are 25 orders a day and the task is taking an hour of your time. What are you going to do when you're shipping 50 orders per day? Elsewhere in this book, you learn about an application that can extract the customer's name and address from your customer invoices and print the name and address on Federal Express airbills, all at the touch of a key.

- *You envision a computer approach that would give you a strategic advantage over your competition.* A Midwestern supplier of machine parts provided its customers with the computer equipment that enabled them to order parts directly from the manufacturer. Because it was so easy and quick to order parts this way, customers started using this ordering system for all or most of the parts they needed, instead of ordering from the competition. Within a year, the firm had virtually driven its competition from the business.

- *The system fails to provide the level of service you want for your valued customers and clients.* Have you found yourself saying, "I'd like to help you, but I just can't find your order form," or "I'm not sure what to tell you; I think it's been ordered, but could you check back in a week?" By making information more readily available and by brining you some of the skills of experts, personal computers can help you provide the level of service your customers and clients deserve.

- *You want to improve the quality of the product you deliver to your valued customers and clients.* You gain time from increased efficiency, and you can use the time you gain in two ways: you can spend the time doing something else, or you can reinvest the time in the task you're doing and aim for higher quality. Suppose that you lay out newsletters for local corporations using the standard, cut-and-paste techniques of traditional layout artists. After you come up with a design, you just can't afford to move it around in an effort to improve it—you'd lose money if you did. And more than once, you have let work leave your office that you weren't too happy with, even though your customers seemed pleased. If you invest in a superb desktop publishing system, it becomes possible to accomplish the job in about half the time. And you can afford to experiment with the design until you're satisfied that it meets *your* standards.

What about the bottom line? Isn't the crucial justification for computerization that it reduces or avoids tangible costs? That reasoning may have been valid when computer systems cost $10,000 or more, but in these days of powerful systems costing only one-fourth that amount, some of the less tangible rationales for computerization take on increased significance. A system that provides better service for your customers, a higher quality product, or a less tedious working environment becomes defensible even if you can't demonstrate a bottom-line benefit. But beware of the computer that starts eating up so much of your time that you can't concentrate on your business! Remember that the goal is not to become a computer programmer, but to use the computer as a tool to improve your business.

TIP

If you decide to try computerizing your small business, start with just *one* application—and make it a relatively modest one, such as setting up a system to respond to routine business correspondence or setting up a mailing list. Don't try to tackle two or more areas simultaneously. As you develop your application, you should consider whether the computer-related activities are taking too much of your time.

Changing the Way You Work

You can't put PCs on everyone's desk and somehow expect productivity to zoom upward. To computerize effectively, you must target the most promising application areas, choose the right software, train yourself and your employees to use it, and guard against computer-related catastrophes such as accidental data loss. This book can help you with these goals.

But if your business is a mess now, when you automate it's going to be an automated mess. The biggest productivity gains you can realize from computerization stem from changing the way you do business, not from buying machines.

Personal computers have the potential to benefit your business, but the key word is *potential*. With a pencil and paper, you can produce an incomprehensible three-page proposal, which no one will read. With a personal computer, you can produce an incomprehensible *16*-page proposal; joining the unread text will be page after page of meaningless and unanalyzed spreadsheet figures.

Businesses all over North America are learning the hard way that the real benefits from computerization don't really come from the technology at all;

they come from changing the way you do business. As you ponder your computerization strategy, consider some of the ways that you can change the way you work:

- *Avoid reinventing the wheel.* Develop and refine template versions of important letters, memos, reports, worksheets, newsletters, business forms, and data management forms. A *template* is a generic version of a document that you can load, modify, and print, without having to repeat all the tedious formatting and design operations that go into creating the document.

- *Combine and simplify.* A Midwestern company orders parts from a supplier, but invariably, something is missing from the shipment. The company nevertheless is billed for everything that was ordered. Under the old system, clerks had to call the receiving department to find out what was received, and what wasn't; once this information was determined, a check was authorized. A mess! Equipping the clerks with computers wouldn't help at all. The computerization strategy? Put computers and accounting staff in the receiving department. The receiving clerks unpack the shipments, click off what's been received using an on-screen checklist, and the computer prints out a check! The suppliers get paid for what they actually ship. This combine-and-simplify approach, called *re-engineering* in business management circles, is finally producing the big productivity gains that were expected all along. But ironically, most of the benefit comes not from the computers, but from the new, more streamlined work patterns that computers make possible.

- *Reorganize work patterns.* Many paper-based processing systems are designed along assembly-line notions: Clerk 1 receives the form, processes it, and moves it down the line to Clerk 2, who processes it, and moves it down the line to Clerk 3, and so on. Business experience proves conclusively that equipping assembly-line clerks with computers is not likely to produce significant gains— and for a simple reason: each clerk still has to get the form, get it into the computer, modify it, print it, and send it along to the next workstation. Huge productivity gains have stemmed from reorganizing such workers into semiautonomous teams, each of which is responsible for *all* phases of the processing. Once a document gets into a team's computer, it stays there until it's done, with no time-consuming, inefficient, intermediate steps of transferring the document to the next computer down the line. An additional payoff: your employees learn new skills, perform more varied work, and express more satisfaction with their jobs.

- *Never type the same information twice.* Computerization provides an excellent opportunity to avoid needless duplication of effort. A simple example: a new customer's name, address, and telephone number are typed just once into a master database, which all other applications (such as word processing, mailing list management, and accounts receivable) access automatically.

- *Make crucial information visible and accessible in simple, clear displays.* In 1984, American Express Co. executives realized that their firm had to improve their credit-authorization services; poor decisions were resulting in losses amounting to hundreds of millions of dollars annually. They developed a computer application called the Authorizer's Assistant that presents the most pertinent information about cardholders on just two computer screens so that human authorizers can quickly and easily scan this information and make a decision. The company estimates that it is receiving a 45 percent to 60 percent annual rate of return on its investment in the system.

- *Use the advanced features of application software.* The least effective organizations use word processing programs as electronic typewriters, ignoring high-productivity features such as macros (recorded series of keystrokes) that can produce huge efficiency gains.

- *Use the technology to produce knowledge, not data.* Using a typewriter, managers can produce a five-page document that lists information without any intelligent analysis. Using a personal computer and a word processor, managers can produce a 50-page document that lists information without any intelligent analysis. But the real benefit of computer technology isn't its unfortunate capacity to *increase* the amount of unanalyzed, meaningless data; it's the computer's much-less-frequently utilized capability to *reduce* information to the essentials. The best computer reports include a very brief executive summary, a statement of the major conclusions, one or two business graphs that vividly show the patterns that have been discovered, and an appendix where the numerical elements are shown in detail. The personal computer uniquely enables the creation of this kind of report.

Because the big payoffs from computerization really come from changing the way you do business, bear in mind that you may be able to reap huge gains by skipping computers entirely and concentrating on improving the way you do business! Computers can play an important role in this process if they can provide the foundation, the staging ground, or the communication linkages that make such improvement possible—but they are not the only means toward this end. Noncomputer solutions—combining forms, moving people's desks closer together, eliminating redundant work, and so on—may produce the same rewards with far less investment.

You can spend the productivity benefits of technology in two ways. You can reduce the amount of work you're doing, or you can put in the same amount of work and raise the quality of your output. *Both* goals are possible and entirely legitimate. Even if you can't prove a bottom-line gain for computerization, it's still worth doing if you can improve the quality of the goods or services you deliver to your customers.

Summary

These are the key points covered in this chapter:

- Computers don't replace paper. Instead, they simulate, automate, and enhance operations you perform on paper.

- Computers bring five potential benefits to your business: automating tasks, learning new skills, making your work more efficient, avoiding errors, and making your output more attractive.

- To select the tasks that you want to computerize, examine the paper-related tasks that you perform in your business.

- The biggest benefits from computerization come from changing the way you do business—not just from using computers.

Software Resources
for Small Business

Effective computerization means understanding what computers can do, focusing on high-payoff tasks, and streamlining the way you do business. And these three points add up to a fourth, and very important, point: you should concentrate now, not on all that snazzy hardware, but rather on *software*—and particularly on *application software*—the programs that transform your computer into a tool for performing a specific task, such as maintaining a mailing list. When you grasp what application software can do, you will know what a computer can do for your business.

Choosing the right software makes hardware selection easy, because most programs have very specific hardware requirements, and some programs are more demanding than others. Your selection of hardware will be shaped by a simple rule: choose the hardware that is required to run your most demanding application program. Actually, choosing hardware is easy. It's choosing the *software*, however, that is difficult. In this chapter, you get plenty of guidance as you develop a map of the software world.

The world of personal computer software is an inordinately complex and confusing world—a jungle of astounding dimensions that would give even an Indiana Jones grounds for caution. More than 75,000 programs are available for IBM-compatible computers, and these programs fall into a welter of confusing categories and application areas.

In this chapter, you survey the world of software, which can be divided into two basic categories:

- *System software:* All programs used to control and maintain a computer system. Commonly used personal computer system software includes Microsoft Corporation's DOS for IBM and IBM-compatible PCs, and Apple Computer's proprietary system software for its Macintosh computers.

- *Application software:* All programs that enable computer users to apply computer technology to their own ends (such as writing a business report or analyzing financial data).

With its focus on application software, this chapter provides the background you need to approach software decisions systematically. For any one business-related computer task, there is often a range of software approaches. Only you can decide which is best for you and best for your business. So this chapter is fundamental. It equips you with the concepts you'll need to profit from Part II of this book, which examines your software options—and their business implications—for a wide range of business tasks.

Defining System Software

System software can be divided into three categories:

- *Operating system:* All programs absolutely essential and indispensable for the computer's proper functioning.

- *User interface:* The portion of system software that displays messages to the user and handles the user's commands. The user interface provides tools to perform tasks, such as preparing disks for use (formatting), copying and deleting files on disks, and starting application programs.

- *System utilities:* Programs for day-to-day system maintenance (such as backing up files or formatting disks) that are provided with the operating system.

Basically, the decision on system software is tied to the hardware and software that you want to use.

If you purchase a Macintosh, you use the system software provided with the Macintosh. If you purchase an IBM or IBM-compatible, you use DOS. If you don't like DOS, you can buy an operating environment to take the place of DOS. The most common operating environment is Windows. Right now, you don't need to know all the ins and outs of system software, but do keep the following points in mind:

- The Macintosh uses a graphical user interface or GUI (pronounced *gooey*). This design depicts files as graphic objects on-screen. Using a mouse (an input device), you can select objects, open menus, move objects, and so on.

- DOS uses a command-line interface. Usually all you see on-screen is a prompt (C>). To perform a task, you must memorize the appropriate command and the appropriate format (called *syntax*). You type the command at the command prompt.

- Microsoft Windows is a graphical user interface similar to the Macintosh. Rather than using the DOS command line, you use Windows to start programs, copy files, and perform other system tasks (see fig. 2.1).

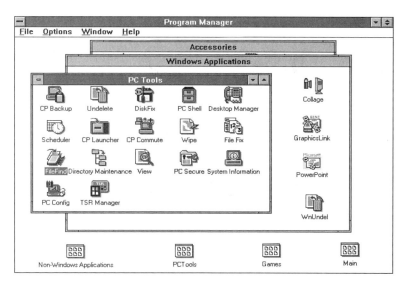

Fig. 2.1. A graphical user interface (Microsoft Windows).

- Graphical user interfaces are easier to learn and use.

- A GUI's user interface functions—the design of on-screen windows, menus, dialog boxes, scroll bars, and the techniques you use to manipulate these features—are made available to compatible application programs so that the user sees a consistent interface, no matter which program happens to be running.

- With the Macintosh and Windows, you can run more than one program at the same time. You can load a spreadsheet program and a word processing program simultaneously, for example. To copy a spreadsheet into the word processing document so that it appears as a table, you don't have to quit one program, save an intermediary file, start another, and insert the intermediary file; you just copy the data you want, switch to the other program, and paste in the data where you want it to appear.

- Application programs are written for specific system software environments. A given program may be written for DOS, for the Macintosh, or for Windows. Some programs are available for two or more system software environments, such as Quicken and Microsoft Works, which are both available for Macintosh and DOS systems. Most programs, however, are available for just one environment.

As you learn in Part III, you must decide which system software environment will run the *most* programs needed for critical applications. For now, that system almost certainly is going to be DOS, because far more business programs are available for the DOS environment than for any other environment. But in the future, many of these programs will run under Windows. Because a suitably-equipped IBM or IBM-compatible computer is capable of running Windows as well as DOS, you will be wise to buy a computer that runs DOS now and is capable of running Windows and Windows applications in the future. For more information on system selection, see Chapter 16, "Designing Your System."

Defining the Five Fundamental Applications

Although people are using computers to accomplish an amazing variety of tasks, five fundamental personal computer applications exist for the business user:

- To write

- To calculate

- To store and retrieve data

- To illustrate

- To communicate with other computers

These areas certainly aren't the only things you can do with computers, but they are the things people do most often. In the sections that follow, you learn more about the five fundamental applications and the procedures you can use to achieve them with a computer.

Word Processing

When you are using word processing functions in a program, you are working with text, and your primary objective is to create a well-written, letter-perfect, and pleasingly printed document—a letter, a memo, a report, or some other piece of written work destined to be printed on paper. (Figure 2.2 shows a document created and printed with WordPerfect, the leading DOS word processing program.) You use four procedures to achieve this objective: entering text, editing text, formatting text, and printing text.

New Drivers School Location

There's been a change in the location for this year's drivers school for the Windy City Chapter, and I know you'll love this one! Instead of going to Blackhawk Farms, we'll be going up to Road America in beautiful Elkhart Lake, Wisconsin.

This way, all you hotshoes will have about 4.5 miles instead of 2.5 miles to thrash your Bimmers around the track. It'll also be easier on your brakes than Blackhawk, due to the longer straights that'll give them a chance to cool off between turns.

The dates will remain the same, May 21 and 22. Lodging, as always, will be available at Siebkens and Barefoot Bay in Elkhart Lake, or at Motels in Sheboygan or Fond du Lac. Remember, you must make your own reservations. Remember also that Siebkens is basically a summertime resort, which means NO HEAT in the rooms. Also no phones and no credit cards. But LOTS of ATMOSPHERE. The rates at both Siebkens and Barefoot Bay are quite reasonable, $24 and $48 (single/double) at Siebkens and $59.95 at Barefoot Bay for either single or double. Driving directions to Elkhart Lake will be included with your registration package, along with a map of the area.

SATURDAY DINNER

There'll be dinner at Siebkens Saturday night, with a choice of fish, duck or prime rib. The cost will be $15 plus tip. We'll have a cash bar also, but remember you'll want a clear head the next morning or your Bimmer will start playing tricks on you. So go easy on the liquid stuff.

If you want to join us for dinner, let Registration know Saturday morning what your choice of entree is, otherwise there'll be no food waiting for you.

PRETECH AT LEO'S

Pretech will as always be at Leo Franchi's Midwest Motor Sports. The date is April 23. This will give you a chance to get anything fixed before the drivers school. A tech sheet is enclosed with the registration package. Be sure to fill it out and bring it along. There is no charge for the tech inspection. We're planning to start at 9 a.m. and go until everybody is done.

If you miss the tech at Leo's, you'll have to go to your favorite mechanic and bring proof of the inspection and any repairs that were made. Remember, NO TECH - NO TRACK.

We look forward to seeing you all at Elkhart Lake.

Enjoy!

Fig. 2.2. A newsletter created with WordPerfect.

- *Entering text:* You can think of a word processing program as a *television-typewriter* because you type the text at a keyboard (typewriter), and the text appears on-screen (television). The big advantage of this approach is that you can get the wording just right before printing.

- *Editing text:* Every word processing program provides tools for inserting text within text you already have typed. With a feature called *automatic reformatting*, the existing text is adjusted to make room for the text you insert. Automatic reformatting also takes care of the gaps left by deletions. When deleting text, you can make use of commands that delete a character, a word, a line, a paragraph, or even a whole line at a time. A major benefit of word processing for writers is the ability to move blocks of text from one place to another; you can use this feature to improve the organization of your written work.

- *Formatting text:* To format text is to use commands that instruct the printer to print text in an aesthetically pleasing way on the page. You can perform formatting tasks such as attaching emphasis to the text (such as **boldface**, *italic*, or <u>underlining</u>), setting margins, indenting text, choosing line spacings, and adding page numbers. In a *what-you-see-is-what-you-get* (WYSIWYG) program, you see the results of your formatting choices on-screen. Less desirable is the use of *embedded commands*—formatting commands you place in the midst of the text, which don't show up until you print the document.

- *Printing:* After you create, edit, and format the text, you need to print the document. At this point, the operation is all but automatic. The program prints the document within the margins you choose and with or without page numbers.

These word processing operations are rudimentary. A full-featured word processing program is likely to include many more features that enhance these operations: spell checking; an on-line electronic thesaurus; automatic hyphenation; on-screen outlining; the capability to sort lists; and the capability to add footnotes, headers, and footers.

Electronic Spreadsheets

An electronic *spreadsheet* or *worksheet* is a computerized version of an accountant's pad. When you are using spreadsheet functions in a program, you are working with numbers (as well as with explanatory text, called *labels*).

A spreadsheet program presents you with a matrix of rows and columns that form individual cells (see fig. 2.3). Each cell has a distinctive cell address which expresses its precise location on the worksheet. Cell B4, for example, lies at the intersection of column B and row 4. In each cell, you can place a value (a number), a label (text), or a formula. Formulas are what make spreadsheets so powerful. A formula can contain constants (such as 2 + 2), but creating formulas using cell addresses (such as A2 + A3) is much better. Because you can refer to the values in other cells by using cell addresses in a formula, you can create a worksheet in which all the values in the whole worksheet are interlinked.

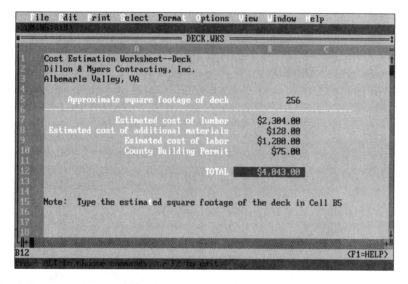

Fig. 2.3. *Viewing a spreadsheet (Microsoft Works).*

The following is an overview of the main operations you perform with electronic spreadsheet programs:

- *Entering data and labels:* You type the numbers and headings in cells. You can edit the data you typed, and you can change the alignment (flush left, centered, or flush right). More recent programs, such as Microsoft Excel for Windows and 1-2-3 Release 2.3 and 3.1, enable you to use distinctive typefaces and type sizes.

- *Entering formulas:* You can create simple addition formulas and complex financial calculations. Formulas can reference cells so that when you change the cell, the formula is recalculated.

- *Copying formulas:* After you enter a column or row of formulas, you can copy them to adjacent columns or rows in such a way that the formulas are adjusted automatically to suit their new location. If you write a formula that sums all the figures in column C and then copy the formula to column D, for example, the copied formula sums column D. This feature saves time by frequently eliminating the need to retype complex formulas (see figs. 2.4 and 2.5).

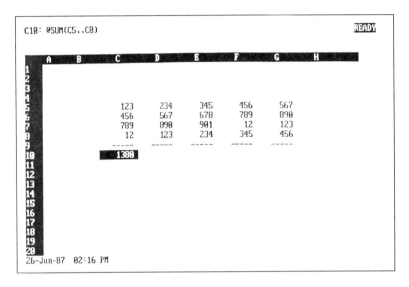

Fig. 2.4. A spreadsheet with one column summed.

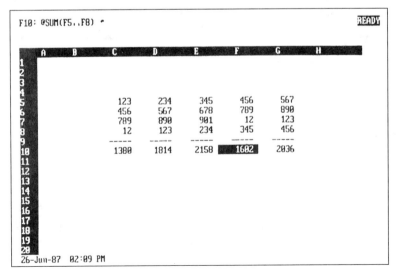

Fig. 2.5. A spreadsheet with copied formulas.

- *Choosing formats:* You can define how you want the numbers displayed; you can choose from currency, percentage, integers only, fixed number of decimal places, and other options.

- *Performing what-if analyses:* The point of creating a worksheet isn't just to find the answer to a problem. When the worksheet is completed, you can type in new values, and the spreadsheet is recalculated almost instantly. This type of analysis, called *what-if analysis*, is a form of data exploration in which key variables are changed to see their impact on the results of the computation.

- *Using a worksheet as a template:* You also can set up a spreadsheet to serve as a generic worksheet, called a *template*, for performing a calculation you must do repeatedly, such as estimating costs. Every time you have some new data to work with, you just read the generic worksheet from the disk file in which you have stored it, type in the new key variables, and in seconds, you see the answer on the bottom line.

- *Graphing:* Included here, rather than under "Graphics," are business graphs (such as bar graphs, column graphs, line graphs, and pie graphs) because these graphs are generated from tables of numerical data. Many spreadsheet programs can generate these graphs almost automatically after you define the areas of the spreadsheet that contain the necessary data.

- *Printing:* You can print the entire worksheet or just one area.

Database Management

Database management provides computer assistance for the kinds of tasks librarians perform in maintaining a card catalog, such as creating the card format, alphabetizing the cards, deleting old cards, and finding a card on a specific subject. When you use a program's database management functions, your primary objective is to store and retrieve information from a *database*. A database is a collection of related information about a subject that has been organized in a useful manner, enabling you to retrieve information, draw conclusions, and make decisions.

The basic unit of information in a database is a *data record*, a complete unit of information about something, such as a book in the library or an employee. In each record, you see *data fields*, or areas in which a particular kind of information is stored.

The following is an overview of the basic operations you perform in database management:

- *Creating the database:* To create the database, you begin by defining the number of data fields you want to use, with specifications for their length and the type of data you want to place in it (alphabetical, numeric, date, and so on).

- *Entering data:* To assist you in entering the data, the program displays a blank *data form* which includes the headings and explanatory text you have chosen as well as the data fields, which are waiting for you to type the required data.

- *Browsing through the data:* With many programs, you can view the data in two ways. In Record mode, you see each individual record on-screen, one at a time, as if you were looking at a five-by-eight card (see fig. 2.6). In List mode, you see several records' worth of information expressed as a columnar table (see fig. 2.7). Most programs enable you to enter data and edit data in both modes.

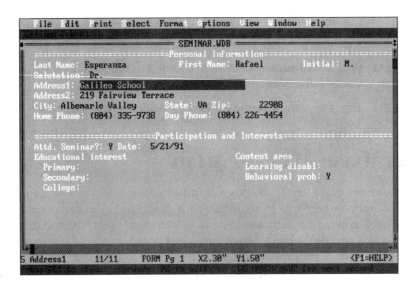

Fig. 2.6. Record mode showing one record (Microsoft Works).

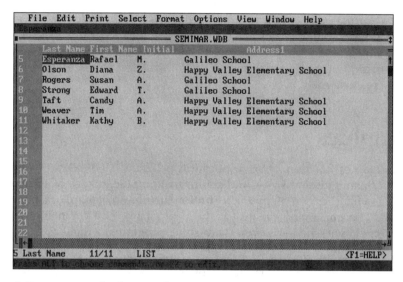

Fig. 2.7. Browse mode showing data in columns (Microsoft Works).

- *Retrieving data:* After you enter the data, you can retrieve it in two ways. You can search for an individual record that contains information you want to see, or you can perform a query. When you *query* the database, you specify the criteria by which you want to group two or more data records. You can tell the program, for example, "Show me all the customers whose bills are more than 30 days overdue."

- *Editing and updating data:* You can modify the information in any data record. Particularly useful, however, is a form of data modification called an *update*, that uses a query. When you perform an update operation, the program finds all the records that meet the criteria you specify, and then the program makes the changes you request in just those records. You can tell the program to find all the records that contain the text *Acme Perfection Products*, for example, in the data field called MANUFACTURER and to multiply the price in the PRICE field by 1.25.

- *Deleting data:* In data deletion, you remove the records that are no longer needed. Because data deletion can have adverse consequences if done accidentally, most database programs make it difficult to accidentally delete records.

- *Printing data:* When you print a database, you produce a report. For archival purposes, it's always a good idea to print all the contents of every record. Ideally, a report reduces the welter of information in the database to just the information you need to draw a conclusion.

Graphics

The graphics function of an application program is concerned with the creation, alteration, display, and printing of graphic images of some sort, such as a hand-drawn picture, a technical illustration, a map, or a business graph. The image you create can be printed by itself or included in a document, worksheet, or even (with some programs) a database.

You can use two types of graphics: bit-mapped and object-oriented. *Bit-mapped* graphics are made up of small squares. Figure 2.8 shows a magnified view of an image created by a paint program. Note how the lines are composed of squares, and that the diagonal lines are uneven (this unevenness is known as the *jaggies*). Enlarging or reducing this type of graphic is difficult. It is also difficult to edit the drawing because each addition you make merely adds more squares to the pattern. Removing a line or a background pattern may be impossible. *Object-oriented* graphics are defined by a mathematical equation. You easily can change the size and shape of an object-oriented graphic. Furthermore, each object you create, such as a line or a circle, can be independently selected, sized, moved, or deleted, so it is easy to edit the drawing.

The following is an overview of the basic operations you perform when you use a program's graphics functions:

- *Choosing a tool:* Graphics programs present a toolbox in which you can choose from a variety of tools that enter distinctive graphics elements (see fig. 2.9). For a bit-mapped program, you are likely to find a pencil, a brush, and an eraser; a spray can (which "sprays" a pattern of dots) and a fill bucket (which fills an enclosed area with a pattern or color); a line tool; a mini-word processor for entering text; and tools for entering rectangles, circles, arcs, and polygons. In object-oriented programs, you find fewer tools: a mini-word processor, as well as tools for entering lines, rectangles, arcs, ovals, and circles (see fig. 2.10).

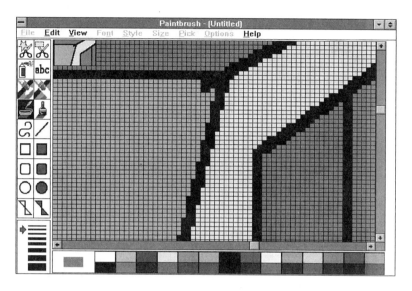

Fig. 2.8. *A paint program (Microsoft Windows Paintbrush).*

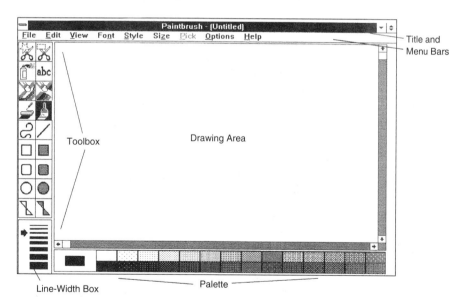

Fig. 2.9. *A toolbox for a paint program (Microsoft Windows Paint).*

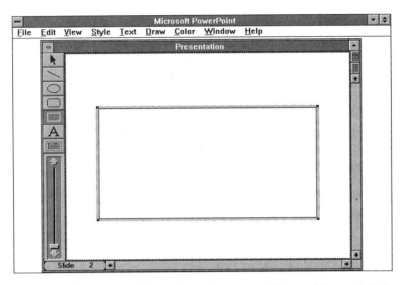

Fig. 2.10. A toolbox for an object-oriented drawing (Microsoft PowerPoint).

- *Painting or drawing:* With a bit-mapped graphics program, you create the illustration by choosing from the wide variety of painting tools; you build up the tapestry of dots on-screen so that it achieves your goal. Fixing big mistakes can be difficult, however, because you cannot manipulate separate parts of the drawing independently. With an object-oriented program, you draw the illustration using the tools that enter geometric shapes. You easily can edit the drawing so that it meets your objectives just by selecting an object and moving or deleting that object.

- *Printing or importing:* When you finish the object, you print or import it into a word processing document.

Communications

A program's communications function enables you to exchange information with other computers. The communications function of an application program makes network or telecommunications resources available to you; it does so by transforming your computer into an electronic version of a walkie-talkie: you *send* messages to other computers, and you *receive* a response. The closest comparison that can be made between the world of paper and the world of electronic communications is between mail (in electronic mail, you send and receive memos and letters) and database management (when you access a central database or an information service, you send queries and receive views).

The simplest link, *telecommunications*, uses your computer's serial port and a modem. A *serial port* enables your computer to exchange data with other computing devices, including printers and optical scanners (which "read" or digitize drawings and photographs). A *modem* modifies the signals coming from the serial port so that they can be transmitted via the phone line, and it also demodifies the signals coming from the phone line so that the serial port can accept them. Equipped with a modem, the entire world telephone system is open to your computer, as long as another properly equipped and expectant computer is waiting at the other end of the line.

Telecommunications is slow; it is used mainly for applications such as exchanging data files and accessing on-line information services, about which you learn more in Chapter 12, "Going Online."

Requiring more equipment is a *local area network* (LAN) that directly wires from a few to a few hundred personal computers into a network capable of high-speed data exchange. To create a LAN, each linked computer (or *workstation*) must be equipped with the necessary network interface circuitry and network software and must be directly wired to the other computers. Most LANs also require that a single computer, equipped with a huge hard disk, be set aside as a *file server*, a machine that contains the computer resources that all the workstations share. Communications resources in LANs include electronic mail, the creation of common databases for storing and retrieving information vital to an organization's functioning, and computer conferencing.

The following is an overview of the basic operations you perform when you use a program's communications function:

- *Choosing communications settings:* No single, set standard is followed for telecommunications, so you frequently must choose a pattern of communications settings (called a *communications protocol*) before you can use a communications system effectively.

- *Logging on:* You choose the commands that activate the modem (or give you access to the network).

- *Choosing an action:* In most systems, you can pursue more than one course of action after you log on. If you're using a local area network, chances are the prompt looks like a DOS prompt (such as F>), and you can treat the network as if it is a gigantic hard disk (you can run programs, copy files, and so on). If the system has E-mail, you choose the command that gives you access to the E-mail software, and then you can read your current messages, reply to them, delete them, and write new messages to others.

- *Logging off:* You choose the command that disconnects you from the communications link. From this point, you can log on to another network or quit the communications function.

Defining the Four Kinds of Application Software

The preceding section discusses the five fundamental applications. In this section, you learn the four ways that application programs emphasize or combine features to meet one or more of these objectives: single-purpose application programs, integrated programs, special-purpose programs, and vertical-market programs.

Single-Purpose Application Programs

In this category are programs that concentrate on just one application, such as word processing or database management. These programs try to provide most or all of the tools a user could conceivably need to carry out the application, such as writing or illustrating. These programs are flexible, capable of applications in a huge variety of varying contexts, and—if the user has the requisite programming skills—can be customized for specific purposes, at the cost of considerable development work.

The best-selling programs in this category are packed with features that aid the fundamental application. A state-of-the-art word processing program, for example, includes just about everything you need to write, edit, format, and print effectively with the computer—including outlining, spell checking, support for a variety of typefaces, an electronic thesaurus, automatic list numbering, and much more.

In their zeal to give you everything you need, programmers may incorporate features strongly reminiscent of other software functions. Most word processing programs, for example, include fairly primitive features for setting up mailing list databases, and many now include table-creation capabilities that set up a spreadsheet-like matrix of cells. These features always are adapted to the program's primary purpose.

A word processing program that incorporates such features, however, is still a word processing program: its primary objective is to provide you with the tools you need to create, edit, format, and print text. To perform what-if calculations, you need a spreadsheet program.

A considerable disadvantage of single-purpose programs is data incompatibility. For example, WordPerfect (a best-selling word processor) cannot read Microsoft Word (another word processor) files directly (although it can do so with the aid of a file transfer utility program). Increasingly, the best word processing programs come with file conversion utilities that enable you to read and write files in several other programs' formats. This feature enhances data interchangeability in offices where two or more programs are in use.

Another disadvantage of single-purpose programs, at least under DOS, is the tedium involved in switching to other single-purpose programs. With DOS, you can run only one major, single-purpose program at a time.

TIP

Beware of the development costs needed to tailor a single-purpose program to a highly specific application objective, such as maintaining a mailing list, handling your firm's accounting, or billing for time expenses. Many of these programs come with their own programming languages which can be used to create customized, special-purpose applications. But don't waste time reinventing the wheel. Investigate special-purpose and vertical-market applications, to be discussed next in this chapter, before deciding to customize a single-purpose application. One of these applications may offer precisely the features you need, making it unnecessary to spend time and money customizing a single-purpose application program.

Integrated Application Programs

In contrast to single-purpose programs, a true integrated program tries to offer two or more single-purpose programs in one program. Microsoft Works, for example, includes a word processor, a spreadsheet, a database manager, business charts, some other graphics functions, and communications. These integrated programs try to deliver many or most of the features users need to tackle two or more applications.

Creating in one program two or more modules that are really the equal of their single-purpose counterparts is difficult to do. Microsoft Works' word processor, for example, doesn't have many of the features standard in single-purpose word processing programs.

Compared to single-purpose programs, integrated programs have two significant advantages. First, transferring data from one application module (such as the spreadsheet) to another (such as the word processor) is easy; the programs are designed to do precisely that quickly and easily. Second, little time or effort is required to switch from one module to another. In Works, you can open a spreadsheet window while you're working with database management or the spreadsheet without even saving your work. Quitting one program and starting another isn't necessary, so the convenience is a major gain.

TIP

If you are attracted by the ease with which you can transfer data from one module to another in an integrated program, remember that a windowing environment such as Microsoft Windows or the Macintosh system software offers the same advantage, but enables you to run full-featured, single-purpose programs.

Special-Purpose Application Programs

A special-purpose application program turns the tables on the design premises of single-purpose and integrated programs. Instead of trying to provide all or most of the tools needed for a general application objective, such as writing or managing data, a special-purpose application program combines limited aspects of two or more software functions to support a narrowly restricted application purpose.

The best way to understand the nature, benefits, and limitations of special-purpose application programs is to examine a range of examples:

- *PageMaker:* This page layout program combines limited word processing and object-oriented graphics capabilities for the single purpose of laying out pages for a publication. By themselves, the word processing and graphics capabilities are insufficient for the application objectives of writing or creating illustrations; the word processing and graphics modules are reduced in scope and modified in function so that they suit the program's narrow purpose: laying out text and graphics for newsletters, price lists, brochures, and other material to be published (see fig. 2.11).

Fig. 2.11. *A price list created with PageMaker.*

You would not really want to *write* a document with PageMaker, for example; the program doesn't include many of the document organization and editing features that make a single-purpose program such as Microsoft Word so useful and powerful for creating and revising text. With its blend of object-oriented graphics, absolute positioning of page elements, and the capability to import and position text accurately, PageMaker goes far beyond the formatting and printing capabilities of word processing software.

- *FastPak Mail:* This special-purpose program was designed specifically for creating and maintaining mailing lists, as well as for printing mailing labels. This program includes limited word processing and database management capabilities tailored for mailing list purposes. You can develop a mailing list application with a word processing program or an integrated program such as Microsoft Works, but FastPak Mail does much more: the program can detect and eliminate duplicates, sort by ZIP code for lower bulk mailing rates, capitalize proper nouns, and print addresses on Federal Express airbills.

- *Timeslips III:* This special-purpose program was designed specifically to meet the time and expense billing needs of professionals who charge by the hour. Like FastPak Mail, the program includes database management and word processing capabilities, but these capabilities are modified and tailored to suit the program's special purpose. Conceivably, you can modify a database management program to accomplish what Timeslips does, but only at the cost of an enormous development effort; Timeslips incorporates that effort, and with very little modification, a professional can set up a highly effective time and expense billing system for a professional practice.

Compared to single-purpose or integrated programs, the major advantage of special-purpose programs is that they incorporate the huge development effort needed to tailor software for a specific application.

Special-purpose programs have one significant disadvantage: reduced flexibility (as compared with single-purpose programs). With a single-purpose database management program such as dBASE, or the database manager within an integrated program such as Microsoft Works, you can create many data fields and name them in any way that suits your business. The database manager in a special-purpose mailing list program such as FastPak Mail is preconfigured with just so many data fields; you cannot add or create your own, so if you want to customize the application, you are out of luck.

TIP

> Because they require little or no development to serve a specific application purpose, special-purpose applications may prove very valuable for your business. Beware of their lack of flexibility, though. You can invest a considerable amount of time learning a special-purpose program and typing data, only to find that its lack of flexibility prevents you from performing a task crucial to the way you do business.

Vertical-Market Application Programs

A *vertical-market application program* is a special-purpose program not only targeted for a specific purpose (such as billing for time and expenses) but also developed for a specific profession (such as medicine, law, accounting, engineering, business consultation, or real estate) or business (video rentals, equipment rentals, or general contracting). Shrink Plus, for example, a program that meets the needs of a psychotherapy practice, provides scheduling, time, and billing support for psychotherapists, including complete expense tracking, insurance company billing, and clinical record-keeping.

Like special-purpose programs, vertical-market programs incorporate the development necessary to tailor them to a special purpose. They also incorporate knowledge about the specific needs of a particular profession or business, and their design reflects further customization and development so that the program suits those specific needs. This development comes at a price, however. Vertical-market programs generally cost much more than special-purpose programs.

If you are thinking about a vertical-market program, you should clearly understand one potentially catastrophic drawback: these programs offer even *less* flexibility than special-purpose programs.

Special-purpose programs, such as FastPak Mail (for mailing lists) and Timeslips III (for time-and-expense billing), may be designed for a specific activity, but these programs also are designed for a mass market. Special-purpose programs, therefore, typically include at least *some* scope for user customization. With Timeslips III, for example, you can choose whether you want to charge your customers sales or service tax, and whether you want to charge them interest on overdue accounts. With comparatively little effort, even a beginner can customize Timeslips III for a wide variety of businesses that bill by time, ranging from basement day care operation to legal practices with dozens of attorneys.

Vertical market programs are not designed for a mass market; these programs are designed only for a tiny slice of the market, and programmers see no need to include a wide range of customization options. Most vertical market programs do offer some scope for user customization, but it usually is far narrower than what you find in a comparable special-purpose program. You must be extremely cautious when purchasing a vertical-market program: if the program doesn't do what your firm needs, it's going to waste your time and money.

No one guarantees that a vertical-market program is based on a solid grasp of your line of work. Vertical-market programmers may have a specific scope of business in mind when they develop the program: some programs are designed for small firms and don't include features that can be of critical value for larger firms, such as tracking employee productivity.

Before you commit your business to a vertical-market package, you should find out what kind of reputation the program has among people in your same line of work, look for reviews in professional and trade magazines, determine the program's focus (is it designed for a relatively large firm? a small one? one user or many?), and carefully examine the program's features and capabilities to make sure that something isn't missing that may prove crucial to your business.

If you believe you can benefit from a vertical-market application program, be aware that these programs are rarely available from computer stores or mail-order software firms. You learn about vertical-market packages in trade-related journals and magazines, which often run objective reviews of these packages.

Comparing Flexibility and Development Cost

A trade-off exists between flexibility (whether you can customize a program) and development costs (how much it will cost you to apply the program to your business successfully):

- *High flexibility/high development costs: single-purpose and integrated programs.* Although flexible and useful for the tasks for which they are intended, single-purpose and integrated programs are expensive and difficult to customize so that they meet a specific business's needs for such applications as accounting, payroll, inventory control, or document production. On the positive side, these programs are often capable of handling large amounts of data, so they can usually accommodate your business's growth.

- *Reduced flexibility/low development costs: special-purpose programs.* Typically, special-purpose programs incorporate a considerable amount of development effort. Even a beginning user can follow the straightforward procedure, which is outlined in the program's manual, necessary to apply the package to a specific business's needs. Although these programs are much less flexible than single-purpose or integrated programs, they typically offer a range of options, among which you may find a feature of crucial strategic importance for your business's needs. But be sure to investigate whether the program can accommodate your business's growth. What happens if your mailing list grows from 500 names to 50,000?

- *Minimum flexibility/minimum development costs: vertical-market programs.* Many vertical-market packages are almost ready to use right off the shelf; you just type in your company's name, the beginning date, and choose Go. Because these programs offer a minimum of flexibility, the lack of a crucial option or feature can result in your wasting a great deal of time and money. Note, too, that there is a risk that you will be left hanging should the software company go out of business. What will happen if you have your business on a product that no one can support or modify?

You can reduce development costs by choosing special-purpose and vertical-market programs, if they suit your needs. But as you've just learned, you should select such programs with caution. Will they accommodate your business's growth? Will the software company survive so that you continue to receive upgrades and support? Before purchasing any program that is going to be central to your business, determine its limits—How many pages of text can you create? How many data records can you store? How large a spreadsheet can you create, given your computer's memory capacity? Make sure these and other limits can accommodate a reasonable estimate of your company's growth for the next five years. If you're considering a little-known vertical-market program, find out how long it has been in business—is it an established firm with a solid user base, or a chancy new venture?

TIP

You can put together a software library that draws from both ends of this continuum. Purchase single-objective programs for the times that you need all the tools necessary for a task such as writing, calculating, or illustrating. Don't waste money and time trying to customize these programs. Investigate special-purpose and vertical-market programs for these applications—but be sure to choose products from established firms, and make sure the programs can accommodate your business's growth.

Developing a Plan of Attack

You need to do some homework before you go shopping for software. The following is a six-step plan of attack for computerizing your small business, with an explanation of just how this book can help you:

1. Develop a *problem statement* that succinctly and accurately analyzes what is wrong with the way you're doing things right now.

Is it taking too long to do something? Is there something you cannot do because you cannot handle the paperwork? Are you making mistakes? Are you unable to locate information? Be as specific as you possibly can.

As you develop your problem statement, don't just enumerate problems. You should see the problem as an opportunity to rethink the way you do business. Your challenge: to figure out a way in which you can apply personal computer technology so that you not only solve the problem but introduce a major improvement in the way you do business.

2. Choose the critical areas to which you want to apply personal computer technology.

This step isn't an easy task if, like most personal computer users, you really don't have a clear idea of just what application software can do. In this book, you find detailed examples of a wide variety of programs, applied to tasks such as maintaining mailing lists (Chapter 4), creating business newsletters (Chapter 9), using an electronic spreadsheet program to develop a cost-estimation system (Chapter 6), and developing a point-of-sale/inventory control system for a small retail business (Chapter 14). As you read the chapters that seem pertinent to your business, you develop a clearer idea of just which areas of your business are the most likely candidates for computerization.

3. Develop a list of the features and capabilities that the software must have in order to suit your business's needs.

After you decide which application area or areas you're going to tackle, develop a list of the features and capabilities you want for the application. Read the relevant chapters of this book to discover what some of the available application programs can do, and learn about others by obtaining information from software publishers, magazine reviews, and computer stores. Then develop a prioritized list of the features that seem to offer opportunities for your business—specifically, opportunities to do what you are doing in a simpler, more logical, more streamlined, or more effective way.

Figure 2.12 shows a problem statement with a list of specifications that a realty company may develop to evaluate options for a mailing list/mailing label application.

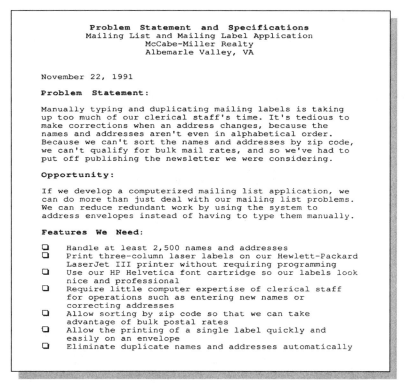

```
              Problem  Statement  and  Specifications
              Mailing List and Mailing Label Application
                       McCabe-Miller Realty
                       Albemarle Valley, VA


      November 22, 1991

      Problem  Statement:

      Manually typing and duplicating mailing labels is taking
      up too much of our clerical staff's time. It's tedious to
      make corrections when an address changes, because the
      names and addresses aren't even in alphabetical order.
      Because we can't sort the names and addresses by zip code,
      we can't qualify for bulk mail rates, and so we've had to
      put off publishing the newsletter we were considering.

      Opportunity:

      If we develop a computerized mailing list application, we
      can do more than just deal with our mailing list problems.
      We can reduce redundant work by using the system to
      address envelopes instead of having to type them manually.

      Features  We  Need:

      ❏    Handle at least 2,500 names and addresses
      ❏    Print three-column laser labels on our Hewlett-Packard
           LaserJet III printer without requiring programming
      ❏    Use our HP Helvetica font cartridge so our labels look
           nice and professional
      ❏    Require little computer expertise of clerical staff
           for operations such as entering new names or
           correcting addresses
      ❏    Allow sorting by zip code so that we can take
           advantage of bulk postal rates
      ❏    Allow the printing of a single label quickly and
           easily on an envelope
      ❏    Eliminate duplicate names and addresses automatically
```

Fig. 2.12. *A realty firm's specifications for mailing list and mailing label software.*

4. Decide whether single-purpose, integrated, special-purpose, or vertical-market software best meets your needs.

   Decide whether you want to pay for the development costs needed to customize a single-purpose or integrated program. Chances are you will be better off with a special-purpose or vertical-market program that meets all your specifications. In many of the chapters of this book, you find illustrations of what it takes to customize a single-purpose program and what you sacrifice by using a special-purpose or vertical-market application.

5. Choose a program.

   You need to evaluate such factors as technical support, warranty, upgrade policies, multiuser licenses, and more. Part V of this book provides plenty of guidance.

6. Purchase a system optimal for the software you have chosen.

   For guidance, see Chapter 17, "Buying and Installing Your System."

Summary

To computerize your small business successfully, forget about hardware for the moment. Concentrate on choosing the right application software for the critical application areas in your business—the areas that must operate efficiently and productively if you hope to turn a profit and keep your customers. Keep the following key points in mind:

- Choose application software first and then worry about the hardware platform for the software you have chosen.

- Application programs are designed to run in specific system software environments, such as the Macintosh System, DOS, and Microsoft Windows. Although some programs are available in versions for two or more system environments, most of the programs useful for your business probably will run under DOS.

- Although people do many things with computers, these are five fundamental applications: to write, to calculate, to store and retrieve data, to illustrate, and to communicate with other computers.

- Four kinds of application programs are available: single-purpose application programs, integrated programs, special-purpose programs, and vertical-market application programs.

- Come up with a plan to pinpoint the areas in which you want to use a computer. Find the appropriate software to accomplish the tasks you want by developing a list of the features and capabilities that the software must have to suit your business's needs.

In Part II, you receive guidance on these issues with respect to a given application area.

Part II

Getting Organized

Includes

Managing Time

Developing a Mailing List

Managing Information

Crunching Numbers

3

Managing Time

If you're like most people who run small businesses, scheduling your activities, projects, and commitments exacts a heavy toll. Daren, who runs a little wine shop that stocks high-quality California, French, and Australian wines, says that every day is a knock-down fight to stay on top of things—and he's losing.

"Customers are asking what's happened to their special orders," says Daren. "The newspaper's just published a list of the 10 best buys in California chardonnays, most of which I don't stock, and I misplaced the clipping. Just today, another customer asked me about recycling bottles and corks, but I keep forgetting to call the Ecology Center to ask where they should take them. And that's not to mention the stack of unpaid bills and unanswered letters." Does Daren's lament sound familiar?

Daren wants to give his customers the best service he can, but as his business has grown, it has come close to overwhelming him with minute organizational details. Can a computer help? As this chapter shows, the answer is "Yes"— *if* you spend all or most of your day near (or in front of) your business computer. A computerized approach to time management will not do you much good if your computer is in Pasadena, and you're in Malibu, wondering what your next appointment is!

Looking At Time Management Software Options

One of Daren's top priorities in computerizing his business is to find software that will help him manage his schedule, his to-do list, and all the minute details of day-to-day information more effectively. He identifies four categories of software that look promising:

- *Appointment schedulers:* An appointment scheduler—such as the Appointment Scheduler utility in PC Tools (Central Point Software)—is a utility program that presents an on-screen version of an appointment diary, complete with day-to-day schedules and to-do lists. With many appointment schedulers, you can use a pop-up mode that informs you of an impending appointment (such as "Chuck from Central Wine Distributors will be here in 10 minutes") even if you're using another program. Appointment schedulers may meet your needs if your business involves many meetings or regularly scheduled appointments with clients.

- *Personal information managers:* A personal information manager (PIM)—such as Lotus Agenda (Lotus Development Corporation)—is a special-purpose database program designed to accept items of information, which you then categorize in any way you want (such as Orders, Reviews, or Recycling). A PIM may meet your needs if you find yourself dealing with a wide variety of information (not just appointments) that has a time-management component.

- *Contact management programs:* A contact manager (also called an activity tracker) closely resembles a personal information manager, except that it's specifically designed to aid people who must track and follow up business contacts over the telephone. Typically, these programs include a database manager for recording names, addresses, and telephone numbers, and an autodialing utility that uses your computer's modem to dial a number for you. (You pick up the receiver when the modem finishes dialing.)

- *Project management software:* Project management programs are special-purpose programs that help you allocate time and resources for projects involving more than one person and more than a few days of effort (such as adding a room and developing a new line of merchandise). A project manager may meet your needs if your business involves many complex projects that you must manage from start to finish.

The boundaries separating these types of time-management software aren't always sharp and distinct. IBM's Current, for example, is three programs in one: it serves as an appointment scheduler, a personal information manager, and a project manager. And note, too, that you sometimes can find time-management aids in unexpected places. Mind Your Own Business (Teleware), an accounting package for the Macintosh and Windows systems, includes a useful business calendar and to-do list. You can search for expiring discounts, pending sales, overdue contacts, and past-due shipments.

This chapter surveys the strengths and weaknesses of each of these four software aids for time management.

Reviewing the Benefits of Computerized Time Management

Depending on which kind of program you're using, you can expect to perform some or all of the following tasks when you're using time-management software:

- *Keeping an on-screen diary of appointments.* The program should be able to detect the current date and show you today's schedule automatically. Creating and editing appointments should be easy.

- *Creating and viewing an on-screen to-do list with priorities you assign.* The list should "migrate" to the next day's calendar if any tasks have been left undone.

- *Setting an alarm that will warn you of an impending meeting, even if you're using another program.*

- *Dialing the telephone number of the person's record you're displaying on-screen.* This feature, called *auto-dialing*, is common in contact managers, and it's very useful for anyone who spends a lot of time talking on the phone.

- *Viewing tasks in a variety of ways.* You will need a personal information manager to consider your tasks from a variety of angles, such as high-priority to-do items, people to call, and projects to tackle. You can ask questions such as "What must I get done today? Who am I supposed to call? What subjects am I planning to discuss with Tom?" And the computer answers them.

- *Planning an entire project.* This function includes allocating people and resources, setting aside blocks of time, tracking the tasks that must be completed, and finding out whether you have exceeded the project's budget. Project management software handles this job.

If you're not in your office for all or most of the day, you have two options that can preserve the benefits of computerized time management:

- *Printing pages in popular appointment book formats.* Many appointment schedulers and contact managers can print address lists, daily and monthly schedules, and other information in pages formatted precisely for popular diaries such as DayTimers.

- *Using a hand-held personal organizer.* Mobile business people who still prefer the computer approach should investigate the Sharp Wizard or the Psion Organizer. Both are small, hand-held scheduling computers that you can carry easily in a pocket or briefcase.

Time management software can help you get organized, but there's an important caveat: computerized time management works best if you're around your computer all day. If you're out and about a lot, you may find that an old-fashioned paper-based appointment diary, such as a DayTimer, suits your needs better.

Scheduling Appointments and Creating To-Do Lists

Appointment schedulers are special-purpose programs that you can add to your software library. Good appointment schedulers are often included in other programs, however, such as Andrew Tobias' Managing Your Money (MECA), which includes budgeting, checkbook reconciliation, tax estimation, a financial calculator, and more. Appointment schedulers also are included with windowing environments and utilities packages, such as Microsoft Windows and PC Tools. The appointment schedulers are provided as part of these packages' desktop utilities.

These appointment schedulers are simple but may meet your needs. In addition, because they come free-of-charge with programs you may want for other reasons, they're an excellent bargain. You may need the additional features that a special-purpose appointment scheduler provides, however. This section explains your options.

Desktop Appointment Schedulers

The ideal computer system is equipped with a full range of desktop accessories, such as a utility for finding files, an on-screen clock, a notepad utility for jotting down notes, a phone dialer, and an appointment scheduler. Microsoft Windows, for example, comes equipped with a simple appointment scheduler, and PC Tools (which includes desktop accessories for DOS systems) includes a very well conceived, full-featured appointment scheduler. If you're using Windows or PC Tools, you may discover that you already have an appointment scheduler that's sufficient for your needs.

Daren has picked up a copy of PC Tools just for its hard-disk backup capabilities, so he decides to investigate the appointment scheduler to see if it meets his needs. Daren installs PC Tools' desktop accessories program, which is called Desktop, in its terminate-and-stay-resident (TSR) mode, so that he can display it on-screen even if he's running another program. (A *TSR program* remains in memory even after you exit the program. You then can run another program, such as Lotus 1-2-3. While you're in another program, you can activate the TSR just by pressing its *hot key*, which is a keyboard command that overrides the current program and displays the TSR program. After you finish using the TSR program, you return to the program you were using, right where you left off.)

After Daren starts PC Tools and chooses the appointment scheduler, he sees the display shown in figure 3.1. PC Tools detects and highlights the current date (November 14, 1991), and the current time (9:56 a.m.), and shows the current daily schedule (the window on the lower right). On the left of the screen is a to-do list.

Daren uses the Make Appointment command to enter a 2:00 appointment with a distributor, which is an appointment that will last two hours. He asks PC Tools to display a reminder alarm on-screen 10 minutes before the appointment, even if he is using another program at the time. Figure 3.2 displays the appointment that he has made. The musical note reminds Daren that he has set an alarm, and the solid line along the left shows the time that has been set aside for the appointment.

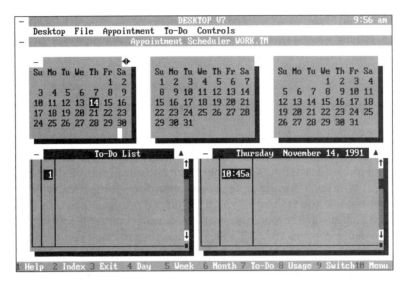

Fig. 3.1. *An appointment scheduler (PC Tools Version 7).*

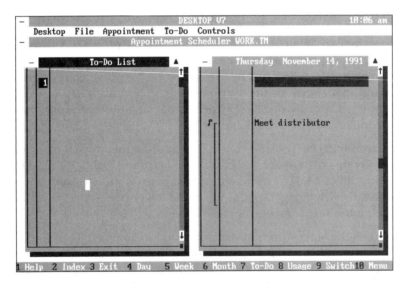

Fig. 3.2. *An appointment set with an alarm (PC Tools Version 7).*

After you set an appointment with an alarm, Desktop pops on-screen to remind you that an appointment is impending. You choose whether you want the alarm to appear 5 or 10 minutes before the appointment. In figure 3.3, you see an appointment that appears while Daren is writing a letter with Microsoft Works. Daren can choose the Snooze option, which displays the message again in five minutes, or OK, which confirms that he is aware of the appointment.

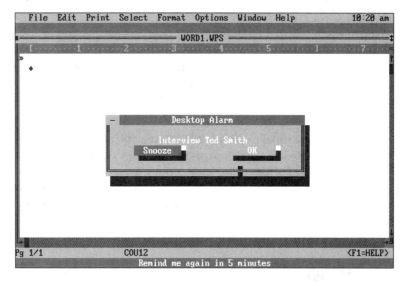

Fig. 3.3. An on-screen warning of an impending appointment (PC Tools Version 7).

Next, Daren adds some pressing items to his to-do list (see fig. 3.4). Desktop enables Daren to prioritize items on this list; doing the special orders comes before calling the Ecology Center.

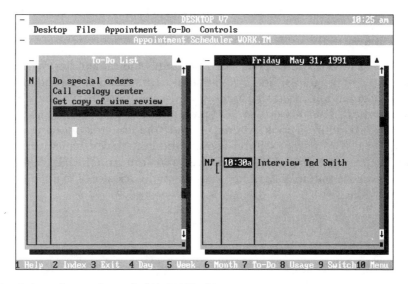

Fig. 3.4. Updating the to-do list (PC Tools).

Vertical Market Appointment Schedulers

If your business involves meeting clients, you should investigate special-purpose and vertical-market appointment scheduling programs, which may offer additional features tailored to your business needs. Therapist Helper (Brand Software), for example, offers counselors an appointment-management package with many additional features, such as managing information about patients.

For information on vertical market applications, talk to colleagues in your line of work and look for ads or reviews in trade or profession-related journalism magazines. Most of these programs aren't known outside the business or profession to which they're targeted—you won't find them, for example, in software stores, and they're seldom reviewed in mass-market personal computer magazines.

Keeping Track of Contacts

If your business has you spending long hours on the telephone with dozens of people, a contact manager (also called an *activity tracker*) may provide an excellent option for you. A contact manager closely resembles an appointment scheduling utility, but with an important difference: it includes a database of names, addresses, and phone numbers, and it can dial a number for you automatically. Most contact managers also include facilities for taking notes and post follow-up notices to your appointment book automatically.

SideKick 2.0 (Borland International) illustrates the capabilities of contact management programs. SideKick's appointment scheduler is wedded to an auto-dialer module that dials a number for you. Suppose that you have made a note to call Tom Roberts at 2:00 p.m. today. You switch to SideKick's Rolodex-like address book, where you find Tom Robert's phone number. With a click of the mouse, you activate the auto-dialer, which dials the number for you. You pick up the receiver, and Tom is on the line. As you're talking on the phone, you make notes that SideKick stores in a file under Tom's name.

TIP

> If you're using DOS, look for a terminate-and-stay-resident (TSR) contact manager that can pop up on-screen, even while you're working with another application. When the phone rings and Tom is on the line, you want to be able to display your notes and your schedule as soon as possible. If the contact manager isn't a TSR program, you have to save your work, exit to DOS, and load the contact manager before you can make notes.

Using a Personal Information Manager (PIM)

Computerized appointment schedulers are easy to understand because they closely resemble the paper-based appointment books that most of us use. Personal information managers are harder to understand, at least initially, because they use the computer's information-juggling features to give you capabilities that just aren't possible when using a real or simulated paper appointment book.

Lotus Agenda, the best-known personal information manager, illustrates how a PIM works. As shown in figure 3.5, Daren begins by typing the tasks he must accomplish in the left-hand column. Because you can type two or three lines of information, the task descriptions are much more informative than the 30 or 40 character descriptions you can type in an appointment scheduler. Now here's where Agenda does something an appointment scheduler cannot do: it gives you many ways to categorize the tasks that you have entered. The task *Call electrician next Monday about replacing circuit breakers*, for example, is categorized under Activity as a call, under Project as maintenance, and under When as 06/03/91. (Incidentally, Agenda works with a sophisticated pattern-matching program that tries to figure out how to categorize the task. If you type *next Monday*, for example, Agenda figures out the date and places it in the When column.)

A personal information manager is so useful and powerful because you can look at information in a variety of ways. With a few keystrokes, you can look at the information as you would in an appointment book (see fig. 3.6), or you can display the information grouped by the person to whom the task pertains (see fig. 3.7).

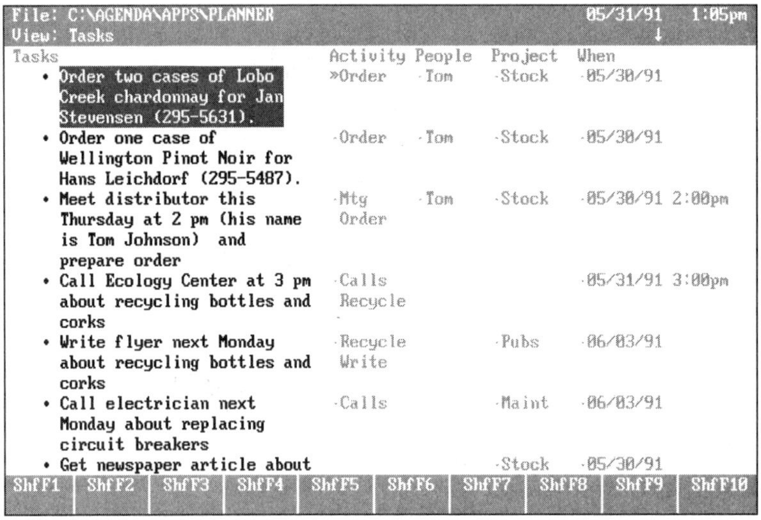

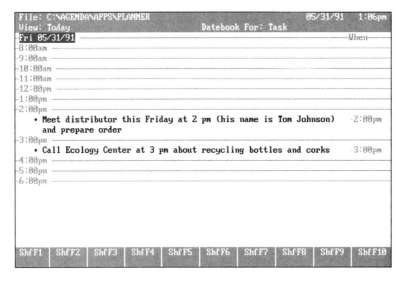

Fig. 3.5. Entering tasks in a personal information manager (Lotus Agenda).

Fig. 3.6. Displaying today's tasks (Lotus Agenda).

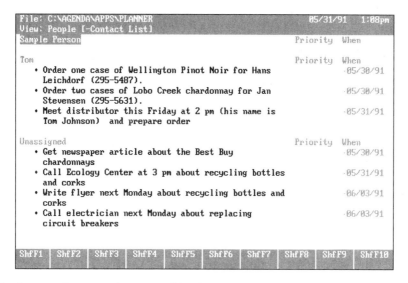

Fig. 3.7. Displaying tasks grouped by the person to whom it pertains (Lotus Agenda).

As Daren explores Lotus Agenda, he finds that he can organize information according to any category that he invents. In a few keystrokes, he can organize his tasks in just the way he wants—calls to make, orders to place, letters to write, flyers to design, issues to resolve. Agenda turns out to be the right choice for Daren's business.

Using Project Management Programs

If your business responsibilities involve managing people who are working on projects that must stick to a budget, you can profit from adding a project management program to your software library. And you don't have to be a million-dollar contractor to benefit from these programs. If you even occasionally find yourself trying to plan a project—such as developing a new line of merchandise, preparing for an advertising campaign, or launching a new service—you may find project management software helpful.

A project management program goes beyond an appointment scheduler or a PIM in that it includes tools for viewing a project's schedule (in the form of an on-screen Gantt chart or time line) and for tracking project expenses (see fig. 3.8). An on-screen view of a project's time line is very helpful for seeing whether enough time has been allotted to a task. Often, the fact that you haven't allotted enough time for a job becomes evident when you see a graphic time line on your computer's screen.

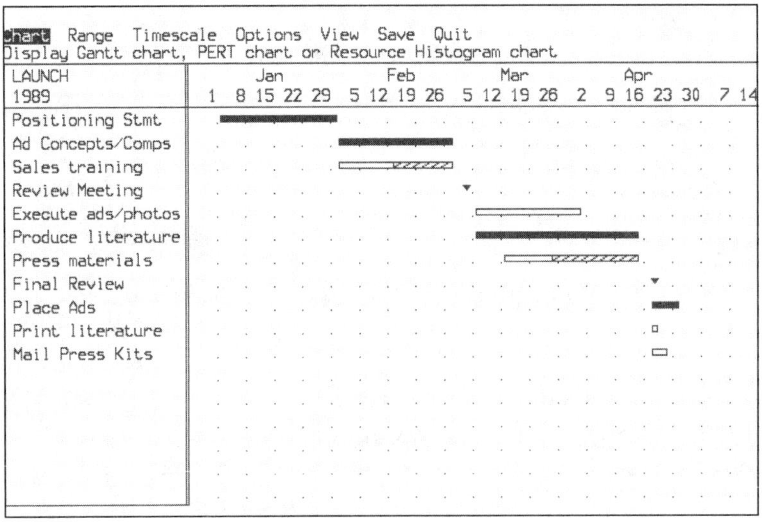

```
Chart  Range  Timescale  Options  View  Save  Quit
Display Gantt chart, PERT chart or Resource Histogram chart.
LAUNCH              Jan          Feb          Mar          Apr
1989           1  8 15 22 29  5 12 19 26  5 12 19 26  2  9 16 23 30  7 14
Positioning Stmt
Ad Concepts/Comps
Sales training
Review Meeting
Execute ads/photos
Produce literature
Press materials
Final Review
Place Ads
Print literature
Mail Press Kits
```

Fig. 3.8. A time line for a project (Project Calc Resources).

To use a project manager, you begin creating an outline of the tasks that must be completed and specifying the resources (people, time, and money) that must be devoted to the task so that it can be completed on time. Then you can switch to an on-screen time line that displays each task with the dates you have chosen. The best programs enable you to manipulate the time line directly, allotting more time for some tasks and less for others. Most programs can display and print schedules for each task or project. Some programs automatically detect scheduling conflicts, overburdened people or resources, and the *critical path* (the tasks that must be completed if the project is to move on successfully).

The time lines and Gantt charts that you can create with a project management program may come in handy when you're proposing a job to a client. If you work up a time line as part of your proposal, you're sending the client a message that you're well organized, that you know how to cope with all the details, that you can devote the resources necessary to the job, and that you are likely to complete the job on time.

Summary

Here's a summary of this chapter's main points:

- *Computerized time management makes sense if you're near your computer all day.* If you're often away, you're probably better off with an old-fashioned, paper-based diary such as a DayTimer.

- *Appointment schedulers are easy to use because they resemble paper-based diaries and to-do lists.* The better programs present an on-screen warning 5 or 10 minutes before an appointment. Appointment schedulers are the best choice if you meet people frequently. Vertical-market programs may offer special advantages.

- *Contact managers combine an appointment scheduler with a database of names, addresses, and telephone numbers.* They also include an autodialer and facilities for taking notes on phone conversations. They're an excellent choice for anyone who spends a lot of time dealing with customers on the phone.

- *Personal information managers (PIMs) record tasks and then enable you to view the tasks in a variety of ways.* PIMs are harder to learn and use, however. PIMs may be the best choice if you routinely perform a wide variety of tasks and need to see quick summaries of them, sorted in different ways.

- *Project management programs help you plan and administer a project.* By portraying the project using an on-screen time line or Gantt chart, such programs help you see whether you have allocated sufficient time and resources to an activity. These programs also include budgeting and cost-tracking utilities. They are an excellent choice for anyone who must manage projects frequently.

Software Suggestions

You will find rich software resources for time management in all three environments: DOS, Macintosh, and Windows. DOS is particularly strong in personal information managers. You will find that the Macintosh and Windows environments excel in the project management area, in large part because a graphics display lends itself naturally to the time lines and graphs that these programs create.

DOS Time Management Programs

- *Harvard Project Manager (Software Publishing Corporation):* A respected project-management program that employs critical-path methods and enables you to directly manipulate on-screen graphic displays.

- *Instant Recall (Chronologic):* An inexpensive contact manager and appointment scheduler that offers autodialing, mailing list/address book, and alarms.

- *Lotus Agenda (Lotus Development Corporation):* By far the most flexible and feature-rich PIM available, Agenda exemplifies the best that personal information management software has to offer. Some people find it hard to learn, mainly because the concepts are unfamiliar. With some practice and experience, these concepts quickly become clear.

- *PC Tools (Central Point Software):* Included in this package of utilities is Desktop, which offers a notepad, an excellent appointment scheduler, telecommunications with autodialer, and much more. You easily can develop a contact manager using Desktop's tools.

- *Project Call Resources (Frontline Systems):* An add-in program for Lotus 1-2-3, this program adds project management and time-line graphing capabilities to this popular spreadsheet program.

- *Time Line (Symantec Corporation):* A project management program with excellent output capabilities, Time Line can produce crisply printed summaries, wall charts, and files that can be converted into 35mm slides.

- *Time Sheet Professional (Timeslips Corporation):* A project-tracking program that is organized around week-at-a-glance views of each project. The people doing the work can record their time and expenses themselves, freeing the project manager of the tedium of data entry that is otherwise required to keep the resource and expense databases up-to-date.

Macintosh Time Management Programs

- *MacProject II (Claris Corporation):* A project management program that uses the Macintosh's graphic display to good effect: you access project-related information by directly manipulating the on-screen time line.

- *QuickDex (Casady and Greene):* A contact manager that functions as a Desk Accessory (DA), so it's always available when you're using other programs.

- *Smart Alarms with Appointment Diary (JAM Software):* This special-purpose appointment scheduler provides the appointment-scheduling capabilities that are missing from the Macintosh system software. You can make appointments and set a variety of alarms, which pop up over other programs that you're using.

Windows Time Management Programs

- *CaLANdar (Microsystems Software Inc.):* One of the accessories provided free of charge with Windows, CaLANdar is a basic appointment scheduler with an alarm, but it lacks a to-do list. When used with Cardfile, a Rolodex-like data manager with an autodialer, this accessory can become a simple but effective contact manager.

- *IBM Current (IBM):* Combines many of the attributes of an appointment scheduler, a personal information manager, and a project management program. You can create and display an appointment diary, look at tasks in a variety of ways, and print time line charts.

- *DeskTop Set (Okna):* An excellent contact manager that includes a programmable auto-dialer and an on-screen phone book. The phone book separates personal and business numbers.

- *Finalsoft Executive (Finalsoft Corporation):* An appointment scheduler and contact manager that also includes many additional features, including a notepad, a database reader, and a to-do list with deadline monitoring.

- *On Target (Symantec Corporation):* An excellent project management program that includes a master calendar, automatic schedule conflict detection, cost tracking, and many other features—all with the easy-to-use Windows interface.

Hand-Held Organizers

- *Sharp Wizard (Sharp Electronics):* This hand-held computer with a two-line display works by battery or AC current and functions as an address, telephone, and appointment book. Also included are a calculator, expense log, message pad, and alarm clock. Optional software add-ins are available, and you can connect the Organizer to your computer through your computer's RS-232 serial port.

Developing a
Mailing List

One of your most valuable business assets is your mailing list, and it doesn't matter whether it's large or small. Either way, a mailing list provides the information you need to send customers information about your business through a still-inexpensive channel: the U.S. Postal Service. Part of getting organized in your business is to do all you can to build your mailing list, to keep it accurate, and to use it frequently to stay in touch with your customers.

With a personal computer and the right software, you have access to a tool—the computerized mailing list—that big companies have used for years to blitz every house in America with tons of junk mail. Now small businesses can use the same technology for mailings on a smaller scale. You'll need to equip your system with software that helps you manage your mailing list and also prints names and addresses on commercially-available peel-and-stick mailing labels (also called *pressure-sensitive labels*). Just about any computer can handle continuous-feed labels, which are drawn through your printer by its tractor-feed mechanism, or sheet labels, which can be used by any printer (such as a laser printer) that can load a full, cut sheet of paper at one time. This chapter introduces your mailing list software options, surveys the benefits of computerized mailing list management, and examines in detail the two software options that are best for small business.

Almost every business can profit from developing and maintaining a mailing list, but it's more important for some businesses than others. If you don't see yourself doing a great deal of mailings, then the major reason for maintaining a mailing list probably has to do with billing. You may be better off with an accounting or billing program that has mailing-list management and label-printing capabilities built in (examples are Timeslips III, a time-billing program, and Pacioli 2000, a complete accounting package). For more information, see Chapter 13, "Billing for Time and Expenses," and Chapter 14, "Keeping the Books."

Exploring Mailing List Software Options

For a small business, the big advantage of maintaining a computerized mailing list isn't to send out 50,000 brochures. Even if you could afford it, what would you do if every 50 brochures resulted in an inquiry that took you 15 minutes to deal with? On the contrary, the small business advantage lies in developing targeted mailings, where you've selected, out of all the names you have, a short, focused list of current customers and promising prospects. So a crucial feature of the software you need is the ability to select just those records that meet the criteria for a specific mailing.

Janet runs an employee training firm, and she discovered this point the hard way. "I deal with a lot of different interest groups," Janet says. "Some of them are interested in communication skills training, while others are interested in health education. I was wasting my time and money sending the same brochures to everyone on my mailing list." Janet codes her mailing list by interest so that when she sends out a brochure, it is aimed at the audience that's most likely to respond.

You have many software options for creating and developing a mailing list. Given the advantage of reducing your mailing to focused groups, though, you can rule out some of these software options right away. Others are hard to learn and require considerable development effort.

The following is a quick overview of mailing list software options:

- *Desktop accessories:* Programs such as Microsoft Windows provide desktop accessories. These sometimes include simple Rolodex-like database managers, such as Windows' Cardfile accessory. These accessories often are useful for contact management, as discussed in Chapter 3, but they are less suitable for mailing list applications: they don't enable you to select just those records that meet your criteria. These programs usually don't do a very good job of printing mailing labels, if they can print them at all (Cardfile can't).

- *Word processing programs:* Full-featured word processing programs, such as Microsoft Word or WordPerfect, can be used to create mailing lists, but sorting and selecting operations are impossible or cumbersome. Worse, these programs are challenging to learn, and you'll have to spend time getting the program to print your labels correctly.

- *Database management programs:* Database management programs, such as dBASE or Personal R:BASE, offer powerful tools for designing a mailing list database, sorting and selecting the information it contains, and printing mailing labels. These programs are hard to learn, however, and you'll have to spend time developing and troubleshooting the mailing list/mailing label application.

- *Mailing list managers:* Special-purpose mailing list managers, such as FastPak Mail, solve the shortcomings of the previous software options. These managers include a special-purpose mailing list database, which makes it easy to sort and select records in a variety of ways, and they also include preconfigured printer settings for just about every mailing label made. These managers have one drawback, however: their databases aren't very flexible in that you can't add your own data fields. Sometimes it's very useful to add your own data fields, as this chapter explains.

- *Integrated programs:* Works (Microsoft Corporation) and Q&A (Symantec Corporation) offer an excellent solution to the mailing list software puzzle. Easy to learn and use, they include database managers that enable you to add all the data fields you want, and they also include preconfigured printer settings for most commercially available mailing labels. These programs are an especially good choice if you want to send personalized form letters—form letters that draw on your mailing list data to generate letters that look as though they had been individually typed.

- *Accounting and billing programs with built-in mailing list management:* This is the best choice for a business that doesn't plan to use the mailing list as a marketing tool and just wants help with sending out the monthly bills.

Because mailing list managers and integrated programs offer the best combination of benefits for businesses that want to take advantage of direct-mail marketing, this chapter closely examines these two options. But don't rule out database management and word processing programs. If you have reason to buy and learn programs such as WordPerfect or Personal R:BASE for other applications, it may be worth your time and effort to develop a mailing list application with them.

Looking at the Benefits of Computerized Mailing List Management

Depending on which program or programs you're using, you can obtain some of the following benefits after you computerize your mailing list:

- *Easy entry and editing of new names and addresses.* Ideally, you should be able to edit the names you have stored in a columnar list. An editable list display makes it easy to go down the list, find errors, and correct them.

- *Flexible sorting capabilities, including last name, ZIP code, and interest code.* You should be able to sort your mailing list quickly in a variety of ways. ZIP code sorting is especially important for bulk mailing, because you get lower rates if the material is sorted by ZIP code.

- *Quick, computer-assisted retrieval of a customer's name and address.* You should be able to find a single address fast; ideally, you should be able to print a single envelope or label quickly.

- *Coding of records so that you can group names together for focused mailings.* You should be able to define at least five different codes, and there should be enough room for naming the codes so that you can use descriptive names.

- *Automatic detection and elimination of duplicates.* This feature is particularly important for large mailing lists.

- *Automatic combining of mailing lists with elimination of duplicates ("merge and purge").* This feature is very important if you have two versions of your mailing list—such as one on your laptop computer and one on your desktop computer—that you periodically want to combine.

- *Automatic printing of reports required by the U.S. Postal Service for bulk mailings.* This is a very desirable feature if you're hoping to take advantage of bulk mailing rates.

- *Automatic printing of U.S. Postal Service bar codes on labels so that your mailings can qualify for lower bulk mail rates.* The U.S. Postal Service has machines that scan envelopes for bar codes. If you have a laser printer, you can print these codes if your software supports bar codes. You get a break on bulk mail rates if you add the bar codes to labels or envelopes.

- *Predefined printer settings for printing on a wide variety of commercial peel-and-stick labels.* Ideally, the program will come with a dozen or more preconfigured printer templates for popular computer labels. It's a hassle to define your own templates, so look for a program that includes preconfigured templates for the labels you're planning to use.

- *Sample mailings to every 5th or 10th name on the list to see what kind of response the mailing generates.* This feature is drawn from professional, mainframe mailing programs. It can be useful if you're doing a lot of direct-mail marketing.

- *Automatic comparison of your mailing list to a U.S. Postal Service database of every valid address in the United States, available on a CD-ROM disk.* It's true! You can purchase a CD-ROM disk that contains every valid address (not names, though) and compare it to your own mailing list. You quickly discover errors. This feature is an advanced one, though, that's of interest only to serious mail marketers.

- *Flexible database configuration that enables you to store much more information than just a customer's name and address.* Very few mailing list managers offer this feature; to get it, you'll have to use a database management program, or an integrated program with a database module. The big question: how much will you lose in development costs?

Setting Up Mailing Lists

As a child, Ken loved to read science fiction and fantasy novels, as well as to collect comic books, and he's turned those interests into a very profitable retail business near a state university campus. Each of Ken's customers tend to express strong interest in just one of the four major areas he stocks: science fiction, fantasy, comics, and role-playing games; only occasionally does a customer express interest in all four. Ken envisions targeted mailings, which would save him money by reaching just the customers who express an interest in one of the areas (or in all of the areas).

To collect the information he needs, Ken invites his customers to fill out a form to add their names to his mailing list, and also to indicate their interests. Already, Ken has developed a list of more than 1,000 people in an area spanning six counties. All of these people are comic book collectors or avid fans of at least one of Ken's product lines. The customers are eager to fill out Ken's questionnaires; they're looking forward to receiving information from Ken.

As he ponders computerizing his mailing list, Ken evaluates two approaches: one using a special-purpose mailing list package (FastPak Mail), and the other using an integrated program (Microsoft Works). Here's what Ken has discovered.

Mailing List Programs

By far the easiest way to create and maintain a mailing list for your business, as well as to print mailing labels, is to use a special-purpose mailing list package, such as FastPak Mail (Bloc Publishing). These packages incorporate the development effort that you would otherwise have to expend to design the data form. The packages also incorporate the even more tedious development effort involved in setting up printing formats for mailing labels, Rolodex cards, Federal Express airbills, and UPS shipping labels. You can sort the records—with FastPak Mail, up to a maximum of 65,000 names and addresses—in a variety of ways, including by company name and ZIP code.

Like most other special-purpose mailing list programs, FastPak Mail offers features that would be hard to match unless you were to hire a programmer to customize a database application. Such features include the following:

- Automatic elimination of duplicate records.

- Automatic capitalization of the first letter of each name (no need to press the Shift key).

- Automatic skipping of unused fields when printing (no easy trick to pull off if you're creating your own mailing list application with a word processing or database management program).

- Capability to repeat a field entry without retyping.

- Capability to generate bulk mail reports (the Post Office gives you a price break on bulk mail if you sort the mail by ZIP code and provide a report of the number of items for each ZIP code).

When you start a mailing list program such as FastPak Mail, you see a predefined data form such as the one shown in figure 4.1. Using the codes, Ken fills out the record shown in figure 4.2 for Julia Kenwood.

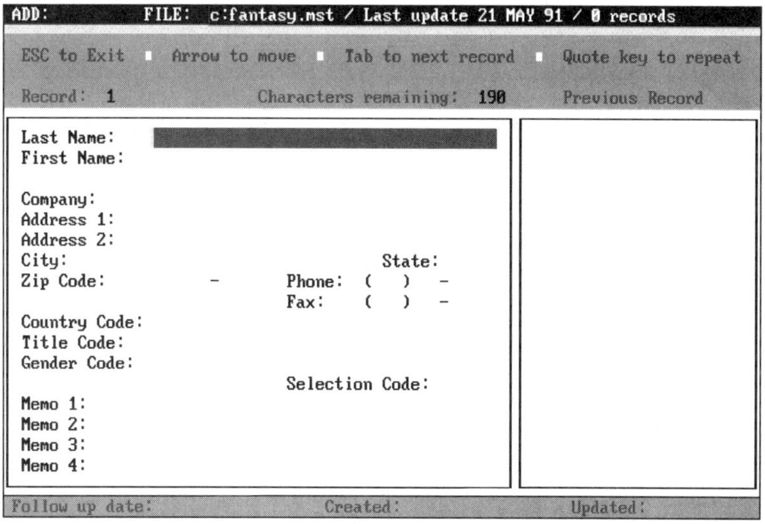

```
ADD:          FILE:  c:fantasy.mst / Last update 21 MAY 91 / 0 records

ESC to Exit  ▪  Arrow to move  ▪  Tab to next record  ▪  Quote key to repeat

Record: 1                    Characters remaining:  190      Previous Record

    Last Name:
    First Name:

    Company:
    Address 1:
    Address 2:
    City:                             State:
    Zip Code:           -       Phone:  (   )  -
                                Fax:    (   )  -
    Country Code:
    Title Code:
    Gender Code:
                                Selection Code:
    Memo 1:
    Memo 2:
    Memo 3:
    Memo 4:

Follow up date:              Created:              Updated:
```

Fig. 4.1. A predefined data form in a mailing list program (FastPak Mail).

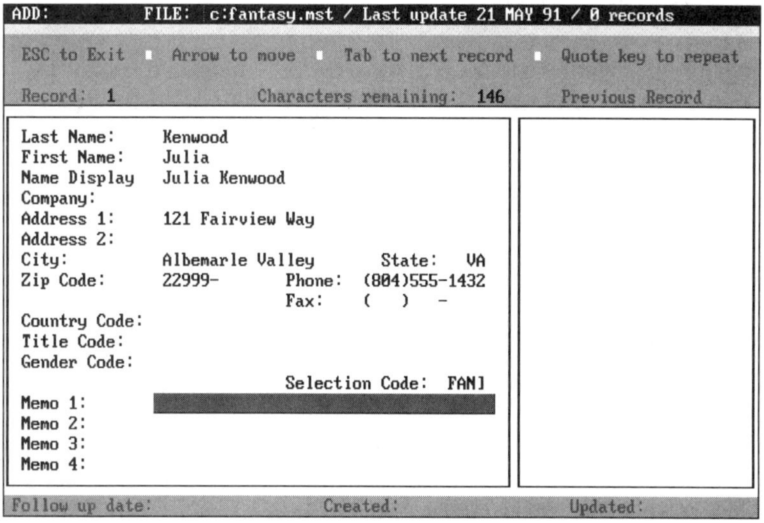

```
ADD:          FILE:  c:fantasy.mst / Last update 21 MAY 91 / 0 records

ESC to Exit  ▪  Arrow to move  ▪  Tab to next record  ▪  Quote key to repeat

Record: 1                    Characters remaining:  146      Previous Record

    Last Name:    Kenwood
    First Name:   Julia
    Name Display  Julia Kenwood
    Company:
    Address 1:    121 Fairview Way
    Address 2:
    City:         Albemarle Valley    State:  VA
    Zip Code:     22999-        Phone:  (804)555-1432
                                Fax:    (   )  -
    Country Code:
    Title Code:
    Gender Code:
                                Selection Code:  FAN]
    Memo 1:
    Memo 2:
    Memo 3:
    Memo 4:

Follow up date:              Created:              Updated:
```

Fig. 4.2. A coded data record (FastPak Mail).

In evaluating FastPak Mail, Ken notes that it's possible to code each data record using a coding scheme such as the one shown in table 3.1.

Table 3.1
Ken's Mailing List Codes

Code	Meaning
SCI	Science fiction interest
FAN	Fantasy interest
COM	Comics interest
ROL	Role-playing game interest
ALL	All interests

After Ken adds names, addresses, and codes to his mailing list, he can print using a wide variety of preconfigured print formats: mailing labels (FastPak Mail is preconfigured for just about every label made, including laser labels), rotary index cards, envelopes, invoices, postcards, and file labels.

Integrated Programs

Ken is impressed with FastPak Mail, but a friend who is in the same business swears by Works (Microsoft Corporation), an integrated program. When Ken looks into Works, he finds that the program's database module offers him much more flexibility in the type of information he can record, but at the sacrifice of requiring him to spend a little time creating the mailing label application.

Database Flexibility

One of the major limitations of a mailing list manager such as FastPak Mail is that you can't add your own data fields. You can code records, but compared to the flexibility a database manager offers, mailing list managers sharply restrict the variety of data you can enter about your customers. If you have a reason to enter more data about your customers than a mailing list package permits, then—as Ken discovered—you have ample reason to consider using an integrated program such as Works.

When Ken discovered that he could enter any data field he wanted to (in addition to the usual name, address, and phone fields), he started thinking about storing additional information about his customers. Ken quickly realized that many of his customers were asking him to look out for comic books they were collecting. If Ken remembered such requests, he made a note of them and watched for the issues when he purchased used comic books, but more often than not, he forgot to write them down or lost the note. So Ken envisioned a data form design such as the one shown in figure 4.3.

```
 File  Edit  Print  Select  Format  Options  View  Window  Help

                            ═══════ DATA1.WDB ═══════
    Last name: Gutierrez
    First name: Manny
    Address1: 171 College Terrace
    Address2: Apartment #110
    City: Periwinkle
    State: VA
    Zip: 22998
    Phone: (804)-555-9090
    ─────────────────────────────────────────────────────────
    Interests  Sci-Fi:   Fantasy:  Comics: Y Games: Y
    ─────────────────────────────────────────────────────────
    Collection information
       Title: Turok, Son of Stone
       Dates: 1959, 1960, 1961
       Willing to Pay: $10/issue

3              3/3       FORM Pg 1   X3.10"  Y3.50"        <F1=HELP>
Press ALT to choose commands; type text followed by colon (:) to create field.
```

Fig. 4.3. A data form design for mailing a list application (Microsoft Works).

As you'll see, the ability to store more data exacts a cost (Ken will have to spend some time developing the mailing label application with Works), but he'll get increased data retrieval capability in return.

Development

Using Works would give Ken an advantage in that he could store more information about his customers and retrieve that information quickly, but this approach has a minor disadvantage. Unlike FastPak Mail, Works lacks the preconfigured settings for printing mailing labels. To print mailing labels or Rolodex cards, Ken will have to follow this procedure:

1. Create a new word processing file and add placeholders, as shown in figure 4.4.

    A *placeholder* tells Works where to print a certain kind of information drawn from the database. In figure 4.4, for example, Ken has shown Works where to print the information stored in the Last Name field in his database.

If this sounds complicated, bear in mind that Works (like Symantec's Q&A, a similar program) enables you to choose the placeholders from menus. This procedure is a lot easier than typing the placeholders yourself, as you must in most full-featured word processing programs.

After Ken chooses the fields, his mailing label document looks like the one shown in figure 4.5.

2. Define the print settings for the mailing labels or Rolodex cards he's using (see fig. 4.6).

   To define the print settings, Ken uses a menu that enables him to choose between single-column and three-column labels, and another menu that enables him to choose additional printing settings.

It isn't a huge job to define the print settings needed to print labels correctly. However, you'll probably have to test the settings several times before you get them right.

Fig. 4.4. Choosing placeholders from a menu.

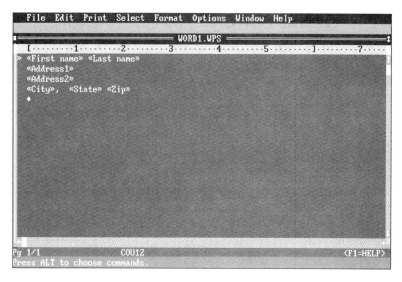

Fig. 4.5. *The completed mailing label document.*

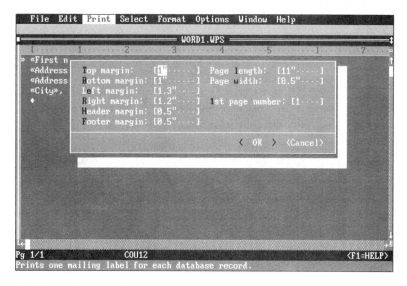

Fig. 4.6. *Selecting the print settings.*

More Retrieval Power

In return for the modest amount of development work Ken must do, he receives a big payoff: increased flexibility of data retrieval. To illustrate this point, suppose that a customer comes in with a copy of *The Green Lantern*, a rare comic published in the late 1950s and early 1960s. He pays the customer $4 for the comic and sits down at Works to perform a query. Here's what he does:

1. With his customer database open, Ken chooses the Query command.

   This command displays what amounts to a blank data form, in which Ken types filters. *Filters* tell Works how to retrieve the data in the database. In figure 4.7, Ken is saying, in effect, "Show me all the records of my customers who are collecting *The Green Lantern*."

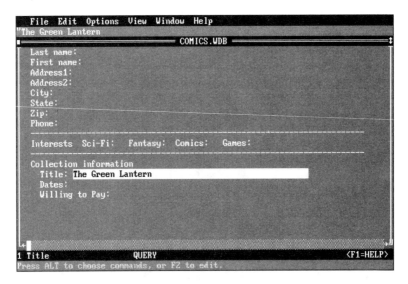

***Fig. 4.7.** Performing a query on mailing list databases.*

2. Ken chooses the command that processes the query. The result is a view of the database: a subset of all his customer records, containing only those customers who are collecting *The Green Lantern*.

And there's a hit! Julia Adams is collecting *The Green Lantern* (see fig. 4.8). Ken makes use of a nifty Works feature that uses the modem Ken has attached to his computer: with the highlight on Julia's phone number, he chooses the Dial This Number command, and Works dials the number for him. He just picks up the receiver as the phone starts to ring!

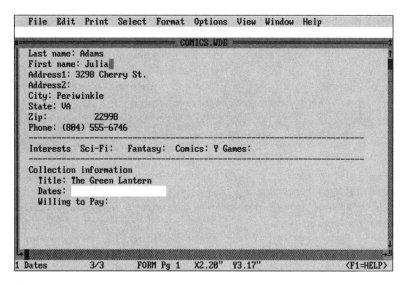

File Edit Print Select Format Options View Window Help

COMICS.WDB

```
Last name: Adams
First name: Julia
Address1: 3298 Cherry St.
Address2:
City: Periwinkle
State: VA
Zip:        22998
Phone: (804) 555-6746
---------------------------------------------------------
Interests  Sci-Fi:   Fantasy:  Comics: Y Games:
---------------------------------------------------------
Collection information
  Title: The Green Lantern
  Dates:
  Willing to Pay:
```

1 Dates   3/3   FORM Pg 1   X2.20" Y3.17"   <F1=HELP>

Fig. 4.8. Viewing a customer record.

Ken decides to go for the Works solution rather than FastPak Mail, but he acknowledges that someone who doesn't need the additional database flexibility is just as well off with a special-purpose mail manager. Works is right for Ken, but bear in mind that the program's database module is weak in comparison with many other programs; it's OK for mailing list applications, but the program would be far from the best choice for many other information-management tasks. For more information, see Chapter 5, "Managing Information."

If you print with continuous, tractor-fed labels frequently, consider adding a label printer to your system. Label printers are inexpensive peripherals that aren't meant to replace your main printer. These printers come into play only when labels are printed, and free users from the tedium involved in removing ordinary paper from the printer, inserting labels, and getting them aligned properly. Another option is to purchase an inexpensive dot-matrix printer that is permanently stocked with continuous-feed, three-column labels.

TIP

Word Processing Programs

Before you settle on a mailing list program, be sure to read Chapter 7, "Tackling Routine Business Correspondence." In that chapter, you learn that there are two big advantages to a close marriage between your mailing list manager and your word processing program. If your word processor can draw names and addresses from your mailing list, you can avoid typing the same name and address twice (once in your mailing list, and a second time in your letter). You also can take advantage of personalized form letters. A personalized form letter sends the same message to all correspondents, but each letter is personalized with each correspondent's name and address, so it looks as though the letter has been typed individually.

To take advantage of the mailing list/word processor connection, choose an integrated program (such as Works or Q&A) or a mailing list manager that includes, or works with, a letter-writing program. An example is FastPak Mail 5.0 (DOS systems), which includes a simple word processing program that is ideal for writing letters, or Address Book Plus for the Macintosh, which is designed to work with Letter Writer Plus.

Summary

Here's a summary of this chapter's main points:

- A mailing list is a valuable business resource, but for a small business, you want software that enables you to select names and addresses for focused mailings.

- The two best software options for small businesses are mailing list managers (such as FastPak Mail) and integrated programs (such as Microsoft Works or Q&A).

- Mailing list managers give you many of the tools of professional, mainframe mailing list programs, such as sample mailings, record coding, and "merge-and-purge." To gain more data-storage flexibility, you can use a database management program instead, but you lose some of these professional mailing list manager features.

- Although you can create a few codes with a mailing list manager, database managers give you much more flexible tools for categorizing your names and addresses. Given the limited mailing budgets of small businesses, it's especially important to target subsets of your mailing list with precision.

Software Suggestions

You'll find the richest trove of mailing list software in the DOS environment, but you can find good software for the Macintosh as well. As of this writing, very little is available for Windows, but by the time you read this book, one or more programs probably will be available.

DOS Programs for Mailing List Applications

- *FastPak Mail (Bloc Publishing):* An inexpensive mailing list manager that offers good value. Advanced features include automatic elimination of duplicates, record coding, automatic capitalization, sample mailings using every *n*th address, dozens of preconfigured templates for mailing labels and envelopes, and many more output capabilities (Federal Express airbills, U.S. Postal Service Express Mail airbills, United Parcel Service C.O.D. labels, postcards, Pendaflex labels, and more). An important plus: Version 5 includes an integrated word processing program that makes this program ideal for letter-writing applications (see Chapter 7, "Tackling Routine Business Correspondence"). You can change field names, and the program prints U.S. Postal Service bar codes.

- *Professional Mail (Arc Tangent)*: A professional-quality mailing list manager. It includes the following advanced features: automatic elimination of duplicates, presorting of mail by mailing class, printing of U.S. Postal Service bar codes and required reports for bulk mailings, automatic generation of sample mailings using every 10th address, and preconfigured templates for a wide variety of mailing labels.

- *Q&A (Symantec Corporation):* An integrated program that combines high-quality word processing and database management modules. Q&A is a better choice than Works if you want to rely on the word processor or database for more advanced work. The database manager includes a lookup function (lacking in Works' database), for example, which makes it suitable for other database applications besides mailing lists. The program includes a good selection of preconfigured mailing label templates.

- *Works (Microsoft Corporation):* An integrated program that includes a database manager, a word processor, a spreadsheet, and telecommunications capabilities. An excellent choice for mailing list management, the program includes preconfigured templates for a variety of mailing labels. The database manager lacks a lookup feature, however, which decreases the database module's usefulness for other database management tasks. See Chapter 5, "Managing Information," for more information on the lookup feature.

- *Zip ++ (Arc Tangent):* Comes on a CD-ROM disk, so you can't use it unless you equip your system with a CD-ROM drive. But here's what you get, and it isn't a misprint: a list, 3.2 gigabytes in length, of every valid address in the United States. Using this disk, you can compare your mailing list against this list of valid addresses, highlighting errors immediately. In addition, Zip ++ supplies the Carrier Route codes and U.S. Postal Service bar codes that you must print to qualify for the lowest bulk mail rates. Designed to work with Arc Tangent's Professional Mail.

Macintosh Programs for Mailing List Applications

- *Address Book Plus (PowerUp):* A mailing list manager with flexible output capabilities; you can print rotary-file cards, mailing labels, and envelopes in a wide range of preconfigured or custom formats. A very important plus: this program works seamlessly with Letter Writer Plus, an excellent choice for business letter writing. See Chapter 7, "Tackling Routine Business Correspondence," for more information.

- *FILE FORCE (ACIUS):* FILE FORCE is a sophisticated database management program that can use more than one database at a time, but it is designed for ease of use. A fast and powerful program, FILE FORCE is ideal for very large mailing list applications, and it includes a good selection of preconfigured templates for printing labels.

- *Kiwi Envelopes (Kiwi Software):* Prints envelopes one at a time from addresses copied from a word processing program. A plus: if your system is equipped with a laser printer, the program prints U.S. Postal Service bar codes on the envelopes.

- *MacEnvelope Plus (Synex):* A mailing list manager with flexible output capabilities; you can print on virtually any commercial label made as well as a variety of envelope sizes, using any of over 100 preconfigured templates for envelopes and labels. Capable of handling up to 100,000 names and addresses, the program handles multilevel sorts and eliminates duplicate names.

- *MacLabelPro (Avery):* Comes from the people who make the labels. Naturally, there are preconfigured templates for every label Avery makes. The program is weak on database management, however; you import the mailing list from another Macintosh application.

- *Works (Microsoft Corporation):* An integrated program that offers (among other modules) an easy-to-use database manager that generates mailing labels easily. Included are preconfigured templates for many popular mailing labels. The database management module is weak, however, and is not recommended for other data-management applications; it lacks a lookup function. See Chapter 5, "Managing Information," for more information on this feature and its importance.

5

Managing Information

W hen it comes to managing routine information such as names and addresses, special-purpose database programs such as mailing list managers or contact managers may do the job well. These programs incorporate a lot of the development effort that you would otherwise have to expend yourself. They do such things as designing the data forms and configuring printer templates. But what about information that is unique to your business?

Here's an example of business information for which no ready-to-run, special-purpose program is available. Charles teaches business courses during the day, but nights and weekends are reserved for a hobby that has become a good business: selling Civil War memorabilia and artifacts on consignment. Charles advertises in several Civil War-related publications, and he needs to answer inquiries quickly. His shoebox full of index cards simply will not do: he's spending too much time sorting the cards, and he cannot find cards quickly enough when a customer calls. Increasingly overwhelmed by the task of managing information in his growing business, Charles may find that database management software addresses his critical application needs.

In this chapter, you learn how to decide whether (like Charles) your business needs the assistance of a database management program, and you learn about the available software options. You also see how Charles develops a database management application for his business.

Deciding Whether You Need a Database Program

If your business deals with unique information, and lots of it, you may reap big benefits from buying a database management program and designing your own custom database. But how can you be sure? And is the development effort worth it? Only you can answer that question, but there are some guidelines that may help you decide whether computerizing your business's information is worth the effort. Do you see your business's situation in any of these statements?

- *The information you're dealing with cannot be handled by a special-purpose program.* Remember the rule: "Don't reinvent the wheel." There is little justification for spending weeks trying to customize a database for accounting operations, such as accounts receivables, inventory, general ledger, or payroll, because you can buy special-purpose programs that are customized for these applications. For more information, see Part IV, "Keeping Business Records." Is the information that you're dealing with really unique, or is there a special-purpose or vertical-market program that may suit your needs?

- *You cannot keep track of the information using manual methods.* Don't bother typing information into a database if you gain nothing by doing so. Why create a database of one or two hundred magazine clippings from a trade journal, when you can store and retrieve them easily from a well-organized file drawer (or a couple of three-ring binders)? You shouldn't consider computerized database management unless manual storage and retrieval methods are threatening your business's ability to grow.

- *You can benefit from looking at the information in more than one way.* A major benefit of computerized database management is that you can sort information on any field. Charles can quickly produce a list of artifacts sorted by price, by battlefield of origin, by artifact type (gun, cap, belt, shoe, and so on), or by year of origin. If you never need to sort information in more than one way, a manual storage and retrieval system may do—or you can simply create a list with a word processing program, most of which can sort by line or by paragraph.

- *You can benefit by having the computer reduce huge amounts of information to show only the relevant information.* Charles has more than 1,000 artifacts in his database, but when a collector calls and says, "I'm interested in just one thing: Confederate guns," his program can quickly narrow the list to the one or two records that qualify. If you never need to reduce information in this way, manual methods may suffice.

- *Maintaining the database is worth the effort.* It takes time to type new records, correct errors, eliminate duplicates, and back up the database regularly. If the database isn't paying off, chances are you will not keep it up, and it will become useless.

If you can recognize your own information-management situation in one or more of the preceding statements, developing a database may be a key step in your quest for improved organization.

Looking At Database Management Software Options

Single-purpose database management programs are divided into two categories: flat file database managers and relational database managers. Here's a brief, nontechnical explanation of the difference—and what it means to you.

Flat-File Database Managers

Flat-file database management programs usually are easy to learn and use, but they work with only one database at a time. This system may raise a serious problem: you are likely to have to enter the same information in more than one place.

Here's an example. Suppose that Charles decides to create a database to keep track of who owes him money. Michael Olezczek orders a Confederate cap, and Charles creates the following record:

LASTNAME:	Olezczek
FIRSTNAME:	Michael
ADDRESS:	129 Oakleaf Way
CITY:	East Shadwell
STATE:	VA
ZIP:	22887
PHONE:	(804) 555-9999
ITEM:	Confederate cap
BILLED:	$595
DATE BILLED:	11/29/91
PAID:	No

Not satisfied to own just a Confederate cap, Michael then orders a Union cap, and Charles creates *another* record:

LASTNAME:	Olezcek
FIRSTNAME:	Michael
ADDRESS:	129 Oakleaf Way
CITY:	East Shadwell
STATE:	VA
ZIP:	22887
PHONE:	(804) 555-9999
ITEM:	Union cap
BILLED:	$395
DATE BILLED:	12/03/91
PAID:	No

Did you notice the typing error? In the second record, Charles typed Michael's last name wrong—there's a *z* missing.

What's the problem here? It's called *data redundancy*—typing the same data in two or more places. Typing the data twice is a waste of time, but that is only one problem. A worse problem is that if you type the data wrong in one or more places, retrieval operations will not be accurate. And what happens if Michael's address changes? You then have to search for all of

Michael's records and change the address. If you miss one record, a bill may go to his old address and not get forwarded. What's the solution to the data-redundancy problem?

Many first-time users of database management programs try to solve this problem by creating more fields on the record, as in the following example (note the fields ITEM1, ITEM2, and ITEM3):

LASTNAME:	Olezczek
FIRSTNAME:	Michael
ADDRESS:	129 Oakleaf Way
CITY:	East Shadwell
STATE:	VA
ZIP:	22887
PHONE:	(804) 555-9999
ITEM1:	Confederate cap
BILLED:	$595
DATE BILLED:	11/29/91
PAID:	No
ITEM2:	Union cap
BILLED:	$395
DATE BILLED:	12/03/91
PAID:	No
ITEM3:	
BILLED:	
DATE BILLED:	
PAID:	

But this design has problems, too. What if somebody orders four items? Charles could add more fields to the database, but some programs don't enable you to add fields without going through a cumbersome and time-consuming operation. And what's worse, Charles is well on his way to violating one of the cardinal rules of computerization: producing clear, easy-to-read screens. This data record is a mess; there are so many fields that Charles can easily make errors filling in the data.

The best way to solve this database design problem is to use a relational database management program or a flat-file program that has a lookup function.

Relational Database Managers

From the user's point of view, the most important aspect of a relational database manager is its ability to work with more than one database at a time. On the surface, this capability doesn't seem like a big deal. But it is, because when you're working with two or more databases, you can eliminate data redundancy.

Charles could use a relational database management program to eliminate data redundancy. A relational database manager can use a common field to link the information in two databases. Charles could create two databases that are linked by a field called CUSTNO (Customer Number). The first database stores information about the customer:

CUSTNO:	451
LASTNAME:	Olezczek
FIRSTNAME:	Michael
ADDRESS:	129 Oakleaf Way
CITY:	East Shadwell
STATE:	VA
ZIP:	22887
PHONE:	(804) 555-9999

The second database stores information about specific transactions. Here's one record:

CUSTNO:	451
ITEM:	Confederate cap
BILLED:	$595
DATE BILLED:	11/29/91
PAID:	No

Here's another record:

CUSTNO	451
ITEM:	Union cap
BILLED:	$395
DATE BILLED:	12/03/91
PAID:	No

As you may have noticed, this design doesn't completely eliminate data redundancy—Charles still must type the customer number (such as *451*) in the CUSTNO field of every record. And because Charles could type the customer number incorrectly, the possibility of error still exists. Still, Charles can detect more easily that he incorrectly entered a three-digit number than an entire name. Best of all, Charles doesn't have to type Michael's name and address twice, and he easily can add more transactions should Michael decide to order more artifacts.

In retrieval operations, a relational database manager can combine the information in the two databases as if it were drawn from one seamless file. It can then produce reports such as the following:

CUSTNO	LASTNAME	ITEM:	BILLED:	PAID?	PHONE
451	Olezczek	Confederate cap	$595	No	(804) 555-9999
451	Olezczek	Union cap	$395	No	(804) 555-9999

If relational database management programs are so great, why aren't more people using them? The answer is that, unfortunately, most relational database management programs seem to have been designed with programmers—rather than end users—in mind. To perform queries and produce reports, it often is necessary to learn how to use a complicated programming language. That drawback is enough to keep most business users away from these programs. (An important exception is Microrim's Personal R:BASE, which is featured later in this chapter.)

NOTE

Technical snobs like to argue about whether a program is truly "relational." In the purest sense, no personal computer program is really relational, as the term is strictly defined by its originator (E. F. Codd, in his book *The Relational Model of Database Management*, published by Addison-Wesley). The pure model is based on an elegant logical theory, but programs that obey the pure model are slow and hard to use. "Relational" programs such as Personal R:BASE include compromises. But unless you're an absolute purist, it's still legitimate to call a program *relational*, as long as the program stores data in tables and displays tables as the result of query operations. Ideally, you should be able to query the database flexibly and continuously, without worrying about where the information came from (or where it is going), until you find the information that you want. A flat-file management program cannot handle such queries, even if it has the "relational capability" of looking up information in other databases.

Flat-File Programs with Lookup Functions

Flat-file database managers can keep only one database in memory at a time, but some programs (like Symantec's Q & A and Ashton-Tate's RapidFile) are able to look up data in another database that is stored on disk. The principle is the same: the information in the two databases is related by means of a common field, such as CUSTNO. You can perform a retrieval operation that draws linked data from a second database.

A flat-file database manager with a lookup function, such as Q & A, offers two advantages: ease of use and a simple solution to the data redundancy problem. But using relational programs still has advantages. With a relational program, you can work with more than two databases at a time. Later in this chapter, you will see an illustration of how useful creating more than two linked databases can be. Relational programs also perform retrieval operations much more quickly than flat-file database managers. If you're storing more than 1,000 records, the speed advantages of a relational database management program are considerable.

Do you really need a relational database manager? The answer depends on how often you would have to type duplicate data in a flat-file program. If your only objective is to keep a database of names and addresses, a flat-file program will be adequate because every record is unique. If you plan to store data that forces you to type some information repeatedly, use a relational program (or a flat-file manager with a lookup function) to eliminate redundancy.

TIP

Database Management Systems (DBMS)

A *database management system* is a full-featured database program—usually a relational one—that includes a programming language and a compiler. In other words, a DBMS is a complete programming environment, which a professional programmer can use to develop a stand-alone database application for a business. This application can handle virtually every aspect of your business, including invoices, inventory management, accounting functions, payroll, accounts receivable, and more. It is expensive, and often tedious and frustrating, to develop such a system with a programmer's aid, however. Before hiring a programmer to develop a customized DBMS application for your business, find out whether special-purpose programs, such as the accounting packages discussed in Part IV of this book, will meet your needs.

Examining the Benefits of Computerized Data Management

You should be able to accomplish almost all of these tasks with any of the flat-file or relational database managers mentioned in this chapter:

- *Define the data fields so that you can store and retrieve information that is unique to your business.* You should be able to rename the data fields, as well as add new ones or delete old ones, after you create the database. Don't buy a program that doesn't enable you to change the data field design after you have entered data, because you probably will need to add or alter data fields. If the program doesn't enable you to make such changes, you have to throw out all your work and start over.

- *Create an on-screen data entry form that facilitates easy, error-free typing and correction of data.* The best programs give you easy-to-use tools to design the screen with colors, lines, and boxes.

- *Enter and edit data easily.* Changes should be easy to make; the program shouldn't force you to learn a new set of complicated keyboard commands.

- *Place filters on each data field to prevent the user from typing the wrong kind of information (such as typing text in a date field).* Using filters (also called *rules*) helps you avoid erroneous data entry. The more kinds of filters you can use, the more likely your database is to be free from accidental data entry errors.

- *Prevent duplicate information from being entered.* This automatic feature is valuable because it helps prevent a potentially serious error: duplicate data entry. This feature would stop a new stock number from being entered the same way as an old stock number, for example.

- *Browse through a columnar list of the information stored in your database and edit this information at the same time.* Seeing a quick, uncomplicated picture of the data stored in your database is helpful. If you see an error while viewing this list, you should be able to correct it right then.

- *Sort the data in a variety of ways, using any data field as the key for the sort.* You should be able to perform a sort easily and define a default sort order so that your records always appear in an organized list.

- *Select only the records that meet the criteria you specify.* You should be able to select records in a variety of ways. Most programs enable you to select records using *relational operators* (such as EQUALS or GREATER THAN) and *logical operators* (such as AND, OR, and NOT). You can ask a program, for example, to show you all records in which the BILLING DATE field is greater than one month ago *and* the PAID field equals *No.* The program selects these records only if both conditions are satisfied—the date is greater than one month ago and the customer hasn't paid.

- *Create printed reports that include subtotals, totals, and averages.*
  You must choose a program that includes automatic report layout
  capabilities, or you will spend a lot of time designing report formats. If the program can lay out a report automatically, you can
  edit the report by removing fields you don't want, which is easier
  than designing the report from scratch.

- *Print mailing labels.* Chances are your database management
  application stores your customers' names and addresses. If you are
  using a database manager that has mailing label capabilities, you
  can skip the mailing list managers discussed in the preceding chapter. Make sure that the program includes preconfigured printing
  templates for popular labels, so you don't have to design the
  templates.

- *Create a complete, menu-driven application customized for your
  business needs.* With some programs, you can create such an application without doing any programming. After you create the application, the user sees a menu of choices customized for your
  business's needs. Applications are useful especially when you want
  someone who isn't familiar with the computer to perform data
  entry or other simple tasks.

The software selection issue boils down to whether you really need
relational capabilities. To help you decide, the next section examines a
relational database manager in action.

Managing Data with a Relational Database Manager

Relational database management programs offer many advantages, but they
typically are difficult to use. An exception is Personal R:BASE (Microrim)—
a DOS relational database management program. Personal R:BASE was
designed from the beginning to make the relational database technology
available to nonprogrammers who want to build their own databases. In this
section, you examine how Charles can set up a simple relational application
for his Civil War artifacts business. You see how simple the underlying
concepts really are, thanks to the clarity and simplicity of Personal R:BASE.

Understanding How a Relational Database Manager Stores Data

In a flat-file database manager such as Q&A, you see your data in the form of data records. In relational database management programs, however, data always is displayed in the form of tables. Each table consists of rows and columns. A row constitutes a complete data record, and the column headers contain the names of the data fields. Figure 5.1 shows Charles' database of Civil War artifacts (for the sake of simplicity, only 9 out of his collection of more than 1,000 artifacts are shown). Having set up this table, Charles can add new artifacts just by inserting a new row and typing.

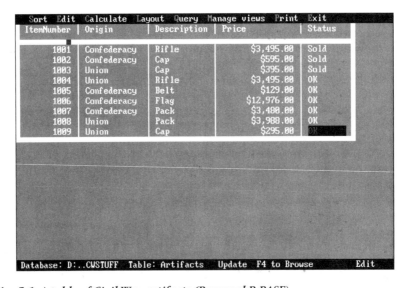

Fig. 5.1. *A table of Civil War artifacts (Personal R:BASE).*

Querying the Database

Suppose that a customer wants to buy a Union cap but wants to spend less than $400. To see whether anything in the collection meets these criteria, Charles uses Personal R:BASE's Query Design screen (see fig. 5.2).

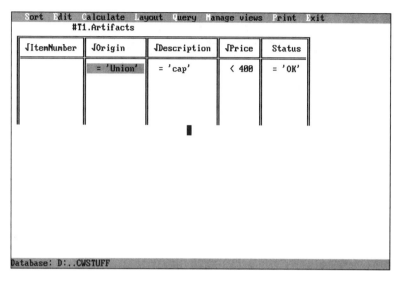

Fig. 5.2. *Adding conditions for the query.*

This screen shows the columns but no rows. Charles uses the program's menus to place conditions in four of the columns, and he selects the columns he wants to appear in the view that results from the query (these columns are shown with a check mark in front of the column's name). The following is a brief guide to what these conditions mean:

= 'Union'	Show only those records for which the Origin column contains the text *Union*.
= 'cap'	Show only those records for which the Description column contains the text *cap*.
< 400	Show only those records for which the Price column contains a figure less than $400.
= 'OK'	Show only those records for which the Status column contains the text *OK*.

The program does not retrieve a record unless the record meets ALL of these conditions.

After Charles gives the command that processes the query, Personal R:BASE displays the screen shown in figure 5.3. Charles does indeed have an artifact that meets the caller's needs: a Union cap priced at $295.

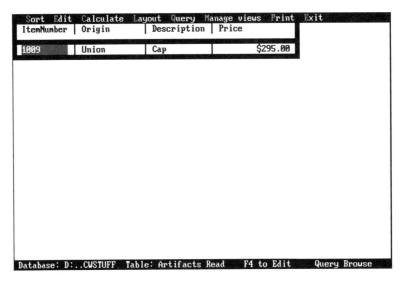

Fig. 5.3. Record retrieval that meets the search criteria (Personal R:BASE).

Drawing Information from Two or More Databases

The query operation Charles just performed can be performed with any flat-file management program. A flat-file database manager cannot easily draw information from two databases.

In addition to the Artifacts table shown in figure 5.1, Charles has created separate tables of customers (see fig. 5.4) and sales transactions (see fig. 5.5).

Charles wants to know who is late paying bills, so he designs a query that displays all the overdue clients' telephone numbers. To begin, he uses Personal R:BASE's menus to display the skeletons of the Sales Transactions and Customers tables. He adds the search conditions to the second table, Sales Transactions. These conditions say *Show me only those records for customers who were billed earlier than May 1, 1991, and who haven't paid their bills* (see fig. 5.6).

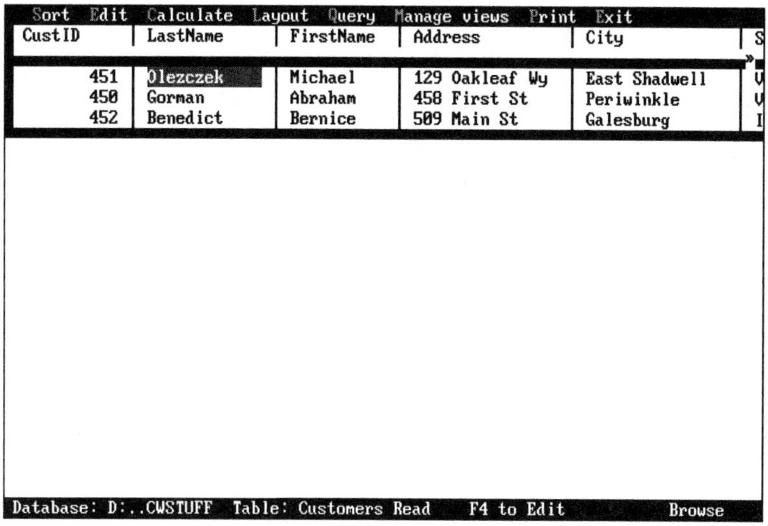

```
  Sort  Edit  Calculate  Layout  Query  Manage views  Print  Exit
 CustID      | LastName  | FirstName | Address       | City          | S
 ┌─────────────────────────────────────────────────────────────────────
 │      451  │ Olezczek  │ Michael   │ 129 Oakleaf Wy│ East Shadwell │ U
 │      450  │ Gorman    │ Abraham   │ 458 First St  │ Periwinkle    │ U
 │      452  │ Benedict  │ Bernice   │ 509 Main St   │ Galesburg     │ I
 └─────────────────────────────────────────────────────────────────────



 Database: D:..CWSTUFF  Table: Customers Read     F4 to Edit       Browse
```

Fig. 5.4. A table of customers (Personal R:BASE).

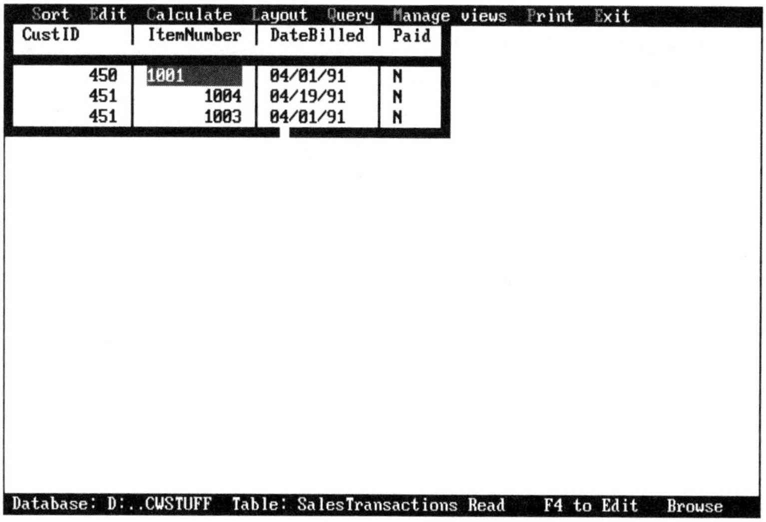

```
  Sort  Edit  Calculate  Layout  Query  Manage views  Print  Exit
 CustID      | ItemNumber | DateBilled | Paid
 ┌──────────────────────────────────────────────
 │      450  │ 1001       │ 04/01/91   │ N
 │      451  │ 1004       │ 04/19/91   │ N
 │      451  │ 1003       │ 04/01/91   │ N
 └──────────────────────────────────────────────



 Database: D:..CWSTUFF  Table: SalesTransactions Read    F4 to Edit   Browse
```

Fig. 5.5. A table of sales transactions (Personal R:BASE).

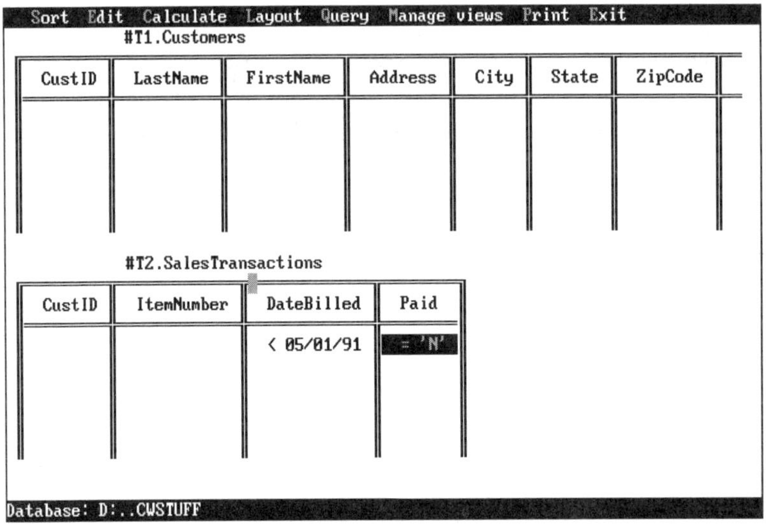

Fig. 5.6. A query design using two tables (Personal R:BASE).

Next, Charles uses a simple menu command to create a link between the CustID fields of the two tables. This link is shown in figure 5.7. Charles also has checked off the LastName and FirstName columns in the Customers Table so that they appear in the view. You cannot see that he also has checked the Phone column, which is just off the right edge of the screen.

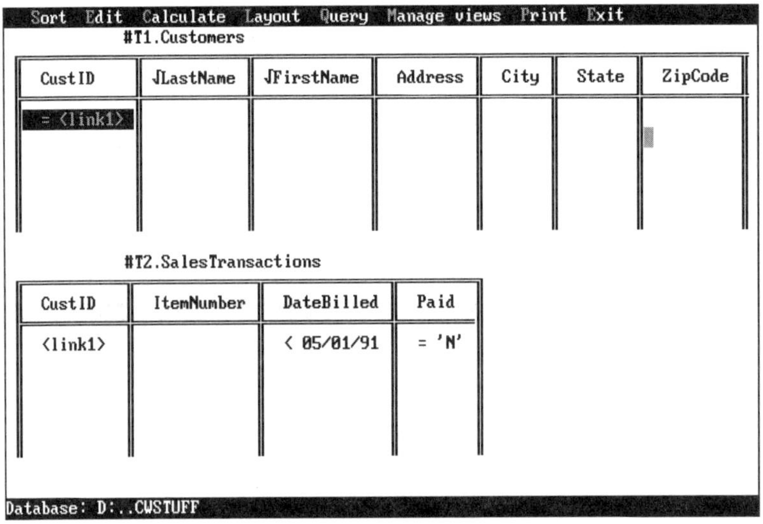

Fig. 5.7. Two tables linked by a common field—CustID (Personal R:BASE).

After Charles gives the command that processes the query, he sees the view shown in figure 5.8. This result has some shortcomings. Charles wants to sit down and call these customers, but he needs to know how much they owe and what items have not been paid for.

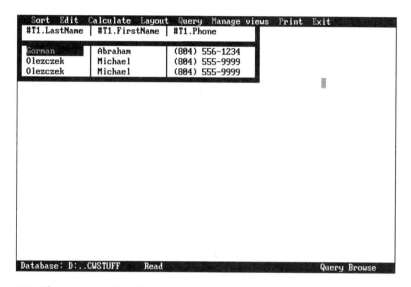

Fig. 5.8. *The view resulting from a two-table query (Personal R:BASE).*

To add more information to this view, Charles returns to the Query Design screen and adds the third table, Artifacts. Then he links the Sales Transactions table to the Artifacts table, as shown in figure 5.9 (note <link2> in the ItemNumber columns of both tables). He also checks off the Description and Price columns in the Artifacts table so these columns appear in the view. After Charles gives the command that processes the query again, he sees the view shown in figure 5.10.

As this example illustrates, anyone can understand how a relational database management program works. The concepts aren't difficult, although (like the concepts of a personal information manager) they are unfamiliar and take a little getting used to. When you break down your information into separate tables, each is simple, clean, and uncluttered. You can create a very complex application with a relational database manager, but because you can use many separate lists, each one is comprehensible and fits nicely on just one computer screen.

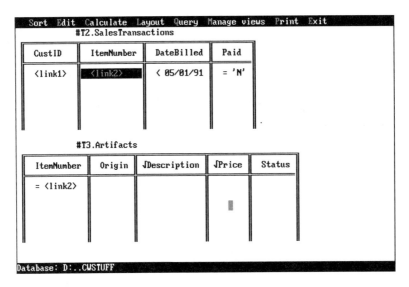

Fig. 5.9. Linking tables.

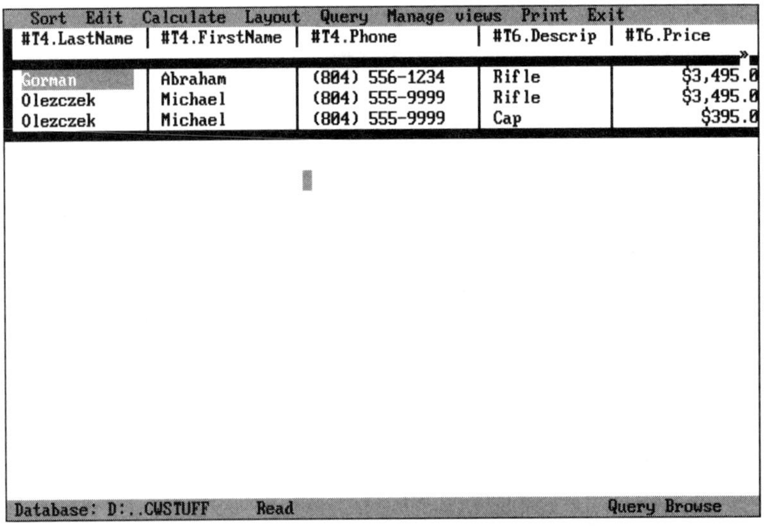

Fig. 5.10. The view resulting from a three-table query (Personal R:BASE).

Creating Reports

Relational databases put information at your fingertips with their capability to display the results of queries on-screen. However, printing the information you have so painstakingly recorded is useful. You do so by creating a report.

With many database managers, this task is difficult at best. Today's better programs, however, include a quick report layout feature, which assumes that you want a report listing all the fields in a database. If you are using a relational database manager, the task is even easier because your tables should be simple (four or five columns at the most). Chances are the quick report layout will work just fine.

In figure 5.11, you see the report layout that Charles uses to print a list of the artifacts currently in his collection (drawing on the Artifacts table). At the top of the screen, you see the *page header*—the information that prints at the top of each page. The row marked "D" is the detail section, where the program inserts the data from the table. At the bottom, below the line, is a Total field, which prints totals.

You cannot tell from the quick layout screen, but this report has been set up with *breakpoints*. When you define a breakpoint, the program breaks down the records by grouping the data in a field, as figure 5.12 (a screen preview of the printed report) shows. Here, the data in the Status field has been broken down into two groups: the artifacts still for sale (the ones with OK in the Status field) and the artifacts that have been sold (the ones with Sold in the Status field). Totals are given for each field.

Personal R:BASE excels in many other areas as well, as Charles discovers. Using the program's application generator, Charles quickly sets up a menu-driven application for his databases. When he chooses this application from the program's initial menu, he sees a menu bar across the top of the screen showing the options he has created. He quickly can select the table to which he wants to add data; instead of the table, however, he sees an on-screen form that makes entering data easier. He also has used the generator to create and save the searches, selections, and reports he frequently uses, and these items are available from the menus. Charles has achieved all of this functionality without writing a single line of program code.

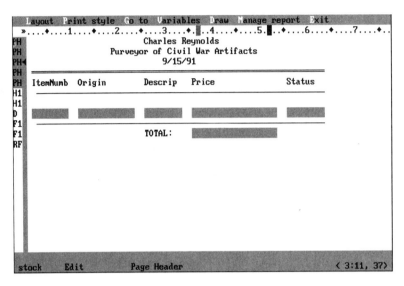

Fig. 5.11. The quick report layout (Personal R:BASE).

```
                    Charles Reynolds
              Purveyor of Civil War Artifacts
                       9/15/91

    ItemNumb  Origin      Descrip    Price           Status

       1009   Union       Cap          $295.00       OK
       1006   Confederacy Flag      $12,976.00       OK
       1007   Confederacy Pack       $3,480.00       OK
       1004   Union       Rifle      $3,495.00       OK
       1005   Confederacy Belt         $129.00       OK
       1008   Union       Pack       $3,988.00       OK

                         TOTAL:     $24,363.00

       1003   Union       Cap          $395.00       Sold
       1002   Confederacy Cap          $595.00       Sold
       1001   Confederacy Rifle      $3,495.00       Sold

                         TOTAL:      $4,485.00

    Press any key to continue
```

Fig. 5.12. A screen preview of a report (Personal R:BASE).

Investigating Other Database Programs

A program such as Personal R:BASE gives a novice user a huge fraction of the power of a database management system (DBMS), but you should understand your limits as you attempt to devise an information-management system for your business. Don't try to tackle too much and remember that special-purpose programs offer benefits that only a professional programmer can extract from a database manager. Special-purpose inventory control programs, for example, offer many special benefits, especially if they are linked to a compatible accounting program. Buying a $59 checkwriting program is a much better idea than spending weeks trying to develop a database application that can print checks!

Summary

The following is a quick review of this chapter's main points:

- Consider a database program if you are dealing with information unique to your business and that information overwhelms you as you try to cope with manual methods.

- Flat-file programs work with only one database at a time, causing problems with data redundancy. For the applications discussed in this chapter, choose a flat-file manager with a lookup function or a relational program.

- With the right database management program, you can store information relevant to your business; locate and edit the information quickly; browse through this information (and edit it if you find errors); sort in a variety of ways; select records that meet criteria you specify; and print reports with subtotals, totals, and averages.

- Today's menu-driven relational packages don't require you to master a programming language to draw information from two or more databases. Although the concepts are unfamiliar, anyone can learn to perform a query with a program such as Personal R:BASE.

- Don't try to tackle too much. Before creating databases with accounting functions, investigate the special-purpose programs discussed in Part IV.

Software Suggestions

DOS is the world capital of personal computer database management systems; you can choose from a wide variety of programs that rival mainframe database managers in speed and complexity. A good selection of programs also is available for Macintoshes, and by the time you read this book, more Windows software will be available.

DOS Database Management Software

- *FoxPro (Fox Software Inc.):* A full-featured, fully programmable database management system (DBMS) that offers an easy-to-use interface. A full set of development tools enables a programmer to develop stand-alone applications, but you need a programmer to get the full benefit from this package.

- *Personal R:BASE (Microrim, Inc.):* An easy-to-use version of Microrim's powerful R:BASE database management system. Designed for individual users, Personal R:BASE retains the relational architecture of its big brother, but it lacks multiuser capability, programmability, security features, transaction processing, and other advanced features. Far more powerful than a flat-file manager, you can create queries that draw from as many as five tables at the same time. The outstanding user's manual and on-screen tutorial provide an education in database design. You also can use a mouse with this program. Speedy and capable, Personal R:BASE is an excellent choice for a database of 5,000 records or more.

- *Q&A (Symantec Corporation):* An integrated program that combines an excellent word processor with an equally excellent flat-file database manager. Ease of use is stressed throughout, and you can choose all or most functions from menus. Included is a lookup function that helps you reduce data redundancy. Like all flat-file database managers, Q&A is slower than relational programs, so it is a good choice only if you are creating a database of about 5,000 records or less.

Macintosh Database Management Software

- *4th DIMENSION (ACIUS Inc.):* A full-featured, programmable relational database management system for the Macintosh. Separately available is a compiler that enables a programmer to create stand-alone applications. You need the assistance of a programmer to get the full benefits of this powerful program. For a single-user, nonprogrammable version, see FILE FORCE.

- *FILE FORCE (ACIUS Inc.):* Like PERSONAL R:BASE, FILE FORCE is a stepped-down version of a professional relational database manager (4th DIMENSION). A relational program, FILE FORCE can use more than one database at a time, and the program includes excellent label-printing capabilities, quick layouts for forms and reports, and many other excellent features. An excellent choice for larger databases (5,000 records or more).

- *FileMaker Pro (Claris Corporation):* A flat-file manager with lookup capabilities, FileMaker Pro is exceptionally easy to use. Incorporating on-screen object-oriented graphics, the program enables you to design attractive forms and reports quickly. Like all flat-file managers, FileMaker Pro is slower than relational programs. This is an excellent choice for a relatively small database (5,000 records or less).

Windows Database Management Software

- *Superbase 4 (Precision Software):* A full-featured, relational database management system (DBMS) for Microsoft Windows, Superbase takes full advantage of Windows' graphic interface. The program makes full use of on-screen fonts and can even store and display graphics images. A row of VCR-like buttons across the bottom of the screen brings pushbutton functionality to database navigation commands. Fully programmable, Superbase requires the assistance of a professional programmer in order for you to get the full benefit from the program.

6

Crunching Numbers

You now have controlled your schedule, developed your mailing list, and put a database manager to work on your business' information. Now it's time to tackle the numbers in your life: not the numbers that you need to track for record-keeping (see Part IV), but those much more vexing numbers—the ones that have questions attached to them. How much should I charge this guy? Should I buy that truck or lease it? What will happen to my profits if I hire someone part-time?

Throughout North America, personal computer users have found a new way to tackle such questions, rather than just going on gut instinct or others' advice: they're using electronic spreadsheet programs. Because an electronic spreadsheet presents an on-screen version of an accountant's worksheet, many people seem to think these programs are best for accounting purposes, such as keeping a general ledger. But special-purpose accounting programs are much better for such applications, as Part IV of this book demonstrates. What makes spreadsheets so useful is their ability to recalculate the whole worksheet if you make changes to key variables.

That's why spreadsheets were developed in the first place. The electronic spreadsheet was first conceptualized by a business school graduate student whose homework involved asking "what if" questions, such as "What will happen to the profit margins if this company succeeds in reducing its manufacturing costs by 5 percent?" Back in those days, the only way you could answer such questions was by going through the tedious process of recalculating pencil-and-paper figures with the aid of a pocket calculator.

Electronic spreadsheets are a boon for anyone who needs to answer number questions. But they have drawbacks as well. As you've already learned, much of the benefit of an electronic spreadsheet program comes from its ability to hide a formula "beneath" a cell; what you see on-screen is the value produced by the formula, not the formula itself. If you typed the formula wrong, you could be getting the wrong results without knowing it. Special-purpose programs have been developed for a wide variety of applications, such as calculating interest or analyzing the results of a survey. Unless you're willing to audit your spreadsheets carefully, you may be better off with a special-purpose program, if one is available for your application.

In this chapter, you learn whether you need a spreadsheet program, and if so, what kind of spreadsheet program you should buy. Also illustrated is the use of a special-purpose number-crunching program, which does an excellent job of tackling number questions that aren't unique to a particular line of work.

Deciding Whether You Need a Spreadsheet Program

Before you spend time learning a spreadsheet and applying one to your business, you should see whether your business' situation resembles any of the following:

- *The numbers you're dealing with can't be handled by a special-purpose program.* If you're trying to decide whether to buy or lease, you may be better off with a special-purpose program such as PercentEdge (Timeslips), which is specifically designed to perform interest-related calculations using proven methods. If you're trying to track business expenses, use a checkwriting or accounting program. Remember: Don't reinvent the wheel. Are the numbers you're dealing with really unique to your business, or is there a special-purpose program that can meet your needs?

- *You can't handle the numbers using manual methods.* If you can figure out how to price a job in your head, chances are you don't need a spreadsheet program to do it. But if you have to consider five or ten different costs that are constantly changing, a spreadsheet program may save you many hours of work.

- *You can benefit from "what-if" analyses.* With a spreadsheet program, you can develop a model of a part of your business—a model that describes how varying costs and other factors affect the bottom line. After you create such a model, you can perform "what-if" analyses to find out how much these variables really affect the bottom line—or, to put it another way, how sensitive they are. When you change a sensitive variable, you see big changes on the bottom line. Changing a less sensitive variable produces a proportionally smaller change in the bottom line. In exploring your model, you may discover that the price you're paying for materials is a lot more sensitive than salary or mileage expenses, so it's worth sending Sam to pick up some bargain parts in a town two hours down the road.

If you see possibilities here, then a spreadsheet may very well be worth buying and learning.

Examining Software Options for Number-Crunching

Spreadsheet programs are so ubiquitous that many people don't realize there are other options for number crunching, and some of them may provide benefits that you would be hard-pressed to match by developing and auditing your own spreadsheet. Here's an overview of the programs you can use for crunching your business' numbers:

- *DOS spreadsheet programs:* The big, blockbuster spreadsheets, such as Lotus 1-2-3 and Quattro Pro, are packed with features, but all this functionality comes with a price: you easily can get lost in the forest. For an occasional "what-if" scenario, these programs may offer far more than you'll ever need. These programs, however, are widely used and well-supported. You will find plenty of books on Lotus 1-2-3 and Quattro Pro. Chances are that you know someone who is using one of these programs. (*Hint:* They can provide free technical help.)

- *Windows and Macintosh spreadsheet programs:* Like DOS spreadsheets, these programs may offer more features than you really need. If you must show your spreadsheets and graphs to others, these programs offer an advantage: you can print your work with many of the features you'll find in desktop publishing programs, such as fonts, graphics, lines, shading, and boxes. (DOS spreadsheets offer these features too, but with less finesse and flexibility than their Macintosh and Windows counterparts.)

- *Integrated programs:* If you've been looking at Microsoft Works for other reasons, look again, because this program comes with an excellent spreadsheet in both its DOS and Macintosh versions.

Works' spreadsheet is featured in this chapter. More challenging, but significantly more capable, is Symphony (Lotus Development Corporation), which incorporates the well-supported, capable spreadsheet from Lotus 1-2-3.

- *Spreadsheet templates:* You can buy ready-to-use spreadsheet files, called *templates*, that have been developed professionally for a wide variety of applications. Many are available free of charge or for a nominal fee from shareware software suppliers. But be fore-warned: many public domain templates are of poor quality or contain erroneous assumptions.

- *Special-purpose number-crunching programs:* Special-purpose programs have been developed for a wide variety of number questions that aren't specific to a particular line of work, such as calculating interest or analyzing the results of a survey. Unless you're willing to audit your spreadsheets carefully, you may be better off with a special-purpose program, if one is available for your application. You sacrifice flexibility, however, for the decrease in developmental effort and the reduced chance of error.

How much spreadsheet power do you need? Very little, for most small business applications. Remember, it's much better to develop a simple, clear spreadsheet that occupies just one screen, than it is to try to develop a huge spreadsheet with dozens of interrelated formulas. The bigger the spreadsheet, the more likely you are to get lost and make mistakes. The Works spreadsheet includes enough number-crunching capabilities to satisfy the needs of most readers of this book.

Examining the Benefits of Computerized Number-Crunching

With an electronic spreadsheet program, you can expect to perform some or all of the following tasks:

- *Creating a worksheet that enables you to deal with the number questions that are unique to your business—the ones you must answer repeatedly.* Your experience is your best guide here. What are the number questions that you need to answer over and over again? Do you give cost estimates? How do you decide how much you can afford to pay for salaries? Benefits? A spreadsheet program is very useful here; chances are that questions of this type involve assumptions that aren't relevant to other lines of work (or even other businesses in the same line of work).

- *Designing the spreadsheet so that the key variables are all accessible for what-if exploration.* As you'll learn in this chapter, the best way to design a spreadsheet is to place all the key variables— the values you need to type to compute the bottom line—at the top of the worksheet, where you easily can change them. (Novice users frequently make the mistake of putting these values in formulas, where they aren't accessible.) If you design your spreadsheet this way, you can not only answer a given number question, such as "What should I charge this guy for this job," but also more exploratory questions, such as "What could I be making on this job if I could get those parts for 25 percent less?"

- *Drawing on a wide range of built-in functions (as well as the four basic arithmetic operations) to assist you as you construct formulas.* A built-in function performs a complex mathematical operation, such as summing a column of numbers. If your work involves engineering or other advanced computations, you should look for a spreadsheet program that has the capabilities you need.

- *Naming areas on your spreadsheet so you can refer to these areas in formulas using names rather than cell references.* The area of a spreadsheet that you define for this purpose is called a *range*. After you name the range, you can refer to the range in formulas rather than typing the cell references. This desirable feature makes formula-writing less confusing, because you can write a formula such as SUM(1992SALES), the meaning of which is immediately apparent from looking at the formula.

- *Saving the developed and tested spreadsheet as a template, so that you can open and use it quickly when the question comes up again.* With a little time and effort, you can develop well-conceived and tested spreadsheets for all the number questions you face repeatedly. If you build decks, for example, you just plug in the number of square feet, the price per foot of treated lumber, and the salary you're paying your helpers; an estimate then appears on-screen.

- *Transforming spreadsheet numbers into a variety of graphs, including bar graphs, column graphs, pie graphs, and line graphs.* This capability isn't examined in this chapter (see Chapter 11,

"Making Presentations," for more information on business graphs). But keep it in mind if you would find it helpful to look at your numbers visually. In the past, spreadsheet-generated graphs weren't well suited to public presentations, but the new generation of graphics spreadsheets (such as Excel and Lotus 1-2-3 Version 2.3) is changing that picture dramatically.

- *Printing your worksheet with a minimum of fuss and hassle.* Every spreadsheet program can print, but not all measure up in the "minimum fuss and hassle" department. An attractive feature if you create wide spreadsheets is the capability to print the spreadsheet sideways (Landscape mode). Lotus 1-2-3 Release 3.1 and 1-2-3 for Windows offer an automatic fit-to-page option that relegates spreadsheet printing hassles to the past.

In the following section, you'll see how you can put these capabilities to work in two ways: the wrong way and the right way.

Crunching Numbers with Electronic Spreadsheets

Electronic spreadsheet programs are single-purpose programs; that means you're on your own when it comes to developing an application. That's an advantage in one sense, because spreadsheets are flexible enough to accommodate a huge variety of calculations that are tailored to the specifics of a particular business. But it's a disadvantage in another sense: you're looking at spending at least some time developing the worksheet, and if you're not careful, you may make an error that would throw off your calculations considerably. An electronic spreadsheet program can be used well if you understand where it's best applied, and also if you understand how and where spreadsheets can go wrong.

The best way to investigate where spreadsheets are best applied, and what can go wrong with spreadsheet calculations, is to examine a detailed example. Here's the scenario. Alan runs a small insulation business. The cost of insulation and labor fluctuate up and down, and so he often finds himself undercharging for jobs. Alan needs a way to estimate costs, but what's more, he needs a way to redo his estimates quickly and easily if the price of materials or labor changes.

Alan picks up a copy of Microsoft Works and starts creating his spreadsheet. As you follow Alan's work, bear in mind that he's about to make every mistake in the book. Alan's first spreadsheet is a disaster; don't emulate it! You'll learn from Alan's mistakes just as he did.

Examining Basic Errors in Spreadsheet Design

To estimate the costs for an insulation job, Alan develops the poorly-conceived worksheet shown in figure 6.1.

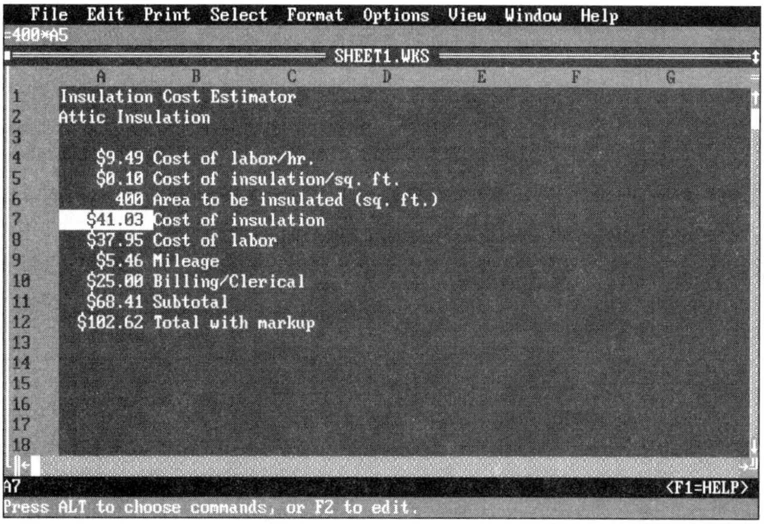

Fig. 6.1. *A poorly-conceived spreadsheet design (Microsoft Works).*

Here are the formulas that Alan has placed in the cells:

- *A4:* To estimate the cost of labor per hour, Alan types the following formula: 5.75*1.65 (the asterisk indicates multiplication). Alan pays his workers $5.75 per hour, and he estimates that he pays an additional 65 percent for social security and other benefits.

- *A5:* Alan pays $8 for a 78 sq. ft. roll of insulation, so he types the formula 8/78 (8 divided by 78) to calculate how much he pays per square foot.

- *A6:* Here, Alan types the number of square feet to be insulated in a particular job (400, in this case).

- *A7:* In this cell, Alan types the number of square feet to be insulated and multiplies this figure by the value in cell A5 (the cost of insulation per square feet).

- *A8:* Here, Alan calculates the cost of labor using the following formula: A6/100*A4. This formula takes the value in cell A6 (the number of square feet to be insulated) and divides it by 100, and then multiplies the result by the value in cell A4 (cost of labor per hour). Alan's reasoning is that it takes his worker about one hour to insulate 100 square feet.

- *A9:* Here, Alan multiplies the mileage to be put on the company truck by 26 cents (a standard mileage rate).

- *A10:* Alan enters a flat clerical/billing fee here to cover his office expenses.

- *A11:* In this cell, Alan uses a built-in formula (SUM) to obtain the sum of cells A8 through A10.

- *A12:* Here, Alan enters a formula to compute his markup (50 percent): A11 * 1.5. This formula takes the value in cell A11 and multiplies it by 1.5.

So what's wrong with this spreadsheet? Plenty. Without realizing it, Alan has broken just about every rule of spreadsheet design. Here's a brief overview of these rules:

- *Don't type constants in formulas.* One of the nice things about spreadsheet programs is that the formulas are hidden; you only see the values they compute. But this virtue can become a liability. It's easy to forget what is in the formulas. If you type constants in the formulas, you may forget that they're there, and proceed willy-nilly with calculations that will produce erroneous results. (A *constant* is a value that you type directly, as distinguished from a value that the spreadsheet calculates from a formula and then displays in the cell.)

- *Place constants in cells, where you can see them and change them, if necessary.* Doing so makes it easy to modify the spreadsheet if these figures must be retyped. Chances are that once you get the formulas right, you'll never have to edit them.

- *Separate data entry areas from calculation areas, and protect the calculation areas.* The values you see on-screen may be generated by formulas rather than constants. If you type a constant over a formula, the program erases the formula, and the result may be an erroneous calculation. As you'll see, there is a way you can protect cells to prevent you or someone else from typing over the formulas and ruining them.

- *Document the spreadsheet so that you will remember how it works.* You can incorporate the documentation as text in an unoccupied area of the spreadsheet. The documentation does not need to be extensive. Just be sure to list all the assumptions that you have made.

To see why Alan (and every spreadsheet user) should follow these four simple rules, consider what happens if Alan tries to compute the cost of another job. This new job calls for 500 square feet of insulation, so Alan types *500* in cell A6. The answer on the bottom line changes to $116.85, but it's the wrong answer. Why? Cell A7 still is computing the cost of insulation using a constant of 400 square feet. Will Alan catch the error? It probably depends on how long it's been since he created the spreadsheet. If he's forgotten how it works, he may not catch the error. If he does catch it, he'll have to edit the formula in cell A7, a much more tedious job than just typing a constant into a cell.

And what if he accidentally types the square footage in the wrong cell? He wipes out a formula, and he'll have to reconstruct it from memory. Alan's spreadsheet must be redesigned from the ground up.

Designing a Better Spreadsheet

Alan realizes the limits of his first spreadsheet design, and having gotten some help from an experienced spreadsheet user, he comes up with a second design (see fig. 6.2). As you'll see, this spreadsheet has become a valuable tool for Alan's business.

A glance at this spreadsheet is all you need to tell where to type the data: column A. Alan has placed every key variable—any constant that could possibly change—in one column. He's most likely to change the Square Feet To Be Insulated and Mileage to Job constants, but there may be other changes, too: for example, Alan may find a new supply of insulation, which offers different-sized rolls (56 square feet instead of 78) at a better price per square foot. Every constant that goes into Alan's price estimates is included in column A.

Because every constant is typed in column A, there's no need for any constants in the formulas in column E: all these formulas reference the constants in column A. The formula in cell E6, for example, reads as follows:

(A5/A7)*A8

To solve this formula, Works first performs the operation within the parentheses by dividing the value in cell A5 (square feet to be insulated) by the value in cell A7 (coverage of 1 roll). Then Works multiplies the result by the value in cell A8 (cost of 1 roll).

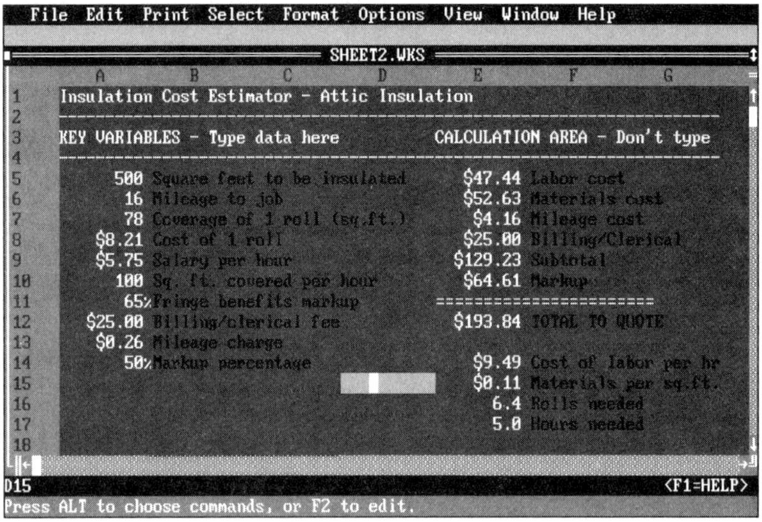

Fig. 6.2. An improved spreadsheet design (Microsoft Works).

Because the formulas in column E contain no constants, there's no need to alter them. Therefore, Alan can choose the Protect command for these cells. The Protect command prevents the user from typing anything in these cells. (If you discover an error, you can "unprotect" the cells. The point of the command is to prevent accidental erasure of a formula.)

To get an idea of how useful this worksheet is, consider the questions that Alan now can answer with just a few keystrokes:

- "I've got an 800 square foot attic job for you, but I'd like to know whether you can finish in just one day."

- "Alan, this guy's offering us 61-foot rolls of R-19 insulation for $5.45. Is it a better deal than what we're getting?"

- "Alan, I'm on my way to the Williamson residence. How many rolls of insulation should I take with me?"

- "Alan, I've been looking over our records, and I don't think our guys are covering 100 feet per square hour, like you're assuming— it's more like 75. You'd better take that into account for the Smith quote you're preparing."

You may feel a little ridiculous sitting in front of your computer with a pocket calculator, but that's just what you should do with every new worksheet you design. Check each result until you're absolutely sure that every formula is working correctly. There's a good chance you'll find an error!

Learning What Spreadsheets Do Well

The insulation spreadsheet example illustrates what electronic spreadsheets do well. Spreadsheets are ideal for the following conditions:

- *The calculations you perform depend on many variables that are unique to your line of work.* In Alan's case, his estimates have to take into account many factors, including the cost of insulation, the cost of labor, the number of square feet to be insulated, and more.

- *You must perform the calculations repeatedly, and you need to see the effects of changing these key variables.* Alan needs this worksheet every time he gives a customer an estimate. It's worth putting the time and effort into perfecting it.

- *Your planning ability is enhanced by exploring the bottom-line impact of changing key variables and assumptions.* Would Alan's business remain competitive if he were to add a 60 percent markup to his costs?

As you refine and improve a spreadsheet, it becomes a model of your business. Alan's objective is to make money in the insulation business. As he develops his spreadsheet, he can ask himself, "To what extent does this spreadsheet accurately reflect my true costs? Is there anything left out?" The more accurately the model reflects reality, the more powerful the spreadsheet becomes as a tool for "what-if" analysis. Alan can start asking questions such as, "Can I really improve my competitiveness in this market by significantly reducing office costs?"

Learning What Spreadsheets Don't Do Well

Electronic spreadsheets are powerful tools for business, as this scenario has illustrated. But this scenario also has illustrated the down side of spreadsheet software:

- *Development costs:* The task of developing a well-conceived, error-free worksheet is far from trivial. It's only worth doing if the worksheet must be used repeatedly, and no other, simpler option is available.

- *The potential for error:* Don't underestimate this one. Electronic spreadsheets are notorious in business circles for containing hidden, subtle errors that can throw off the bottom line significantly. In one celebrated case, a company sued its former chief executive officer for an acquisition that turned out disastrously; the ex-CEO had used the wrong formula in a spreadsheet he designed to forecast the acquisition's payoff.

- *Special-purpose programs may be better:* There's no justification for reinventing the wheel in business. You could spend hundreds of hours customizing a Lotus 1-2-3 worksheet so that it becomes a complete accounting application for your business—but why bother when you can buy a high-quality accounting package such as Pacioli 2000 for only $59?

The next section illustrates all three of these points by exploring the special-purpose program alternative.

Crunching Numbers with a Special-Purpose Program

Alan's business is booming—so much so, in fact, that he must turn down jobs more and more frequently. Although it wouldn't be hard to hire an additional worker, the problem is that Alan only has one truck (it takes a pretty big truck to haul the insulation around).

Alan is considering buying another truck, but he's far from sure it's a wise investment. He's found a used truck that he can buy for $11,400, but this amount is earning 7.8 percent annually in a certificate of deposit. Alan estimates very conservatively that he could earn an additional $500 monthly if he had the truck around for additional jobs. He thinks he can keep the truck running well for three years, but because it's already pretty old, he doesn't expect to be able to sell the truck three years from now for much more than $2,500. Is it better to leave the money in the bank?

The problem that Alan is facing is a classic financial analysis problem, one that calls for a comparative analysis of the net present value of two alternative streams of cash flow. In one case, Alan keeps his $11,400 and gets a steady if modest stream of interest from a bank account. In the other case, Alan forks over his $11,400, but gets a much more impressive stream of $500 monthly coming in for three years, just because he's got the truck around; he also gets $2,500 from the sale of the truck.

After his experience with the cost estimator worksheet, Alan isn't sure he completely trusts his ability to produce an error-free worksheet. His spreadsheet program has a Net Present Value function (@NPV), and he realizes that he can develop a spreadsheet to analyze the problem, but Alan also is aware of the development costs involved in creating his own spreadsheets. Alan realizes that the financial question he's facing isn't unique to his business; it's a common problem, faced by many businesses. It really doesn't require his effort to develop a unique spreadsheet, full of unique variables that no other business has to cope with. There are many special-purpose programs that can deal with these common business problems, and Alan decides to try one of them: PercentEdge (Timeslips Corporation).

PercentEdge is designed specifically to calculate interest in every conceivable way, including a way that's of interest to Alan: computing the net present value of his proposed truck purchase. In brief, the net present value formula provides a way to compare alternative investments that involve different kinds of cash flow. Among PercentEdge's several capabilities is an unusually flexible and reliable net present value screen.

What does Alan gain by using a special-interest program?

PercentEdge is a special-purpose program that brings to personal computers the procedure used by the best professional accountants. Of course, spreadsheet programs can compute net present values of alternative investments. But because this decision is so critical to his business, Alan doesn't want to take a chance on choosing the wrong formula or messing up the analysis with an incorrect cell reference. So Alan gains accuracy and reliability as well as saving the time he would spend developing the worksheet.

To begin, Alan types the current date (9/1/92) in the As Of box, and he also types the rate he could earn on the certificate of deposit (7.8 percent) in the True Rate box. In the Single Payments area, he types the first, initial investment (9/1/92), a negative amount (–11,400), and the proceeds from the sale of the truck three years later ($2,500). In the Periodic Payments area, he types the range of months in which he expects to receive additional income from the truck, and specifies the amount he expects to receive ($500). After he presses Enter, PercentEdge computes the figures shown in reverse video (see fig. 6.3).

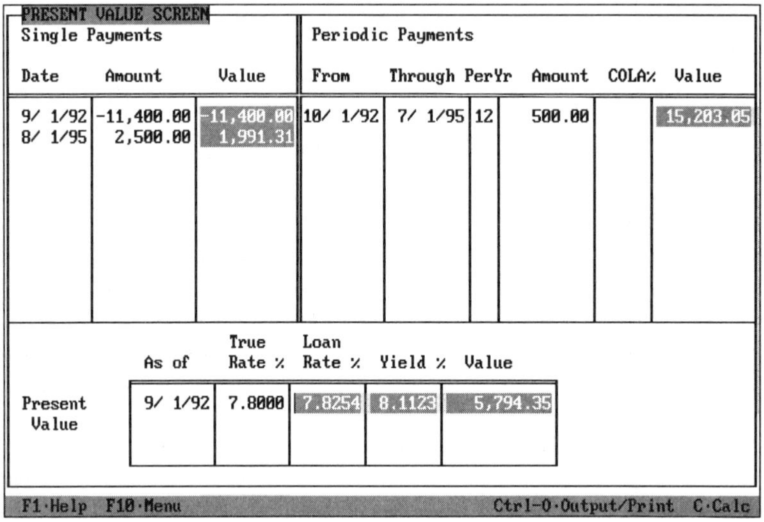

```
┌─PRESENT VALUE SCREEN────────────────────────────────────────────────┐
│ Single Payments              │ Periodic Payments                     │
│                              │                                       │
│ Date      Amount      Value  │ From    Through PerYr  Amount COLA% Value │
│                              │                                       │
│ 9/ 1/92 -11,400.00 -11,400.00│10/ 1/92  7/ 1/95 12    500.00    15,203.05│
│ 8/ 1/95   2,500.00   1,991.31│                                       │
│                              │                                       │
│                              │                                       │
│                              │                                       │
│                              │                                       │
│                              │                                       │
│                              │                                       │
│                  True    Loan                                        │
│           As of  Rate %  Rate % Yield %  Value                       │
│                                                                      │
│ Present   9/ 1/92 7.8000 7.8254 8.1123  5,794.35                     │
│ Value                                                                │
│                                                                      │
│                                                                      │
├──────────────────────────────────────────────────────────────────────┤
│ F1·Help  F10·Menu                        Ctrl-O·Output/Print  C·Calc │
└──────────────────────────────────────────────────────────────────────┘
```

Fig. 6.3. The completed analysis (PercentEdge).

What is of interest here is the figure ($5,794.35) shown in the Value box at the bottom of the screen. Because this figure is greater than zero, PercentEdge has found that the investment is earning better than 7.8 percent. How much better? Alan finds he'd have to find a savings account that pays 36 percent to beat his investment in the truck. The truck looks like a pretty good investment (from a purely financial point of view).

Alan is a little nervous about this cheerful forecast. How dependent is it on his assumptions? Alan types *350* in the Amount column of the Periodic Payments area, to see what happens if the truck brings in only $350 per month instead of $500. The results on the bottom line are still pretty encouraging (see fig. 6.4). The investment is still better than putting the money in the bank. Continuing his exploration, Alan finds that the *break even point*—the point at which the truck investment equals the certificate of deposit—gives Alan a monthly income of about $310.

After reviewing his records, Alan becomes increasingly convinced that the $500 figure he chose initially was conservative enough, and that there is a solid chance that he'll take in much more than the break even amount ($310) after he buys the additional truck. His conclusion: the truck is a good investment, from a financial viewpoint. Of course, Alan must consider what additional costs and problems he'll incur by expanding the scope of his business, but that's a problem for his judgment, not the computer's.

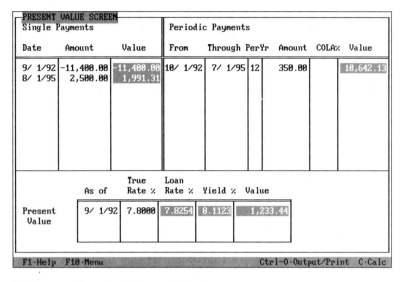

Fig. 6.4. A second analysis (PercentEdge).

Summary

Here's a summary of this chapter's main points:

- An electronic spreadsheet may be valuable if the problem you're working on (1) involves many variables that are unique to your business; (2) must be solved repeatedly, with changes in the key variables; and (3) has potential for "what-if" analysis.

- Use a spreadsheet program with caution. Don't type constants in formulas; place them in cells instead. Separate data entry areas from the calculation areas, and correct the calculation areas. Be sure to check the formulas with a hand calculator to make sure that they're working right.

- If you're trying to solve a number-crunching problem that isn't unique to your business, you can avoid error and save development costs by purchasing a special-purpose program such as PercentEdge. Remember: Don't reinvent the wheel.

Software Suggestions

Excellent full-featured spreadsheet programs are available for all three environments (DOS, Macintosh, and Windows), but you'll find more special-purpose programs for DOS.

DOS Number-Crunching Programs

- *1-2-3 (Lotus Development Corporation):* One of the most successful programs of all time, Lotus 1-2-3 defines the spreadsheet standard. A supple and feature-laden program, its unique menu system—once widely imitated—is showing signs of age. Lotus 1-2-3 is challenging to learn, but there is plenty of support available: books, templates, and even video tapes. Chances are you know someone who uses Lotus, too, so help is nearby.

- *Business Plan Builder (Jian Software):* Works with most DOS spreadsheets and word processing programs. You use it to develop and print a complete business plan, which you can take to banks and investors.

- *Investimator (Jian Software):* A collection of Lotus 1-2-3 and Excel-compatible spreadsheet templates for a variety of business transactions, including cash flows, income statements, and returns on investments.

- *Microsoft Works (Microsoft Corporation):* An integrated program with a good word processor, a flat-file database manager, telecommunications, and an excellent spreadsheet.

- *Minitab (Minitab):* A personal computer version of the famed mainframe statistical analysis program, Minitab is an excellent choice if you frequently perform marketing surveys (and have the statistical competence to interpret the results).

- *PercentEdge (Timeslips):* Featured in this chapter, calculates just about anything that has to do with interest, including mortgage rates, present values, annuities, savings projections, and amortization schedules.

- *Quattro Pro (Borland International):* A full-featured spreadsheet program that has steadily gained market share against Lotus 1-2-3 in the DOS market, Quattro Pro offers a much better interface.

- *SPSS/PC+ (SPSS):* A personal computer version of another famed mainframe statistical program, SPSS/PC+ provides sophisticated data analysis tools if you perform marketing surveys. You'll need statistical competence to understand the results, however.

- *Survey Master (Plain Jeyne):* A menu-driven program that guides you through the creation of a questionnaire, the determination of a sample, and the analysis of survey data.

Macintosh Number-Crunching Programs

- *Excel (Microsoft Corporation):* Excel is a full-featured spreadsheet program that takes full advantage of the Macintosh's graphic user interface.

- *Microsoft Works (Microsoft Corporation):* An integrated program with a good word processor, a flat-file database manager, telecommunications, and an excellent spreadsheet. The Macintosh version includes object-oriented graphics that you can use to dress up spreadsheet printouts.

- *Wingz (Informix):* Highly regarded by Macintosh experts for its HyperTalk-like scripting language, which you can use to create applications with your own, on-screen buttons. If you like Hyper-Card, you'll love Wingz. The program also has excellent graph-generating capabilities.

Windows Number-Crunching Programs

- *Excel (Microsoft Corporation):* A full-featured program that takes full advantage of the Windows interface, Excel provides one of the best rationales for using Windows. Frequently-accessed operations, such as summing, are initiated by clicking tools on the Toolbar, which is located at the top of the screen. An outstanding choice for anyone who wants to create spreadsheets or graphs to show to customers, Excel takes full advantage of Windows' graphics and font capabilities.

- *1-2-3 for Windows (Lotus Development Corporation):* A full-featured version of the famed DOS spreadsheet program, 1-2-3 for Windows abandons 1-2-3's menu system (once widely imitated) to take full advantage of the Windows interface. If you are interested in using 1-2-3, but you are afraid of a steep learning curve, 1-2-3 for Windows is a logical choice.

Part III

Communicating with Clients and Customers

Includes

Tackling Routine Business Correspondence

Writing Reports and Proposals

Getting Into Desktop Publishing

Designing and Using Business Forms

Selling Your Ideas with Presentation Graphics

Going Online

7

Tackling Routine Business Correspondence

In a small business or sole proprietorship, secretarial help is rare. "I find myself writing at least a couple of letters a day, and sometimes five or six," complains Tom, a medical illustrator who runs a successful freelance business. "I write to clients, publishers, graphics service bureaus, suppliers, community groups, government agencies, and colleagues in my professional association. If it weren't for my PC, I would spend more time writing letters than creating illustrations!"

A personal computer also can help *you* deal with the correspondence blues. It's hard to imagine a small business that cannot benefit from word processing software. With even a simple word processing program and a good printer, you can produce clean-looking, error-free letters and reports that reflect favorably on your business. Finding the *right* word processing program for your purposes is another matter. The system that is right for an academic writer or a novelist may not be right for a small business.

This chapter considers your word processing software options from one important business angle: your need to produce good-looking, letter-perfect business letters. A good program for business letter writing includes easy links with mailing lists, offers facilities for using *boilerplate* text (stored passages of frequently used text), and can crank out *personalized form letters* (standard letters sent to many people, but each one has the correspondent's name, address, and salutation added so that the letter appears to be personal).

133

TIP

If your writing needs extend to business reports and proposals, be sure to read Chapter 8, "Writing Reports and Proposals," before deciding on a word processing program.

Exploring Word Processing Software Options

Word processing programs can be categorized in several ways. The following is a list of word processing software that stresses the most important dimension for this chapter's purposes: the usefulness of these programs for composing and printing business letters:

- *Executive word processing programs:* Originally designed for busy executives who wanted an easy-to-use program for writing occasional memos and reports, these programs are not well-suited to small business applications. Typically, they include few of the features that can help you automate letter-writing tasks, such as interfaces with mailing list managers or facilities for cranking out personalized form letters, and some features are actually more difficult to use than other programs. An exception is Symantec's JustWrite for Windows, an executive word processing program that couples ease of use with some impressive advanced features, such as mail merge and built-in outlining.

- *Mailing list/letter writers:* These programs are designed to work with (or include) special-purpose mailing list managers, such as the ones discussed in Chapter 4, "Developing a Mailing List." These programs are close to ideal for small business use because they enable you to draw addresses from your mailing list (and add new addresses when you are writing to a new correspondent). However, these programs do not work well if you need to write lengthy, complex documents, such as reports or proposals.

- *Integrated programs:* Programs such as Q & A (Symantec Corporation) and Works (Microsoft) also are close to ideal for business letter-writing applications because they enable easy data interchange between the word processing module and the mailing list. Note, however, that Works isn't ideal for lengthier documents, but Q & A's word processor is the equal of many full-featured word processing programs.

- *Full-featured, character-based DOS word processing programs:* These programs are the famous heavyweights of personal computer word processing (Microsoft Word for DOS, WordPerfect for DOS, and WordStar). They are excellent choices for anyone who must write lengthy, complex documents, such as proposals and reports, but they have drawbacks for business letter writing: they don't offer an easy interface to capable mailing list managers; they are hard to learn; and for your money, you don't get to see your typeface choices on-screen (unless you switch to a screen preview mode, which may not be actively editable).

- *Full-featured graphics word processing programs:* These programs—Ami Professional for Windows, Word for Windows, Word for the Macintosh, WordPerfect for Windows, and WordPerfect for the Macintosh—are the Cadillacs of word processing. Operating at all times in a graphics mode and taking advantage of the graphical user interface, these programs show you on-screen virtually everything you see when you print, including graphics. Do you need all these features? Some of the advanced features may be difficult to understand and use—they may even require programming aptitude. If you are writing business letters, a program that is designed to make a specific advanced feature (such as mail merge) available to beginners may be more important than having on-screen fonts. These programs are an excellent choice, however, if you need to write reports and proposals.

If you don't need to write reports and proposals, choose a mailing list/letter writer or an integrated program such as Works or Q & A. If you need to write reports and proposals, you need to buy enough word processing power to tackle these projects, and you have to choose a full-featured program. With full-featured programs, you still can create links with mailing list managers and crank out form letters, but doing so is more difficult.

These special-purpose programs can aid letter-writing tasks:

- *Business letter libraries:* You can buy on-disk libraries of hundreds of business letters for every conceivable business situation, including refused credit, acknowledgment of employment application, and many more. The best packages feature letters written by professional business communication experts.

- *Document conversion utilities:* These programs are useful for converting documents created with one word processor so that they can be used by another. The best conversion utilities salvage all or most formats in the conversion process.

- *Grammar and style checkers:* Grammatik and RightWriter, for example, can identify many common errors in punctuation, grammar, usage, and style.

Increasingly, these utilities are finding their way into word processing programs. IBM's Signature, for example, can read documents created by a wide variety of word processing programs, and Professional Write for Windows includes a grammar and style checker.

Benefitting from Word Processing Software

A word processing program makes entering and revising text much easier; the text stays in the computer's memory, where it is almost instantly available, until you are ready to save and print. Big businesses have learned, however, that word processing technology doesn't automatically make everyone a more productive writer. On the contrary, some people just don't seem to be able to resist fussing with their letters and memos, and in more than a few businesses, productivity has actually gone down after word processing technology was made available.

The real gains from word processing technology don't come from increased aid of revision. These gains come from focusing the technology on a specific, critical application area, such as dealing with business correspondence in a timely manner. Depending on which program you choose, you can perform some or all of the following tasks specifically useful for business letter-writing tasks:

- *Composing a letter using a template document that already contains your return address, today's date, your font choices, and the formats appropriate to a business letter.* You can create a template with just about any word processing program. Be sure to look for a program that can insert today's date automatically.

- *Creating a library of boilerplate documents on disk.* If your word processing program can load template documents in a read-only mode, you can create a library of documents tailored to a wide variety of business situations. You can create the letters yourself or use a business letter library.

- *Getting your correspondent's name and address from the database rather than typing them.* One of this book's basic rules for effective computerization is never type the same information twice.

It is amazing that so few word processing programs enable the easy exchange of information between a mailing list manager and a word processing document.

- *Drawing names and addresses from a mailing list and printing dozens, hundreds, or even thousands of personalized form letters.* You can pull this trick off with a mailing list/letter writer program, an integrated program such as Works or Q & A, or a full-featured program. If you choose a full-featured program, however, get ready for a steep learning curve.

- *Proofreading your document for errors in spelling, grammar, punctuation, and usage.* Almost all word processing programs include spelling checkers; you can buy an add-on grammar, punctuation, and usage checker.

Creating Template Documents

With any word processing program, you can create and save a generic version of a letter, such as the one shown in figure 7.1. In this document, created with Microsoft Works, you see the firm's return address centered at the top of the page, a command (*date*) that inserts the current date when the document is printed, a salutation, and a complimentary close. To write a letter, you flesh this document out with text and print the letter.

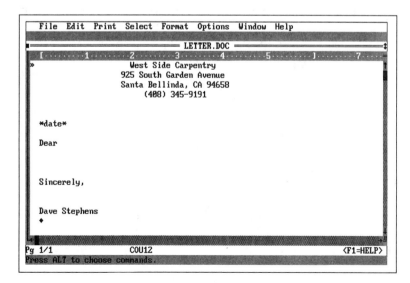

Fig. 7.1. A template document (Microsoft Works).

The only drawback to using a template document such as this one is that you may overwrite it with the completed text. If you do, the next time you open this document, you do not see a skeleton of a letter. You see a complete letter. To avoid this, you have several options, depending on the program you are using:

- *Open the file as a read-only file.* Available on the Open File menus of many programs, this option usually doesn't restrict you from altering the file on-screen, but you cannot save the changes using the same file name. You cannot overwrite the file. (To save your work, you just specify a new file name.)

- *Create a template document.* Some word processing programs enable you to create special files called *template documents*, which always open in the read-only mode. After you open the document on-screen, you can modify it, but you cannot save the document using the same template file name. (To save your work, you can save the document with a different file name.)

To use templates, look for a word processing program that can at least open documents in a read-only mode. Programs like Signature that include special facilities for storing and opening templates are especially useful for business letter writing.

TIP

To avoid overwriting template files, adopt a policy of *never* saving the letters you write. Just print two copies: mail one, and file the other copy in a good, old-fashioned chronological correspondence file. Little justification exists for saving a letter on disk. After you mail it, a letter is *fait accompli*; you cannot revise and send the letter again. Business writers who insist on saving every letter they write quickly fill up their disks with files they never use again.

Using a Library of Boilerplate Letters

Chances are you write the same letters over and over again. You answer inquiries about warranties, extend credit, turn down job applicants, ask customers to pay their late bills, and more. *Remember:* Don't reinvent the wheel! After you come up with a well-written letter on a specific subject, transform the letter into a boilerplate letter. A *boilerplate letter* contains standardized, well-considered text of proven effectiveness for a given situation, such as turning down an employment application or granting credit.

You can add boilerplate letters to your system in two ways. First, you can create generic versions of your own letters. In figure 7.2, you see a boilerplate letter that explains West Side Carpentry's treated lumber guarantee. This illustration is a generic version of a letter actually sent to a customer.

The second way to create a library of boilerplate letters is to buy an on-disk business letter library. A business letter library contains hundreds of disk files with generic business letters written for a wide variety of business situations. You can open these letters with your word processing program and customize the letters. The following is a list of some of the letters that come with FastPak Mail, a mail manager discussed in Chapter 3:

> Correction of billing error
> Follow up on sales letter
> Good credit reference
> Inactive customer sales inquiry
> Incomplete credit information to open account
> Is there a reason for delay in payment?
> Job inquiry turndown letter
> Must have cash with order
> New salesman taking over account
> Notice of credit being placed on hold
> Please give us a quote
> Request for extension of time to pay
> Response from supplier turning down credit
> Sorry for the late delivery
> Sorry we can't give you open credit
> Thanks for opening a new charge account
> Thanks for the order
> Thanks for the order but some items unavailable
> Thanks for your inquiry
> We appreciate your prompt payment
> We want to make sure that you are satisfied
> What do we need to open a charge account
> Wondering why you haven't used your account

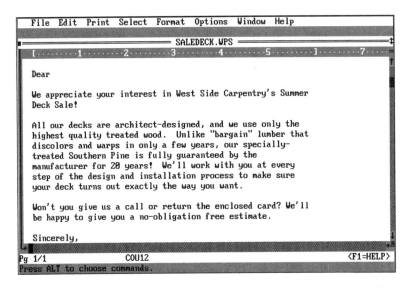

Fig. 7.2. *A template document with wording appropriate to a specific subject (Microsoft Works).*

Creating a library of template letters is definitely worth your time. An exchange of first-class letters constitutes a legal contract enforceable in a court of law. Dave Stephens, the proprietor of West Side Carpentry, must be very careful to make sure that he includes the words *by the manufacturer* when talking about the guarantee on his wood; if he leaves out this phrase by mistake, he can be held liable if one of his decks warps. Creating a library of carefully worded letters isn't just a convenience; a letter library also is an excellent idea from a legal standpoint. For letters dealing with sensitive matters, such as employment rejection, you may want to have an attorney look at the wording you propose to use.

TIP

Look for a business letter library written by professional business communicators. The best program, American Handbook of Business Letters, is an on-disk version of the authoritative book by the same name, which is published by the American Management Association.

Getting Names and Addresses from Your Mailing List

One of the biggest limitations of today's personal computer technology is that information isn't widely available across applications. On too many systems, users have spent too much time developing a mailing list—no easy way exists for getting a name and address into a letter. Programmers and system designers are working on this problem, but for now, you have to plan in advance to avoid some duplicate typing. In this section, you learn how you can use an integrated program such as Works to transfer names and addresses from your mailing list to letters.

The close integration between Works' database manager and word processor helps to explain the program's success. Creating a mailing list database with Works is easy, as explained in Chapter 4. An example of a Works mailing list database is shown in figure 7.3.

The key to getting the name and address from the mailing list into a letter lies in *placeholders*. When you put a placeholder in a letter, you tell Works to go to the database and find the kind of information specified. If you put the placeholder <<LastName>> in your letter, Works can go to the database and find the text that you have typed in the LastName field.

The following procedure demonstrates how Dave Stephens quickly composes a letter to Sally Anderson, who has written asking about the guarantee on the lumber Dave uses:

1. He adds Sally's name to his Works mailing list.

2. He uses Works' Query command to select just one record: Sally's.

3. He retrieves the boilerplate letter, to which he has added the place-holders shown in figure 7.4.

4. He chooses the Print Form Letter command, and Works prints the letter shown in figure 7.5.

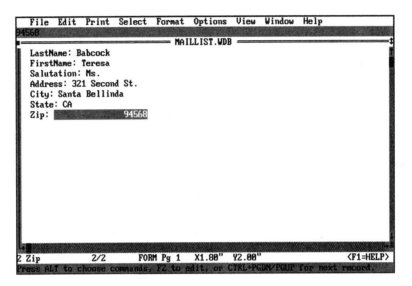

Fig. 7.3. A record in a mailing list database.

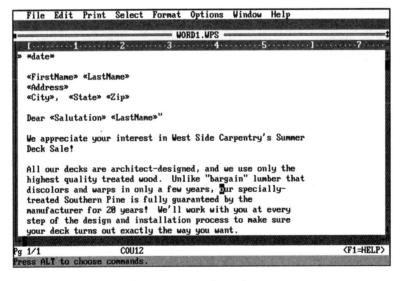

Fig. 7.4. Placeholders in a letter (Microsoft Works).

```
                    West Side Carpentry
                    1127 Woodfield Road
                    West Garden, VA 22987
                       (804) 555-9876




7/13/91


Sally Anderson
2118 Country Vistas
Periwinkle, VA 29876

Dear Ms. Anderson:

We appreciate your interest in West Side Carpentry's Summer
Deck Sale!

All our decks are architect-designed, and we use only the
highest quality treated wood.  Unlike "bargain" lumber that
discolors and warps in only a few years, our specially-
treated Southern Pine is fully guaranteed by the
manufacturer for 20 years!  We'll work with you at every
step of the design and installation process to make sure
your deck turns out exactly the way you want.

Sincerely,


Dave Stephens
```

Fig. 7.5. A letter with the name and address inserted (Microsoft Works).

You can perform this trick with word processing programs other than Works:

- *Mailing list managers/letter writing programs:* These software combinations are designed for this application, so transferring information from the mailing list to a single letter is easy. Make sure that you can select just one name and address at a time.

- *Full-featured word processing programs:* The big disadvantage of these programs is that you must maintain the mailing list in an ordinary word processing file. Often, you are forced to keep the whole name and address on a single line, which you cannot see on-screen at the same time. Operations such as sorting, editing, and selecting are much more difficult than they are with a database management program.

You can keep the mailing list in a database management program, where the list can be easily managed, but you have to write the data to a special ASCII file before your word processing program can read it. This process is such a hassle that you probably will prefer to type the address twice.

Printing Personalized Form Letters

In the preceding section, you learned how you can get a word processing program to draw a single name and address out of a mailing list and place the name and address in a business letter. You can use exactly the same technique to send out personalized form letters to many or all of the people in your mailing list.

Defining a Form Letter

A *form letter* is a letter that conveys the same text to many people. Even though many good reasons for writing such a letter exist, a form letter is impersonal; the letter begins with a salutation such as *Dear Customer*, and the reader knows right away that he or she is reading the same letter that dozens, hundreds, or thousands more are reading. Unless the message is especially valuable or pertinent, chances are the letter will wind up in the trash can without so much as a glance.

Knowing that form letters usually are ignored, big firms have been using computers to crank out *personalized form letters* for years. Thanks to personal computer technology, small businesses also can use form letters. A personalized form letter closely resembles an ordinary form letter, in that you send the same text to many people. A personalized form letter, however, is addressed to a specific person and includes a salutation (such as *Dear Dr. Anderson*). When a personalized form letter is produced well, it looks like a private letter—a letter written by one person to another. Most people know better in these days of computerized mass mailings, and yet they still appreciate someone taking the time and trouble to put their name and address on the letter.

With Works, sending personalized form letters is easy. You use the database module to select a view containing the names and addresses you want, and then you create a letter with placeholders, like the ones in figure 7.4. Works prints one letter for each name and address in the mailing list. If you select all the mailing list records, Works prints one letter for everybody.

The more information you keep in your database about your customers, the more ways you can exploit the database/form letter connection. To illustrate this point, imagine that you are running a small gourmet wine shop, and you ask your customers to fill out a brief questionnaire indicating their wine interests and preferences. Suppose that you have just gotten a shipment of 10 cases of an outstanding Australian chardonnay. A quick query in your database produces just 12 records of people who are interested in Australian chardonnays, but are they ever interested! Letters to all 12, for a cost of five cents per page of laser output and 29 cents for postage, probably will result in a very desirable goal: selling all 10 cases within about three days.

Notifying Customers of Overdue Bills

The following example is a useful variation on the preceding technique. Suppose that you add a couple of data fields to Dave's Works database so that a blank data record looks like the following:

LastName:

FirstName:

Address:

City:

State:

ZIP:

Phone:

DateBillSent:

BillAmount:

BillPaid:

Every time you send out a bill, fill out the screen as follows:

LastName: Tyler

FirstName: Connie

Address: 456 Shady Oaks Lane

City: Salisbury

State: VA

ZIP: 22955

DateBillSent: 8/29/91

BillAmount: $3,295.40

BillPaid: N

Once a month, perform a query of this Works database that asks, in effect, "Show me all the customers for whom the BillPaid field contains N and the DateBillSent field contains a date more than one month ago." Quickly, Works produces a view of the database containing only those records that meet the criteria. You then can open a form letter that asks for immediate payment and print the letters; Works inserts the date of the bill, the amount overdue, and the customer's name and address.

Proofreading for Errors

Almost every word processing program comes with a good spelling checker, and you should use it. Spelling and typographical errors detract from your business's image. Be forewarned, however, that spelling checkers cannot find all spelling mistakes. In particular, a spelling checker cannot help you if you use a correctly-spelled word in the wrong place. The following sentence contains two such errors: "I can not install a deck their" (the correct words are *cannot* and *there*).

In addition to spell checking, you are well advised to add a grammar and style checker such as Grammatik (Reference Software) or RightWriter (Que Software) to your system. These programs can detect a surprisingly large proportion of the flaws commonly found in business correspondence, such as inappropriate legalese (*whereas*), stilted or archaic language (*enclosed herewith*), sexist phrases (*a man and his wife*), doubled words (*the the*), punctuation errors, worn-out cliches, and many more. RightWriter can detect the following problems, for example:

Ambiguity
Archaic expressions
Capitalization errors
Colloquial expressions
Conjunction errors
Difficult sentences
Long sentences and paragraphs
Misleading euphemisms
Missing parentheses
Missing punctuation
Misused words
Negative sentences
Offensive expressions
Possessive errors
Quotation errors
Redundancy
Run-on sentences
Sentence fragments
Sexist expressions
Slang
Split infinitives
Subject-verb agreement
Vague expressions
Weak sentence structure
Wordiness
Wrong verb forms

These programs also can evaluate your document for its readability. You should assume that the people reading your business letters will have the equivalent of an eighth or ninth grader's reading ability.

Summary

The following lists summarizes this chapter's main points:

- The word processing software that is right for technical reports or proposals may not be the best choice for business letter writing. To write business letters, you need a program that offers easy data transfer from a mailing list.

- The programs that offer the easiest transfer of names and addresses from mailing lists are integrated programs (such as Works or Q&A),

and mailing list manager/letter writing packages (such as FastPak Mail Version 5.0). Full-featured programs also can do the job, but you should expect a steeper learning curve.

- Don't reinvent the wheel. Create a generic letter template that comes on-screen with your return address and today's date. Build a disk library of boilerplate letters for a variety of business situations.

- Avoid typing the same information twice. Type names and addresses just once—in your mailing list. Then insert them in the letters you type.

- Keep in touch with your customers by using personalized form letters. If you add a few extra fields to your mailing list database, you can greatly increase the number of things you can do with personalized form letters.

- Check the spelling of every letter you write, and check the spelling again with a grammar and style checker.

Software Suggestions

Excellent software options for letter-writing applications are available in the DOS and Mac environments, and by the time you read this book, more options will be available for Windows. The grammar and style checkers RightWriter and Grammatik are available for all three environments.

DOS Software for Business Letters

- *American Handbook of Business Letters (American Management Association):* A disk full of boilerplate, this package contains hundreds of professionally written letters in ASCII text, which is readable by any DOS or Windows word processing program.

- *FastPak Mail 5.0 (Bloc Publishing):* Highly recommended: includes outstanding mailing list management and an integrated word processing program. The user interface is compliant with Common User Access standards.

- *Microsoft Word 5.5 (Microsoft Corporation):* A full-featured program with an exceptionally well-designed, Common User Interface-compliant screen display. An outstanding choice for reports and proposals due to its excellent outlining capabilities. However, Word's mailing list management is much weaker than WordPerfect's.

- *Personal Law Firm (Bloc Publishing):* A stand-alone application that doesn't require a word processing program, this program interactively creates 30 types of legal documents and letters, including bills of sale; demand letters; letters of offer to purchase; notices of contract breach, rejection of goods, release of lien, termination of contract, and more.

- *Signature (IBM Corporation):* A full-featured program that, like Word, features a well-designed screen display. Signature is harder to learn and use than Word, but the program has better features for template letters. Mailing list management isn't as strong as WordPerfect's. A good choice for reports and proposals.

- *WordPerfect 5.1 (WordPerfect Corporation):* By far the most popular full-featured DOS word processing program, WordPerfect is a powerhouse package that can perform a huge variety of business writing tasks, including all the ones discussed in this chapter. If you are willing to learn WordPerfect, you will find that the program has mailing list capabilities that go far beyond those of most other full-featured word processing programs. You can even select a view of just those records that meet criteria you specify, like you can with a database program.

Macintosh Software for Business Letters

- *Letter Writer Plus (Power Up):* Designed to work with Address Book Plus, a mailing list manager, this program enables you to compose and print letters, memos, and envelopes while you are using any Macintosh program. This program can draw one or many addresses from Address Book Plus, making it useful for form letter applications.

- *Microsoft Word (Microsoft Corporation):* A full-featured program, Microsoft Word is an outstanding program for lengthy documents, such as reports and proposals. However, its mailing list management is weak and form letter commands are difficult to learn.

- *WordPerfect for the Macintosh (WordPerfect Corporation):* A full-featured program that offers excellent mailing list management. Significantly easier to learn and use than its DOS counterpart.

- *QuickLetter (Working Software):* A mailing list manager/letter writing program that offers quick data interchange between the mailing list and the word processor.

Windows Software for Business Letters

- *Ami Pro (Lotus Development Corporation):* A full-featured word processing program best suited to lengthier documents, such as reports and proposals.

- *JustWrite (Symantec Corporation):* An executive word processing program that couples ease of use with an impressive array of features, including mail merge, outlining, and integrated text and graphics.

- *Microsoft Word for Windows (Microsoft Corporation):* Closely resembling the Macintosh version of Word, Word for Windows is a powerhouse package best suited for reports and proposals.

8

Writing Reports
and Proposals

I f you are planning to write long, complex documents with your computer, a simple word processing program (like the word processing
module in Microsoft Works) may not be adequate for the task. Mike writes
grant proposals for a small, nonprofit organization that sponsors research
on learning disabilities. He uses Microsoft Word for Windows. "Without a
program as powerful as Word, I'd write a lot fewer proposals" he says. "I get
organized using Word's outliner, and more advanced features come into
play at every step, including footnotes, automatic table-of-contents generation, cross-references, and indexes. I can develop a proposal quickly, and I
can renumber tables, generate a new table of contents, and update the page
numbers in the index with just a few keystrokes."

Small businesses are at the usual disadvantage when competing in the
report-writing sweepstakes: no clerical or editorial help. Too many small
businesses do not bother to compete for government business (or jobs with
larger firms) that require extensive reporting: they don't have the time to
put together a proposal or write a 30-page technical report when the work
is finished. As this chapter shows, a small business can rightly regard a full-
featured program (such as Word or WordPerfect) as a storehouse of report-
and proposal-writing features, which can reduce the costs of preparing
these lengthy, complex documents.

You may think that you don't need much computing power if you are just performing word processing tasks. You can make do with a basic system. That may be true if you are running Works to write letters and memos, but if you are writing major reports and proposals, you need a full-featured DOS word processing program, such as Word or IBM Signature. These programs enable you to choose between a faster text mode, in which many document elements are not visible on-screen, and a considerably slower graphics mode, in which you see all or most document elements on-screen—including typefaces, type sizes, headers, footers, and footnotes. To run these programs in the graphics mode, however, you need as much computing power as you need to run Windows—at the minimum, an 80386 computer running at a reasonably fast clock speed (such as 16 MHz).

Exploring Your Software Options for Writing Reports and Proposals

You'll find exceptional word processing programs in all three personal computing environments—DOS, Macintosh, and Windows. The DOS powerhouse programs, such as Word 5.5, WordPerfect, and IBM Signature, are character-based programs that do not normally show fonts, font sizes, and graphics on-screen. (You can display these graphic elements with all three of these programs, but it is far from convenient to do so.) If your reports and proposals will include two or more fonts, a variety of font sizes, or graphics (such as charts or illustrations), you should think seriously about a Macintosh or Windows word processing program. Macintosh and Windows environments are designed to work in a graphics environment, making it much easier to combine text with graphic elements.

Exploring the Benefits of Full-Featured Word Processing Programs

Some users look at a word processor and see only an electronic typewriter. What you should see is a treasure-house of report-writing resources. These resources include many with which you probably are familiar: automatic footnote numbering and placement, document reorganization with block moves, automatic page numbering, and so on.

This section, however, discusses the high-productivity features that too many writers don't fully use. This chapter surveys 11 underused features that high-productivity writers are using to crank out reports and proposals:

- *Outlining:* Plan ahead and then reorganize the document after you write it by rearranging headings on an outline.

- *Electronic thesaurus:* Find the right word with a just a few keystrokes.

- *Glossaries:* Insert lengthy, often-used passages and blocks of standardized text (such as a company description), at a keystroke.

- *Tables:* Use spreadsheet-like table generators to lower the time you spend formatting tables, or import spreadsheets directly from programs such as Excel or Lotus 1-2-3.

- *Macros and styles:* Automate often-used command sequences and store complex formats so that you can retrieve them at a keystroke.

- *Automatic numbering:* Don't number anything manually—items in lists, tables, or figures. Let the program do the numbering. If you move text around, the numbers change automatically.

- *On-screen sorting:* Let the computer sort your lists in alphabetical or numerical order.

- *Redlining:* As many as three out of five business documents result from a team effort. If you write collaboratively, you can take advantage of useful tools that help you track and approve the revisions that others want to make to a document you have developed.

- *Table of contents and index generation:* Compile an index and table of contents, complete with page numbers, from words or headings that you have coded in your manuscript.

- *Print previewing:* Before you waste time printing a document with a serious omission (such as lack of page numbers or headings positioned at the bottom of a page), preview the pages on-screen.

Organizing Your Document with Outlining

It isn't easy to write a crisp, well-organized business letter—and the longer the document, the more challenges you'll face as you try to get your document organized. So if you write some long documents, read on: Computer software can help you organize a lengthy report or proposal.

The goal of helping writers organize lengthy documents motivated the very first outlining program, ThinkTank, in the early 1980s. In ThinkTank, you could type headings and subheadings as in a word processor but with key differences. First, you could collapse all the subheadings under a heading, and you could expand the text again to see what was under the heading. Second, you could change the level of a heading laterally, indenting it to the right to diminish its position in the hierarchy of outline levels or indenting it to the left to raise its position in the hierarchy. Third, you could move a heading vertically—including all its associated subheadings—up or down on-screen. With these tools, you could quickly create and restructure a detailed outline.

ThinkTank, however, had one major drawback. Coming up with a good outline is great, but you need to maintain the structure as you write. Frequently, you need to make changes in your outline as you discover new dimensions of your subject while writing. To solve this problem, Microsoft embedded an outliner in the structure of Microsoft Word (in all three of its incarnations: DOS, Macintosh, and Windows).

For anyone who writes lengthy reports and has trouble getting documents organized, Word is a blessing. In Word, no distinction is made between the outlining document and the word processing document: they're one and the same. In outline mode, you look at your document as if you were looking at a table of contents—with two, three, or more levels of headings and subheadings (see fig. 8.1). You can collapse the text so that only the headings and subheadings are visible. In document mode, you see the headings and subheadings, but they are formatted the way you want them (centered, flush left, or whatever), and you also see the text (see fig. 8.2).

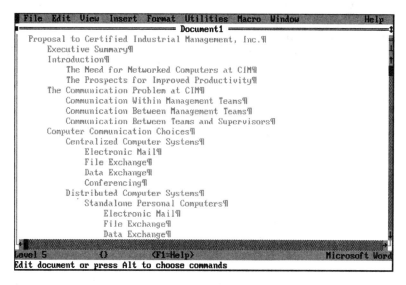

Fig. 8.1. *Outlining mode (Microsoft Word 5.5).*

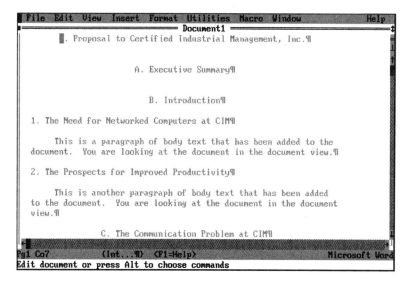

Fig. 8.2. *Document mode (Microsoft Word 5.5).*

Just being able to look at your document in two different ways is helpful; in outline mode, you see the overall structure of your document. What makes Word's outlining capabilities so powerful is that you can restructure your entire document by rearranging headings in the outline. When you move an outline heading, Word moves all the subheadings and text. If you decide that the section titled "Overview of Project Methodology" belongs in Chapter 2 instead of in the introduction, you can make the change in just a few keystrokes. The whole operation is much easier, and much less prone to error, than trying to rearrange your document with repeated block moves.

Finding the Right Word

If you often find yourself struggling to find just the right word to express a shade of meaning, help is just a keystroke away with most full-featured word processing programs, which offer an electronic thesaurus. At the touch of a key, you see synonyms for the word you have highlighted on-screen (see fig. 8.3).

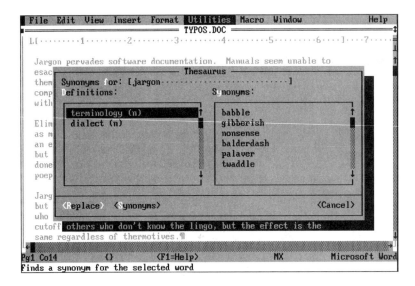

Fig. 8.3. An electronic thesaurus (Microsoft Word 5.5).

An electronic thesaurus can come in handy when you are struggling to find the right word. In place of a vague jargon word such as *analysis*, for example, an electronic thesaurus offers dozens of more specific words, including *experiment, exploration, test, inquiry,* and *trial*. To use the thesaurus, you highlight the word and choose the command that opens the thesaurus. Synonyms appear automatically. When you choose the word you want and press Enter, the program replaces the highlighted word.

Using Glossaries

Do you type lengthy passages of text over and over again? If so, you can save time by creating and saving *glossaries*, which are stored blocks of boilerplate text that you can retrieve quickly. To retrieve the text with some programs, you type the passage's name, such as *company_description*, and choose the command that inserts the glossary with that name.

You can use glossaries to:

- *Enter commonly used phrases:* If your firm's name is lengthy, devise a glossary to enter the name automatically. Instead of typing *Albemarle Valley Engineering Services, Inc.*, you just type *AVES* and choose the glossary command; the program replaces *AVES* with *Albemarle Valley Engineering Services, Inc.*

- *Enter boilerplate passages:* Create and standardize a company description, which you can enter at a keystroke into every proposal you write. You can use the same trick for any other block of text that you know you will reuse.

Many programs enable you to assign glossaries to keys. Entering a two-paragraph company description becomes as easy as pressing a key combination such as Alt-Shift-C.

TIP

Using Macros and Styles

Writers of lengthy reports and proposals must frequently repeat tedious operations, such as paging through documents to inspect page breaks or entering a long series of formatting commands. As long as you can do so with a minimum of programming fuss, you should automate everything you can. With macros and styles, you can automate items in two ways:

- *Using macros:* A *macro* is a list of program commands that you have saved on disk, where they can be retrieved at a keystroke. When you retrieve a macro, the program carries out these commands, just as if you were typing them at the keyboard.

- *Using styles:* A *style* is a list of formats that you have saved on disk, where they can be retrieved at a keystroke. When you retrieve the style, the program applies all the formats to the text you have selected.

What is the point of creating macros and styles? Huge productivity gains. If you find yourself choosing a complicated command sequence over and over again, the process is a likely candidate for a macro. Why fuss with the keyboard or spend time choosing six or seven layers of menus when you can automate the whole process with a macro?

Suppose that you add the same header to every report or proposal you write. (A *header* is a word or phrase that appears at the top of every page. Headers often include page numbers). Why not create a macro that enters the header and page numbers, instead of creating the header for each new document?

Styles offer comparable gains. To create a heading, for example, you center the text, apply the boldface characteristic, choose the Helvetica 14 font, and code the heading so that the program does not break a page beneath it. This process includes four separate formatting commands! Instead, you can create and save a style called Heading 1, and assign that style to a key.

Styles and macros are not hard to create. To record a style, you choose the formats you want, highlight the formatted text, and choose the command that records the style. To record a macro, you turn on a macro recorder that monitors everything you do. You choose the commands you want, and when you are finished choosing the commands, you turn off the macro recorder. In both cases, the program then prompts you to choose the key to which you want to assign the style or macro.

Using Automatic Numbering

Many reports and proposals require that items, such as lines, paragraphs, or tables, be numbered sequentially. Numbering items manually is a drag, and if you add or delete material, you may throw the numbers off. Full-featured word processing programs include automatic numbering capabilities that enable you to number the following elements:

- *Paragraphs:* In a word processing program, a paragraph is any block of text that ends with an Enter keystroke. By this definition, a paragraph can be an item in a list, such as a bibliographic citation. If you can type an item as a paragraph, most programs can number the item.

- *Figures and tables:* Some programs (such as Microsoft Word) include features that enable you to create more than one numbering series, which are numbered independently (for example, your five figures are numbered as figures 1 through 5, and your 14 tables are numbered as tables 1 through 14). You can use one series for figures, a second series for tables, and a third for illustrations. Instead of numbering these elements yourself, you enter the series code. When your document prints, the program inserts numbers in place of the series codes.

Sorting Data

Reports and proposals frequently include lengthy lists, such as specifications or references. With most full-featured word processing programs, you can have the program sort such items alphabetically or numerically. You just highlight the text you want sorted and choose the sort command. Most programs enable you to sort in ascending order (A, B, C, or 1, 2, 3) or descending order (C, B, A or 3, 2, 1).

When used with *column selection*, which enables you to highlight a rectangular block of text on-screen, the sort feature of Microsoft Word enables you to restructure a table in many ways. In figure 8.4, for example, a column has been selected in a table. Figure 8.5 shows the results of an ascending numerical sort that uses this column as a *key*, or a guide for the sort. Notice that Word does not scramble the data; the $14.36 in figure 8.4 stays with its heading (Paper) and the value under Apricot.

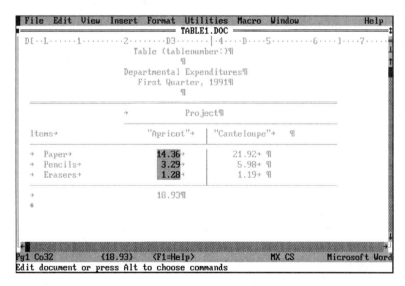

Fig. 8.4. *Selecting a column of data in a table (Microsoft Word 5.5).*

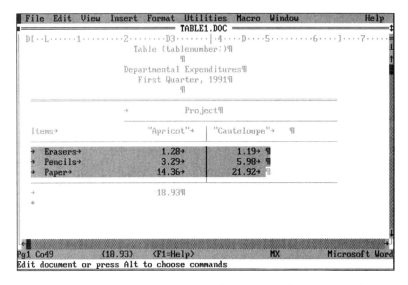

Fig. 8.5. A table after sorting the graphics department data in ascending numerical order (Microsoft Word 5.5).

Doing On-Screen Math

If you frequently type tables, there's no need to get a hand calculator to add up columns of figures. Most of the full-featured word processing programs discussed in this chapter include on-screen math capabilities.

A common use of on-screen math is adding up columns of numbers in a table. Microsoft Word typifies the process: you select the data you want to add and choose the Calculate command (see fig. 8.6). With a few keystrokes, you enter the results where you want them to appear (see fig. 8.7).

TIP

If you are working in an engineering field, look for a program that can help you type and print complex equations, complete with non-ordinary elements such as integrals and summation signs. Two good possibilities are Microsoft Word for the Macintosh and WordPerfect 5.1 for IBM PCs and compatibles. Both come equipped with excellent *equation editors,* program modes that enable you to compose (and view on-screen) multiline equations.

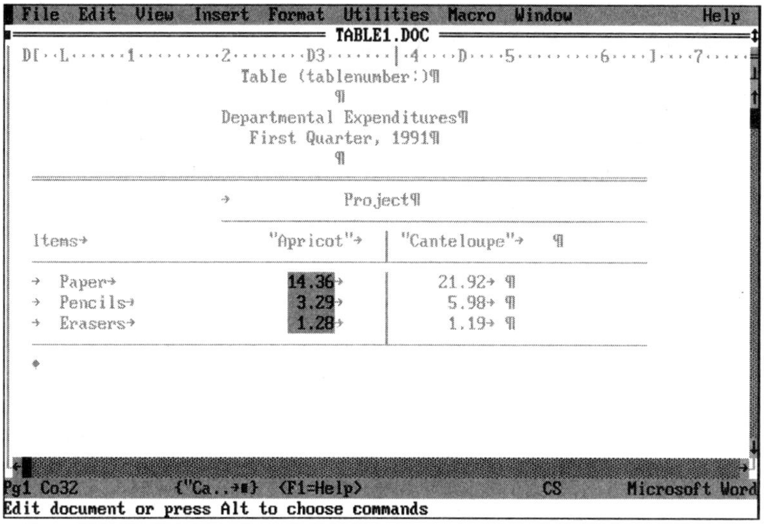

Fig. 8.6. Selecting the data to be totalled (Microsoft Word 5.5).

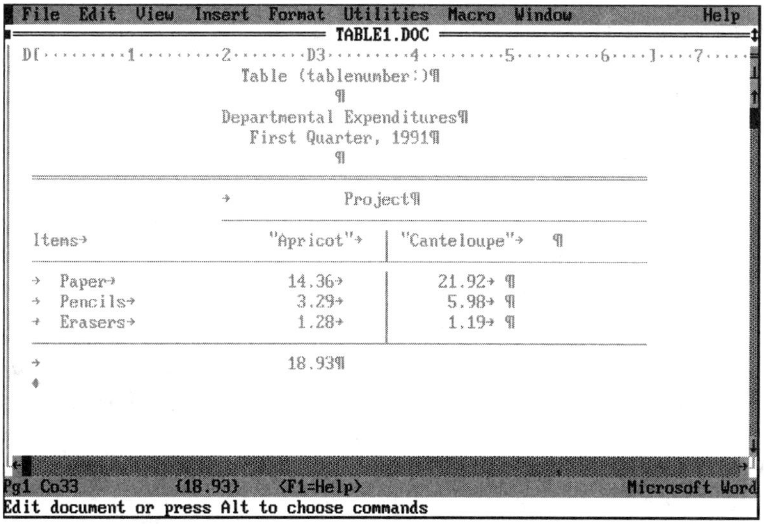

Fig. 8.7. Adding the total to the bottom of the column (Microsoft Word 5.5).

Using Redlining

Two heads may be better than one, but when two people are trying to write the same document with a computer, determining who did what can be impossible. *Redlining* is a program mode, offered in most full-featured word processing programs, that displays editing changes and enables reviewers to confirm them. When you turn on the redlining mode, the text you insert appears in a distinctive format. The text you delete doesn't disappear; deleted text appears as strikethrough text.

After the document has been edited in this way, the reviewer uses a document-review command that finds every change (every insertion and deletion), and enables the reviewer to accept or reject the change. If the reviewer accepts the change, the inserted text loses its distinctive formatting, and the deleted text disappears.

Generating a Table of Contents and Index

To compile a table of contents or an index for your document, you must code the text. Figure 8.8 shows the codes you use to code words for inclusion in a Microsoft Word index. When you finish coding the document, Word compiles an index, adds the page numbers, and places the index at the end of your document. You create a table of contents in the same way—you code the headings, and when you finish the document, Word compiles the table of contents, adds the page numbers, and places the table of contents at the beginning of your document.

To make the index process go faster, WordPerfect offers *concordance indexing*. Instead of coding the words, you type all the words you want indexed in a separate file, called a *concordance file*. WordPerfect then draws on this file as a basis for the indexing operation, which is automatic. WordPerfect scans your document, and when the program finds a word that matches one of the words in the concordance file, WordPerfect codes the word for inclusion in the index.

Word offers a feature that speeds the task of generating the table of contents. Instead of coding each heading, you display the headings in outline mode. You collapse the subheadings until you have displayed just the levels of the headings that you want to appear in the table of contents. Word then uses this outline display as a guide for constructing the table of contents. No manual coding is needed.

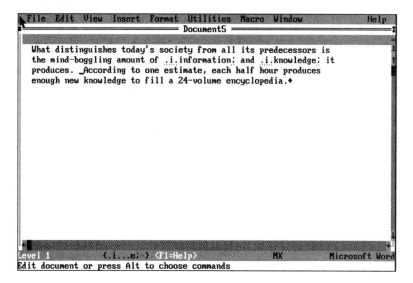

Fig. 8.8. Words coded for inclusion in an index (Microsoft Word 5.5).

For a document of 25 to 40 pages, generating a table of contents or an index manually is too difficult *the first time*. Suppose that you go to your client, and she says, "It's great but take out the section on such-and-such." If that section is on page 3, all the page numbers are thrown off for the rest of the document. If you have coded the table of contents and index entries, you can regenerate the table of contents and the index quickly. If you haven't used these codes, you are in for a profit-chomping, time-guzzling ordeal.

Previewing Your Document

Few computer frustrations are as irritating as printing out a lengthy document, only to find that you have forgotten to add headers, page numbers, or some other needed element. If you have been moving text around, Murphy's law predicts that a heading will end up at the bottom of the page, with no text under it. To check your document before printing, use the print preview mode that most full-featured word processing programs offer.

When using the print preview feature, you see all document elements—even the ones that the program cannot manage to display on-screen while you're editing. Figure 8.9 shows you how your document will appear on the page.

TIP

With many programs, you can prevent *widowed* headings—headings left alone at the bottom of the page. Just format the heading with the command that prevents the program from entering a page break after a paragraph.

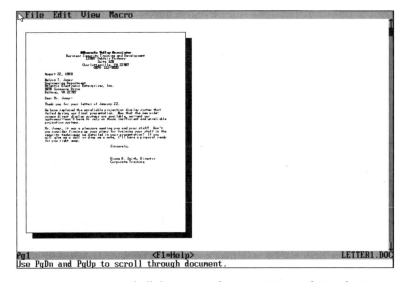

Fig. 8.9. *A print preview of all document elements (Microsoft Word 5.5).*

Summary

If you are planning to write lengthy or complex documents such as reports or proposals, you can use a full-featured word processing program's advanced features to improve your productivity. These features include the following:

- *Outlining:* Use a program's outlining mode to plan (and, if you are using Word, restructure) your document quickly.

- *Electronic thesaurus:* Look up the right word without leaving your computer.

- *Glossaries:* Add lengthy phrases or blocks of text at a keystroke.

- *Tables:* Create tables quickly with the table generator or import spreadsheets directly from spreadsheet programs.

- *Macros and styles:* With just one keystroke, enter lengthy command-choosing sequences or multiple formats.

- *Automatic numbering:* Number lists, tables, and figures automatically and have the program renumber them so that you can make changes to your document.

- *On-screen sorting:* Quickly sort a list in alphabetical or numerical order, whether ascending or descending.

- *Redlining:* Use the redlining mode to alert your collaborators where you have inserted and deleted text; your collaborators can review the changes and accept or delete the changes.

- *Table of contents and index generation:* Generate a table of contents and an index from coded headings and words in your text, complete with page numbers. If you change your document, you can regenerate the table and index quickly.

- *Print previewing:* Check for formatting errors before you waste time, paper, and (if you are using a laser printer) expensive laser toner.

Software Suggestions

You'll need a full-featured word processing program to tackle reports and proposals. DOS programs are fast, capable, and well-supported—there are many people who are using programs such as Microsoft Word 5.5 or WordPerfect 5.1. If you're planning to include graphics (fonts, font sizes, charts, or illustrations) in your documents, though, you'll be wise to choose a Macintosh or Windows program.

DOS Word Processing Programs for Reports and Proposals

- *Microsoft Word (Microsoft Corporation):* A powerful and capable program, Word recently received a facelift that gives the program a much-improved user interface, making it by far the most approachable program in this category.

- *WordPerfect (WordPerfect Corporation):* An exceptionally versatile program, WordPerfect is widely used—you probably know someone who's using it! But expect a steep learning curve. You'll have to edit hidden codes to gain full control of the program.

- *Signature (IBM Corporation):* Based on the highly regarded XyWrite, Signature features a much-improved, industry-standard user interface, replete with pull-down menus, dialog boxes, and mouse support. For this reason, the program is easier to learn than WordPerfect, but expect a steep learning curve—as in WordPerfect, you'll have to edit hidden codes to gain full control of the program. Signature is even more feature-packed than WordPerfect and features an editable graphics mode, in which you can see your font and font size choices on-screen.

Macintosh Word Processing Programs for Reports and Proposals

- *Microsoft Word (Microsoft Corporation):* Considered by many to be the finest word processing program available, Word combines the Macintosh's legendary ease of use with a feature list comparable to the DOS powerhouse packages. Very highly recommended.

- *WordPerfect for the Macintosh (WordPerfect Corporation):* The first release of this program failed to take full advantage of the Macintosh environment, but subsequent versions addressed this shortcoming and won acclaim from Macintosh software reviewers. Even so, the program retains its insistence that users edit hidden codes when they need to delete or alter formats.

Window Word Processing Programs for Reports and Proposals

- *Ami Pro (Lotus Development Corporation):* A well-regarded, full-featured program that takes full advantage of the Windows environment. Offers many features that make the program suitable for some desktop publishing uses.

- *Word for Windows (Microsoft Corporation):* The market leader among Windows word processors, Word closely resembles its Macintosh counterpart and is highly recommended.

Getting Into
Desktop Publishing

J ust a few years ago, using a personal computer meant producing ugly
output from noisy, dot-matrix printers. With laser printers now available
for less than $1,000, even a small business or sole proprietorship can save
big on document production costs by doing some desktop publishing in-
house. The documents you can expect to desktop publish with a personal
computer include sales brochures, price lists, menus, newsletters, forms,
instruction manuals, and more.

Desktop publishing is the use of a personal computer and laser printer to
generate typeset-quality text, often blended with graphics. To do desktop
publishing, you need a program that can merge text and graphics on the
same page. In the early years of desktop publishing (the late 1980s), that
meant using a *page-layout program*, a program especially designed to
prepare pages filled with text and graphics (such as PageMaker). Many word
processing programs have taken on some of the characteristics of desktop
publishing software. If you have a full-featured word processing program
such as Microsoft Word, you already may possess some desktop publishing
capabilities.

Small businesses can really use desktop publishing. Suppose that Amer
runs a pizza shop. He spends $800 to have new menus designed, and the
design comes back from the artist late. Misspellings are all over the place.
The artist claims that he could not read Amer's handwriting and wants
more money to fix the mistakes.

If you must prepare documents such as brochures, fliers, display ads, price lists, newsletters, or menus, desktop publishing can save significant amounts of money. As Amer's example illustrates, desktop publishing enables you to control the schedule—at least through the design and typesetting phases. You easily and quickly can correct errors, right up to the moment the document is printed. These significant advantages explain why desktop publishing is one of the fastest-growing business applications of personal computers.

This chapter introduces desktop publishing and surveys desktop publishing software, programs for illustrating your documents, software and hardware for scanning and retouching photographs, and the many ways you can add fonts to your system. You learn how your business can benefit from desktop publishing with even a modest investment.

Examining Desktop Publishing Software Options

You can desktop publish simple but attractive documents with word processing programs, but page-layout programs give you many more features for page design. The following sections explain each of these differences.

Full-Featured Word Processing Programs

Some of the best full-featured word processing programs, such as Microsoft Word in all three versions (DOS, Windows, and Macintosh) and Ami Pro (Windows), can position graphics in absolute, fixed locations on the page and can display text and graphics simultaneously. You also can draw lines, make boxes, and place text in multiple, "snaking" columns. *Snaking columns*, also called *newspaper columns*, are found in newspapers, newsletters, and magazines; the text runs down to the bottom of the column, and then "snakes" up to the top of the next column (see fig. 9.1). These programs give you a full complement of tools for writing and editing the text of the document, including spelling checkers.

PageOne 1

PAGEMAKER:
WHERE DESKTOP PUBLISHING BEGINS

ALDUS CORPORATION, in Seattle, Washington, leads the desktop publishing industry with PageMaker, page layout software that allows individuals and businesses to produce professional-looking publications in-house. PageMaker's introduction into the market has met with a great deal of industry recognition, particularly from the press. *Infoworld*, the computer industry's influential magazine, gave it the Best Software Product of the Year Runner-Up award for 1985.

THE PHRASE, "DESKTOP PUBLISHING," was coined by Aldus founder and president, Paul Brainerd, who saw that page-layout software would be invaluable to anybody who wanted to produce printed communications, from newsletters, order forms, and annual reports, to proposals, manuals, and magazines. Given the advances in graphics-oriented microcomputers and laser printers, the introduction of PageMaker meant that, for the first time, people could afford to create visually appealing publications with ease.

PAGEMAKER LETS PEOPLE WORK electronically the way professional designers work with conventional pages. With the click of the mouse, or a simple keyboard command, the computer screen becomes a blank page on a pasteboard, accompanied by a toolbox of design aids. A person arranges the page as desired, establishing margins, creating columns of varying widths, adding page numbers, and so on. Then the person fills the page with text and graphics created with other software programs, using on-screen rulers and dotted lines for accurate placement.

INDIVIDUALS AND CORPORATIONS alike have turned to PageMaker as the most reliable way to publish high-quality, low-cost materials, from brochures to 300-page books and technical manuals.

Desktop Publishing Sales in Billions of Dollars

Desktop publishing is expected to grow into a multibillion dollar industry, especially now that it has been introduced into the PC market. What was a $1-billion boom in 1985 may soar past the $5-billion mark in 1990.

Fig. 9.1. A newsletter with snaking columns.

Word processing programs do have drawbacks for desktop publishing. Their options for drawing lines and boxes are limited. Sometimes you can see the text and graphics simultaneously only in a sluggish page preview mode, which may not be editable. Rearranging page elements becomes very tedious in such cases. With most word processing programs, creating a page-layout design that repeats on every page of your document is impossible (complete with borders, headlines, and rules).

Page-Layout Programs

Page-layout programs are designed to help you design the appearance of each page of your document. Unlike a word processing program, a page layout program always works in page preview mode and is fully editable. In addition to the page-layout capabilities of word processing programs such as Word or Ami Pro (absolute positioning of text and graphics on the page with text flowing around the positioned object), these programs include more line, box, and shading options. You can include halftone and shading effects; repeat page designs, which appear on every page of your document; use on-screen rulers for precise placement of text and graphics; automatically align inserted elements; and use a full repertoire of fonts and type sizes for display and body type. Figure 9.2 shows how desktop publishing software (PageMaker, in this example) shows text and graphics in an on-screen, editable display. Note the rulers, which enable precision alignment of the document elements. The latest generation of desktop publishing programs can produce subtle effects such as rotating text and wrapping text proportionally around a graphic (see fig. 9.3).

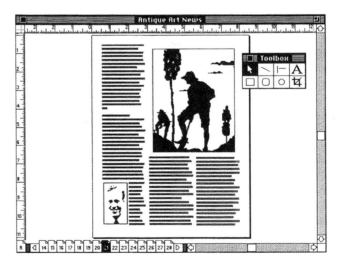

Fig. 9.2. An editable page layout.

The selected graphic showing
its custom text-wrap boundary.

Dragging the graphic
into place on the page.

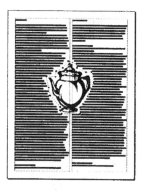

Surrounding text automatically
reflows itself around the graphic.

The final page after enlarging
and repositioning the graphic.

Fig. 9.3. Wrapping text around a graphic (PageMaker).

Page-layout programs do have their drawbacks. They aren't designed for writing. Very few include spelling checkers and facilities for creating and editing the text. You probably will want to create the document's text in a word processor, and when you're sure it's letter-perfect, you can import the text into your page-layout program.

Another disadvantage of page-layout programs such as PageMaker and Ventura Publisher is their high price. However, you now can buy "entry-level" desktop publishing programs that lack some of the features professional layout artists need (such as First Publisher). These programs may suffice for a small business's modest desktop publishing needs.

Illustration Programs

If you want to integrate text and graphics, you'll need graphics. One source for graphics is commercial *clip art*, which gives you a library of pictures on a disk (see fig. 9.4). (For a discussion of clip art, see Chapter 11, "Selling Your Ideas with Presentation Graphics.") But chances are you'll need to create your own illustrations.

Fig. 9.4. Clip art (T/Maker).

Here's a brief survey of your software options:

- *Paint programs (Windows Paint, SuperPaint, MacPaint):* A paint program turns your computer's screen into a palette for creating bit-mapped images, in which you're able to turn thousands of tiny on-screen dots on or off. You can choose from many predesigned shades and textures, and you can use a variety of tools, including a *paint brush*, a *spray can*, and a *pencil*.

  An experienced and talented user of such a program can create beautiful effects, but the pictures are difficult to edit and often don't print very well: the on-screen dots are tied to the screen's resolution, which the printer may not match. And the picture that is created can't easily be scaled.

- *Drawing programs (MacDraw, Micrografx Draw):* A drawing program uses object-oriented (vector) graphics to help you create images out of lines, rectangles, circles, and ovals. The picture is easy to edit because each shape can be independently sized and manipulated. Even better, the picture always prints at the printer's maximum resolution. But these programs have limited capabilities for more complex illustrations, and their typesetting capabilities are limited. The printed drawing may appear very nice but have crudely printed type.

- *Illustration programs (Adobe Illustrator 88, Corel Draw, DrawPerfect):* These professional-quality graphics programs take full advantage of the capabilities of the printer you're using, including the high-definition fonts as well as object-oriented graphics.

Photographs

In a small business, you're more likely to include photographs—pictures of houses for sale, a portrait of this month's top employee, a picture of a hot new product—than to get involved in professional illustration. To add photos to your documents, you'll need to equip your system with a scanner.

A *scanner* is an electro-optical device that connects to your computer via its serial port or a special board that plugs into one of your computer's expansion slots. A scanner "reads" an illustration and creates a bit-mapped (*digitized*) image that is stored in a disk drive file (see fig. 9.5). Most desktop publishing programs can access these files and incorporate them into reports, price lists, newsletters, and other documents.

For personal computers, two kinds of scanners are prevalent:

- *Hand-held scanners:* These scanners "read" a three- or four-inch swath of a page, which is enough for most photographs. The cheapest scanners create unsatisfactory bit-mapped files, which you won't want to include in documents you give your customers. The best hand-held scanners produce Tagged Image File Format (TIFF) files, which are high-resolution files capable of subtle gradations of gray.

- *Flatbed scanners:* These desktop scanners are capable of scanning an entire page, and are significantly more expensive than hand-held scanners.

If you just need to scan an occasional photograph, you can rent a scanner at a graphics service bureau for as little as $10 per hour.

TIP

Fig. 9.5. *A scanned image.*

Don't expect miracles from the scanned photographs you print with a laser printer. In professional graphics, photographs are set using many shades of gray, but laser printers can't print gray—they just print black and white. To simulate the subtle gradations of a photograph, scanner software records the image using a technique called *dithering*, in which tiny dots are offset against one another to simulate a limited range of gray shades. But the trick is quite obvious, even to an untrained eye. Still, scanned and laser-printed photographs are okay for informal brochures, price lists, information sheets, and modest newsletters.

TIP

An image enhancer (such as Digital Darkroom) can dramatically improve the printed appearance of scanned photographs. Such programs also enable you to perform retouching, add airbrush effects, and add special effects.

Looking At the Benefits of Desktop Publishing

Depending on the software you choose, you may be able to realize some or all of the following benefits:

- You may be able to save significant amounts of money that would otherwise go to graphic artists and typesetters. Some businesses have found themselves paying up to $2,000 per page to typeset a complex technical manual. Such costs may amount to as much as 15 percent of the total manufacturing costs in technical industries.

- You can assure that the project will be done on time. When you contract typesetting work outside your firm, you're relying on the honesty and diligence of others—but they may not be honest or diligent.

- You easily can display text and graphics on the same page. You can create good-looking price lists, product descriptions, and brochures—all illustrated with scanned photographs or illustrations.

- You can anchor pictures to an absolute, fixed position on the page so that text flows around them automatically. This capability makes it easy to design a page for such purposes as brochures and newsletters. You figure out where you want the graphics to go, and nail them down. Then you pour text into the areas that remain available, and the program automatically fills up the free space with the text.

- You can make last-minute changes. With a good desktop publishing program, the page design is kept in memory until you print, so it's easy to correct spelling errors, alter the design, change fonts, and even change the text—right up to the moment you print.

- You can create a wide range of documents that enable you to stay in touch with your customers—including catalogs, newsletters, product bulletins, news flashes, fliers of all kinds, sale notices, illustrated brochures, and more. Put that mailing list to good use!

Learning How Computers Handle Fonts

If you're planning to take advantage of desktop publishing, you'll need to know more about how personal computers handle fonts. There is a distinction, puzzling to new users, between *screen fonts* (the typefaces that appear on-screen) and *printer fonts* (the typefaces that generate printed output). Because screen fonts and printer fonts typically rely on totally different technologies, there is no necessary relation between the two: What you see on-screen may have little to do with what is printed. For desktop publishing, the best systems make this distinction irrelevant by matching screen fonts and printer fonts as much as possible. Here's a brief explanation of this distinction.

Screen Fonts

A basic distinction is drawn between screen fonts and printer fonts. A *screen font* displays type on-screen, while a *printer font* makes the type available to the printer. Just what this distinction means to you depends on the operating environment you're using (DOS, Windows, or Macintosh).

On DOS systems, there's a noticeable difference between the screen font and the printer font. Most DOS programs are *character-based programs*, which means they rely on the screen font that is permanently encoded in the computer's read-only memory (ROM). This font is a *monospace* font that closely resembles the output of an office typewriter. (The term *monospace* refers to the use of a fixed character space for every character in the font. The narrow *l*, for example, gets the same space as the wide *w*, as in `Mellow`.)

Can a DOS program take advantage of your printer's font resources? It all depends on how well the program supports your printer. A big drawback of DOS programs is that DOS leaves printer support up to each individual program. To cope with the multitude of printers on the market, publishers of DOS software must add hundreds of printer drivers to their programs. (A *printer driver* is a file that contains printing specifications for a particular make and model of printer.) Some programs provide better printer drivers than others. In a DOS system, for example, you may find that WordPerfect fully supports all your printer's font resources, while other programs do not provide such support and cannot use the printer's full range of font resources.

A few DOS programs, such as IBM Signature, can display fonts on-screen when running in the computer's Graphics mode, in which the computer displays a screen image completely made up of individual dots. These programs come with screen fonts that closely resemble the fonts a laser printer can print. If you quit one of these programs and start another DOS program, however, you'll find that you're back to the Character mode, with its monospace typewriter font. A big advantage of Windows and Macintosh systems is that screen fonts (and printer fonts) are available for all your programs.

One of the most important technical advantages of Windows and Macintosh systems is that screen fonts and printer drivers are handled at the operating system level, instead of leaving font support up to individual programs. Most Windows and Macintosh programs can use all the screen fonts that are installed in your system. If you install additional screen fonts, they become available, too. If you want to produce good-looking output from a variety of programs, including spreadsheets and database managers, Windows or Macintosh systems offer a decisive advantage.

Printer Fonts

A *printer font* is a font available for printing the document by placing it in the printer's memory. No matter what font you see on-screen, it won't print unless it's made available to the printer in some way.

You can handle the task of making the font available to the printer in several ways:

- *Using built-in fonts:* All printers have at least one built-in font (also called a resident font). This is the computer's default font—the font the computer will use unless your program commands it otherwise. On most laser printers, the default font is Courier 12. (Courier is a monospace font that resembles the output of a fine office type-writer.) Today's printers typically offer more than one built-in font. Built-in fonts have a technical advantage in that they're almost instantaneously available to your printer, and they don't wear out.

- *Using cartridge fonts:* Many printers, especially Hewlett-Packard and HP-compatible printers, have cartridge slots that accept font cartridges. Many cartridges offer only two or three fonts, but some manufacturers offer cartridges that make many more available. The 25 Plus/Charisma Font Cartridge, available for HP and HP-compatible laser printers, makes more than 150 fonts available to your printer. Like built-in fonts, cartridge fonts are almost instantaneously available to your computer.

- *Using soft fonts:* If your printer has its own memory, you can keep fonts on disk in your computer and transfer them to your computer when it's time to print. This operation is called *downloading*. A major disadvantage of soft fonts is that the printer's memory clears when you shut the printer off, so that you must wait one or more minutes for the downloading operation to occur. In Windows and Macintosh systems, the downloading process is automatic; if you choose a soft font, the system downloads the font without you performing any action. DOS programs don't perform this operation unless automatic downloading capabilities have been built in to the program. Microsoft Word and WordPerfect both offer automatic soft font downloading.

Many printers combine all three ways of making fonts available. The Hewlett-Packard LaserJet IIIP, for example, has many built-in fonts and accepts font cartridges. In addition, it has its own memory so that you can download soft fonts.

TIP

If you're shopping for a laser printer, look for one with many built-in fonts and sufficient memory (at least 1M) to use them. Built-in fonts save you the expense of cartridges or soft fonts, and because they're instantaneously available to your printer, there's no lengthy downloading process necessary before you can use them.

Bit-Mapped Fonts vs. Outline Typefaces

Computers employ two very different technologies to store and reproduce fonts—whether screen fonts or printer fonts (see fig. 9.6):

- *Bit-mapped fonts:* In a bit-mapped font, each character in the font is stored as a dense configuration of dots, like an Impressionist painting by Seurat. Curved edges may show an unattractive distortion called the *jaggies*. Bit-mapped fonts resemble bit-mapped graphics in this respect, and they have all the other disadvantages of bit-mapped graphics; you can't scale them up or down without introducing horrible distortions, and they take up huge amounts of storage space because you need one complete set of characters for every font. When you buy a bit-mapped font, you get a complete set of characters in one size or a range of sizes, such as Times Roman 10, Times Roman 12, and Times Roman 14. And those are the only type sizes you can use.

- *Outline typeface:* In an outline typeface (also called a scalable typeface), each character is generated by a complex mathematical formula. Like object-oriented or vector images in computer graphics, the characters produced by outline fonts print with graceful and undistorted outlines because the formula generates the characters and scales them to any size you want within a given range (such as 4 to 127 points). For this reason, it isn't necessary to store one complete character for each character in a font. (That's why it's more accurate to call scalable typefaces outline typefaces: when you buy an outline typeface, you get a huge range of potential fonts in just about any size you specify.)

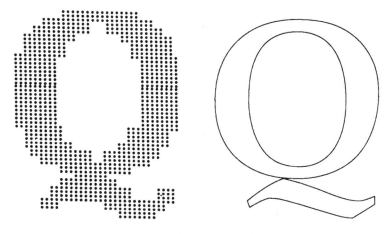

Fig. 9.6. *A bit-mapped character and an outline character.*

If it sounds as if outline fonts are technologically superior, you're right: they are—except that they place enormous demands on your system's processing capabilities. In an outline font, every character must be generated from a complex mathematical formula. To generate these characters (and other page elements), the computer must load a *page description language* (PDL) interpreter, which accepts a program's output and generates the information needed to print the font. If your computer must load the PDL and perform the calculations itself, printing speed suffers. That's why top-of-the-line laser printers include their own computer circuitry, including a microprocessor and a built-in PDL interpreter. These printers cost a lot of money—at least $2,000—because buying the printer is like buying a second computer. The alternative is letting your computer do all the processing, at the sacrifice of printing speed.

By far the most popular page-description language for personal computers is the PostScript language (from Adobe). Adobe has developed hundreds of beautiful outline typefaces, but the company levies big license fees for printer manufacturers who include PostScript interpreters in their printers' circuits. As a result, PostScript-compatible laser printers cost more than other printers capable of printing outline typefaces. To avoid Adobe's licensing fees, non-PostScript outline font technology is becoming widely available. Hewlett-Packard's PCL5 page-description language brings outline typeface technology to its inexpensive LaserJet IIIP printers, and Apple's TrueType technology brings outline typefaces to its non-PostScript printers—as does Adobe Type Manager, which brings scalable font technology to Windows printers.

PostScript still has its defenders, largely because it's the most comprehensive package of outline typeface technology available. If you're really serious about desktop publishing (you're planning to go into the desktop publishing business, or you're taking over all your company's publications), you'll be well advised to equip your system with a PostScript-compatible laser printer. If you just want to produce occasional brochures and price lists with nice-looking type, though, you may not need PostScript's capabilities. For specific tips and advice on choosing the right printer for your system, see Chapter 16, "Designing Your System."

Using Desktop Publishing in a Small Business

As you've learned in this chapter, you'll need to do some planning if you want to set up your system for a serious desktop publishing application. But there are degrees of technology. What are your goals? Do you just want to print letters and reports with nice-looking fonts? Do you want all your documents, including some simple price lists and brochures, to use beautifully-printed fonts with a typeset appearance? Do you want to get into page design, blending text and graphics and producing professional-looking newsletters and catalogs? In the following three scenarios, you see a range of ways in which you can apply the technology that underlies desktop publishing.

Roger, a consulting engineer, does only one thing with his business computer that his clients see: the technical reports he writes when he finishes a project. For Roger, WordPerfect under DOS is just fine. WordPerfect does an excellent job of printing his documents with the nice-looking fonts that come with his Hewlett-Packard LaserJet IIIP, and Roger is quite satisfied with his system. He doesn't mind the fact that his spreadsheet and database output don't have these fonts; this output is only for his use. For Roger, desktop publishing is irrelevant; his needs do not extend to page-layout software, PostScript printers, and illustrations.

Deborah runs a small restaurant in a charming country inn, and in keeping with her rural location, she changes her restaurant's menu frequently to take advantage of fresh local ingredients. Every other day or so, she finds herself writing out a new menu by hand, a task that can take a half hour or more if she wants it to look nice. Although her flowing script is appealing, she doesn't like giving her customers menus that are obvious photocopies of the original, and once in a while she makes a spelling mistake that she doesn't catch until a customer points it out.

Deborah is planning to computerize her business, and as she examines her needs, she decides that she'll produce several documents with her computer—not just menus, but wine lists, brochures, and even employment application forms. Deborah decides to purchase a Windows or Macintosh system with a PostScript-compatible laser printer so that she can take advantage of the ability of these systems to display and print fonts with most programs. In the end, she chooses a Macintosh system with Microsoft Word, which she uses to prepare her simply-formatted, tasteful menus (see fig. 9.7). Deborah doesn't really need a page-layout program to produce her menu; she's not blending text and graphics, and she doesn't need to manipulate a page design extensively to find an attractive solution.

If you are contemplating a Windows system, consider the Hewlett-Packard IIIP laser printer, which offers optional scalable font technology that is widely supported by Windows applications.

TIP

Fair Oaks Inn

Wine by the Glass
  Fair Oaks Select California Chardonnay, $3.95
  Fair Oaks Select California Sauvignon Blanc, $3.45
  Fair Oaks Select California Cabernet Sauvignon, $4.25

Appetizers
  Gougere, 3.95
  Paté Maison, 3.95
  Paté de Campagne with Walnuts, 4.95
  Crab and Lobster Platter, $9.95

Soups
  Bououillabaise, 3.95
  Minestrone Verde, 3.95

Salads
  Our Famous Caeser Salad, $2.95

Entrees
  Linguini with Herbed Shrimp, $12.95
  Beef Stew with Cumin Seasoning, $14.95
  Blanquette de Veau with Dill Seasoning, $16.95
  Chicken Breasts Dijonnaise, $12.95
  Tortellini with Gorgonzola Cream Sauce, $11.95

Sweets
  Chocolate Mousse, $1.95
  Apple Mousse with Apple Brandy, $2.95
  Red Raspberry Pie, $2.95
  Linzertorte, $2.95

  We accept Visa, MasterCard, and American Express. No personal
  checks, please.

  September 16, 1991

Fig. 9.7. A simple menu typeset with Microsoft Word.

Suzanne likes to stay in contact with prospective real estate clients, and she's found a great way to do it: she publishes a newsletter. She's put together a Macintosh system with a full-page display, a high-resolution, hand-held scanner, and a PostScript printer. She's also running PageMaker and Digital Darkroom. Her newsletter includes many boilerplate articles about fixing up houses to sell them quickly and how to understand the mysteries of closing costs and mortgages. What really gives her newsletter life, however, is the two-page illustrated spread of current and interesting properties.

When Suzanne sees photographs of especially appealing houses that have come on the market, she scans them, enhances them in Digital Darkroom, and includes them in her newsletter with brief descriptions.

Unlike Deborah, who didn't need a page-layout program, Suzanne does: every time she designs her newsletter, she has to move the pictures around until she achieves a pleasing balance on the page. That's possible with Microsoft Word, but it isn't easy.

Summary

Here's a review of this chapter's main points:

- Desktop publishing can save significant amounts of money that would otherwise go to graphic artists and typesetters. It also gives you more control over your printing schedule and enables you to make last-minute changes.

- Full-featured word processing programs can handle some page-layout tasks, but they can't repeat designs on all pages, rearrange page designs quickly and easily, automatically align page elements to on-screen rulers, or provide a full complement of lines and shadings.

- To include illustrations in your document, you may need an illustration program or a scanner. You can significantly improve the printed appearance of photographs by enhancing them with an image-enhancement program.

- Most DOS programs are *character-based*, which means they rely on the computer's built-in, typewriter-like characters. Some DOS programs can take full advantage of your printer's font resources, but others can't.

- In Windows and Macintosh systems, screen fonts and printer drivers are handled at the operating system level rather than being left up to individual programs. That means you see screen fonts, and you can print with your printer's full range of font resources, with all or most programs.

- There are three ways to make fonts available in your printer. Best of all are built-in printer fonts. Equally fast, but subject to wear, are font cartridges. Less expensive are soft fonts, but your computer must download them to the printer if they've been erased from the printer's memory.

- Bit-mapped fonts require little processing power, consume a great deal of disk space, and offer a limited range of type sizes. Outline fonts must be generated by the computer, which consumes processing resources, but they're scalable within a given range (such as 4 to 127 points) and produce graceful, even curves (rather than the "jaggies") when printed.

- You can take advantage of desktop publishing technology at a variety of levels. The simplest and cheapest way is to add fonts to your system so that your word processor's output looks better. If you're more serious, you can add PostScript printing technology, scanners, page-layout programs, and image enhancers.

Software Suggestions

For serious desktop publishing applications, you'll be looking for a Macintosh or Windows system.

Macintosh Desktop Publishing Software

- *Adobe Type Library (Adobe Systems, Inc.):* 194 beautifully-designed PostScript typefaces, available separately or on a compact disk (CD).

- *Adobe Type Manager (Adobe Systems, Inc.):* Takes the "jaggies" out of large fonts when displayed on-screen and improves the appearance of print output on non-PostScript printers.

- *Digital Darkroom (Silicon Beach):* An image enhancement program that can dramatically improve the printed appearance of scanned photographs, as well as add special effects.

- *Freehand (Aldus Corporation):* A sophisticated illustration program that requires a PostScript Printer.

- *PageMaker (Aldus Corporation):* The leading professional desktop publishing program in the Macintosh environment. PageMaker requires a PostScript printer.

- *Publish it! Easy (Timeworks, Inc.):* An entry-level page-layout program.

- *SuperPaint (Silicon Beach):* Combines painting and drawing capabilities.

Windows Desktop Publishing Software

- *Adobe Type Library (Adobe Systems, Inc.):* 194 beautifully-designed PostScript typefaces, available separately or on a compact disk (CD).

- *Adobe Type Manager—Windows Version (Adobe Systems, Inc.):* Takes the "jaggies" out of large fonts when displayed on-screen.

- *CorelDraw (Corel Systems Corporation):* An outstanding illustration program that is as powerful as it is easy to use.

- *Image-In (Image-In, Inc.):* A program that enhances the printed appearance of scanned photographs.

- *PageMaker (Aldus Corporation):* The Windows version of the sophisticated, pathbreaking Macintosh page-layout program.

- *Ventura Publisher (Ventura Software):* A page-layout program designed for lengthier documents, such as technical manuals, quarterly reports, and lengthy catalogs.

10

Designing and Using Business Forms

Every business uses forms—invoices, employment applications, quarterly reports, and many more—that employees and customers fill out on paper. If your business can use preprinted, standard forms you can buy from a business supply store, there's very little need for you to invest the time and money needed to design your own forms with the computer. If your business is like many small businesses, however, you probably need at least some forms that require a custom design.

Marjorie and Gary run a successful convention coordinating business, which requires custom forms. "I send forms to hotels, to make sure they've got the facilities we need, and others to my customers, to find out what *they* need," Marjorie says. "In the past, I had no choice: I went to a print shop and paid several hundred dollars for custom designs. But even this approach didn't solve the problem. If my needs changed, I was stuck with 3,000 printed forms I couldn't use!"

Marjorie and Gary solved their problem with a PC and FormTool Gold (Bloc Publishing), a special-purpose program designed for creating and printing business forms.

If your business uses custom forms, you'll find that it's easy to design your own forms with the computer. In this chapter, you survey your software options for designing forms. As you'll see, you may not even require a special-purpose *forms design program* to create and print simple forms: some word processing programs include line and box-drawing features you can use to create simple forms. But there's a real advantage to using form design programs, which provide tools not only for creating the forms, but also for editing them once you've created them. If you must fill in pre-printed forms (such as Federal Express airbills), you can use *form-filling programs* to make short work of this task. The sections to follow introduce these programs in detail.

Exploring Software Options for Designing Forms

You have a wide choice of software options for designing forms:

- *DOS word processing programs:* Most full-featured DOS programs, such as Microsoft Word and WordPerfect, include simple features for drawing horizontal and vertical lines, as well as entering boxes. These programs construct the lines and boxes out of the built-in graphics characters in the DOS character set. You can use these features to create simple forms.

  Once you've created a form this way, however, it's very difficult to edit it without making a mess of the lines and boxes.

- *DOS form-design programs:* These special-purpose programs use the same graphics characters that word processing programs use, but there's a key difference: form-design software includes commands that greatly facilitate *editing* the form once you've created it. You can insert, delete, and move lines and boxes quickly and easily, and when you type characters, you don't make a mess of the lines you've entered.

Moreover, these programs often come with large libraries of ready-to-use forms (such as the one in figure 10.1), many ofwhich can be modified quickly to suit your needs. A list of many of the ready- to-use forms included with FormTool Gold follows.

Ready-to-Use Forms Included with FormTool Gold (Selected)

Alert for Bad Checks
Business Car Use
Change Order
Credit Application
Customer Contact and Marketing Report

Customer Order Tracking Report
Daily Cash Register Reconciliation
Employee Payment Record
Employee Referral Form
Facsimile Usage Log Sheet
Invoice/Statement
Packing List
Parts List
Prospect Tracker
Purchase Order
Quotation
Request for Quotation
Retail Order Form
Special Supplies Request
Subcontractor Backcharge
Time and Labor Report Form
Warranty Service Journal
Weekly Sales Summary
Weekly Summary of Business Activities
Wholesale Order Form
Work Order/Sales Slip

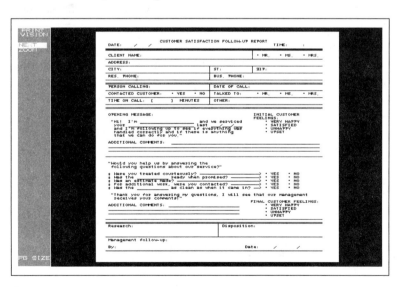

Fig. 10.1. *A screen preview of a ready-to-use customer satisfaction survey form (FormTool Gold).*

- *Windows and Macintosh graphics programs:* In the Windows and Macintosh environments, you can use painting or drawing programs such as Windows Paint or SuperPaint (for the Macintosh) to create and edit business forms quickly and easily. A program with object-oriented graphics capabilities, such as SuperPaint, facilitates editing because each line or box can be independently sized, edited, or moved. If you have a desktop publishing program such as PFS: First Publisher or PageMaker, you can design and edit forms easily.

- *Windows and Macintosh form-design programs:* These programs— such as PerFORM PRO for Windows (Delrina) and Informed Designer for the Macintosh (Shana Corporation)—are the Cadillacs of form design: they combine all the advantages of DOS form-design programs, including a library of forms you can modify, with the convenience of object-oriented graphics.

Which of these options is best for you? If you use several forms in your business, you'll be wise to choose a program that enables you to edit the forms easily (and that rules out most word processing programs for this application). Form-design programs offer considerable advantages: they're special-purpose programs that are designed specifically for creating, editing, and printing forms, and they come equipped with a large library of forms you can modify quickly and easily.

If business form design is a critical application area for you, there's a decisive advantage to Windows and Macintosh systems. DOS form designers require you to learn a lengthy series of complicated commands to manipulate the lines, boxes, and text; with Windows and Macintosh systems, you can manipulate individual form elements by dragging and sizing them with the mouse.

Benefitting from Computerized Form-Design and Form-Filling Software

Here's an overview of the benefits you can expect from form-design and form-filling software:

- *Savings on form layout and design costs.* By designing your own forms, you save the money you would otherwise have to pay to a professional artist or design studio.

- *Early revision of the form if it turns out to have errors.* If you pay a professional to design a form, you will pay extra for revisions. With your computerized forms stored on disk, revision is fast, simple, and free. You can make all the changes you want until your form is just right.

- *Increased access to vital information.* A by-product of your use of well-designed, custom forms will be an increase in your access to vital information about your customers, your transactions, your inventory, and all the other matters for which you design forms. The use of forms ensures that you obtain all the information that's needed to perform your business's tasks efficiently.

Creating a Custom Form

Mark is the owner of a small custom framing business, and when people order frames, it's essential that he get the information correctly. If Mark fails to obtain some of the information he needs, he may not know how to proceed with the job unless he calls the customer. If the job is done incorrectly, the customer may reject it, leaving Mark with no choice but to throw away all the materials and start over. So Mark's first step in designing his form is to figure out exactly what information he needs.

Mark begins by looking at the orders he has taken in the past few months. He has been scribbling the orders down on a pad of paper, which worked pretty well as long as *he* was taking the order (although Mark himself has made some errors). On a few occasions, Mark scribbled down what he thought the customer was ordering, but it turns out that the customer expected a different frame or mat when the item was picked up. And Barbara, who works for Mark part-time and is just learning the business, doesn't always remember to ask the right questions, despite the fact that she's an excellent employee.

Mark needs a business form—a *custom* business form—that will serve three purposes: making sure the information is taken correctly, making sure *all* the information is taken, and giving the customer a chance to review and confirm his or her choices.

Creating the Form

Looking over the orders, Mark makes a list of the information he needs and quickly works up a sketch of the form on paper. Then he turns on his IBM-compatible computer and starts FormTool Gold, a DOS form design program. As if he were using a word processing program, he types his firm's name and address (see fig. 10.2).

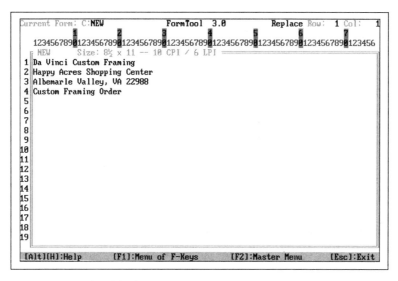

Fig. 10.2. FormTool Gold's form design screen.

Where FormTool Gold differs from a word processing program, however, lies in the ease with which the user can enter lines, grids, and boxes. Working quickly, Mark transforms his paper sketch into a well-designed form, as shown in figure 10.3 (what you see on FormTool Gold's screen) and figure 10.4 (a printout of the entire form).

Editing the Form

After creating the form, Mark prints a few copies, and he and Barbara try taking some orders. Right away, they notice some problems. There isn't enough room for the customer's last name. And on a couple of the forms, it's hard to read the numbers that Mark has written in the Order No. and Moulding Style Number fields. So Mark decides to edit the form, making more room for the last name and adding grids to the areas where numbers are written. (*Grids* are small boxes that separate the numbers people write, making them much easier to read.) Figure 10.5 shows Mark's form after he makes the changes, which takes him just a couple of minutes.

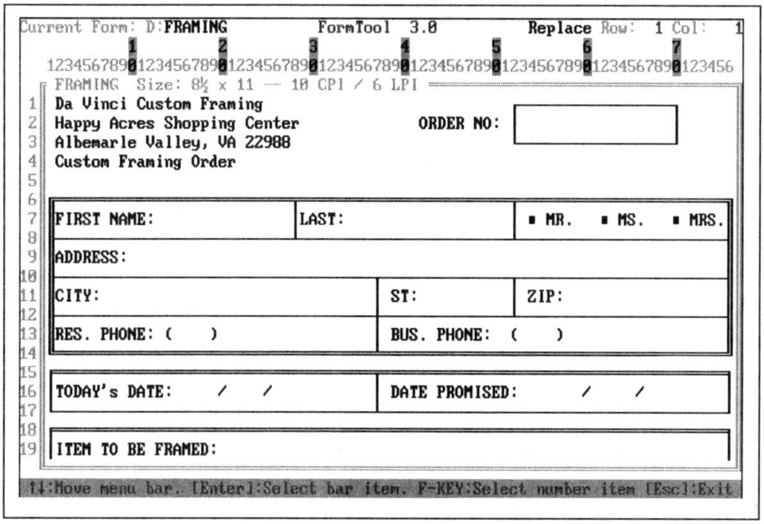

```
Current Form: D:FRAMING          FormTool  3.0         Replace Row:  1 Col:   1
              1         2         3         4         5         6         7
    12345678901234567890123456789012345678901234567890123456789012345678901234567890123456
   ┌ FRAMING  Size: 8½ x 11 ── 10 CPI / 6 LPI ══════════════════════════════
 1 ║ Da Vinci Custom Framing
 2 ║ Happy Acres Shopping Center          ORDER NO: ┌──────────────┐
 3 ║ Albemarle Valley, VA 22988                     │              │
 4 ║ Custom Framing Order                           └──────────────┘
 5 ║
 6 ║
 7 ║ FIRST NAME:          LAST:              ▪ MR.   ▪ MS.   ▪ MRS.
 8 ║
 9 ║ ADDRESS:
10 ║
11 ║ CITY:                   ST:         ZIP:
12 ║
13 ║ RES. PHONE: (    )        BUS. PHONE: (    )
14 ║
15 ║
16 ║ TODAY's DATE:      /    /      DATE PROMISED:       /    /
17 ║
18 ║
19 ║ ITEM TO BE FRAMED:
    ↑↓:Move menu bar [Enter]:Select bar item F-KEY:Select number item [Esc]:Exit
```

Fig. 10.3. Mark's form (design screen).

Filling Out Printed Forms

Ruth and Kirsten run a modest but growing mail order business and they ship their products—prerecorded cassette lectures and books—via Federal Express. What's slowing them down is the job of typing Federal Express airbills. Because Ruth and Kirsten have a Federal Express account, the company gives them airbills preprinted with Ruth and Kirsten's company name, address, and account number, but they still must type the customer's name and address. And if they type the name or address incorrectly, they must throw out the form and start over.

Ruth and Kirsten are spending increasing amounts of time hunched over the office typewriter. Worse, by the time Ruth and Kirsten get around to typing the Federal Express airbill, they've already typed the name and address twice: once on an invoice, and a second time on a packing slip. Kirsten feels as if she's memorized the names and addresses of everyone who has ordered from their firm.

Ruth and Kirsten know that they need computer help, but what's more, they also see an opportunity to streamline and improve the way they do business. What they need is an application that lets them type the name and address just once, instead of three times, and automatically transfers the name and address to computer versions of the invoice, packing slip, and Federal Express forms. Ruth and Kirsten find what they're looking for in Form Filler (Bloc Publishing)—a DOS form-filler program.

```
Da Vinci Custom Framing
Happy Acres Shopping Center        ORDER NO:  [                ]
Albemarle Valley, VA 22988
Custom Framing Order

FIRST NAME:                     LAST:            [] MR.   [] MS.   [] MRS.
ADDRESS:
CITY:                           ST:        ZIP:
RES. PHONE: (    )               BUS. PHONE: (    )

TODAY's DATE:      /    /        DATE PROMISED:       /    /

ITEM TO BE FRAMED:
[]  Print         [] Painting        [] Drawing         [] Watercolor
BRIEF DESCRIPTION OF SUBJECT:


APPROXIMATE VALUE:
UNFRAMED SIZE:                  FRAMED SIZE:
SPECIAL CROPPING NOTES:

   MAT 1 COLOR      MAT 1 TEXTURE      MAT 2 COLOR      MAT  2 TEXTURE
   [] White         [] Plain          [] White         [] Plain
   [] Off-White     [] Linen          [] Off-White     [] Linen
   [] Beige                           [] Beige
   [] Light grey                      [] Light grey    OFFSET:
   [] Deep grey                       [] Deep grey

GLASS     [] None        [] Non-Glare         [] Regular

MOULDING STYLE NUMBER:   [                ]

COST ESTIMATE:
I have read the above information and confirm that it accurately
reflects the order I have placed.  I agree to pick up the framed
item within 30 days of the estimated completion date.
           SIGNED:   [                        ]

           DATE:     [                        ]
```

Fig. 10.4. *Mark's form (printout).*

```
Da Vinci Custom Framing
Happy Acres Shopping Center        ORDER NO: [  ][  ][  ][  ]
Albemarle Valley, VA 22988
Custom Framing Order

FIRST NAME:           LAST:                  [] MR.   [] MS.   [] MRS.

ADDRESS:

CITY:                    ST:           ZIP:

RES. PHONE: (    )        BUS. PHONE: (    )

TODAY's DATE:    /    /       DATE PROMISED:    /    /

ITEM TO BE FRAMED:
[] Print        [] Painting       [] Drawing        [] Watercolor

BRIEF DESCRIPTION OF SUBJECT:


APPROXIMATE VALUE:

UNFRAMED SIZE:              FRAMED SIZE:

SPECIAL CROPPING NOTES:


MAT 1 COLOR   MAT 1 TEXTURE   MAT 2 COLOR    MAT 2 TEXTURE

[] White     [] Plain     [] White      [] Plain
[] Off-White [] Linen     [] Off-White  [] Linen
[] Beige                  [] Beige
[] Light grey             [] Light grey   OFFSET:
[] Deep grey              [] Deep grey

GLASS    [] None      [] Non-Glare      [] Regular

MOULDING STYLE NUMBER:  [  ] - [  ][  ][  ]

COST ESTIMATE:

I have read the above information and confirm that it accurately
reflects the order I have placed.  I agree to pick up the framed
item within 30 days of the estimated completion date.

           SIGNED: [                    ]

           DATE:   [                    ]
```

Fig. 10.5. Mark's form after making changes (printout).

Using Form-Filler Programs

You can buy computer forms from almost any business forms supplier. The reason they're called *computer forms* is that they're continuous forms, like the tractor-fed paper used with dot-matrix printers. And like tractor-fed paper, computer forms are supplied with punched-hole edges so that the printer can pull the forms through the printer. Unlike the forms you print with a form-design program, computer forms come with three- or four-part carbons.

A form-filler program displays an on-screen version of a computer form, enabling you to type (and correct) the needed information on-screen before you print the form. In addition, the program also provides tools that calculate sums, sales taxes, and totals, all at the press of a key. When the form is complete on-screen, you choose the Print command, and the printer fills in the form correctly. Even better, the program can transfer the name, address, and other data to another on-screen form at the press of a key. You type the data just once.

As you may have guessed, care is need to make sure that the on-screen version of the form—called a *template*—has precisely the same spacing as the printed version—the one that's in the printer. Without such care, the printed data will not print correctly. As do other form-filler programs, Form Filler approaches this problem in two ways:

- *Using templates for preprinted forms:* You order preprinted computer forms from a computer forms supplier, using the order booklet enclosed with Form Filler. The dozens of forms available include invoices, statements, packing slips, checks, and more. For each of these preprinted forms, Form Filler displays an on-screen template that is already precisely aligned with the printed version. This option is an excellent choice because all the development work needed to create an on-screen template is already done for you.

  In addition to ordering your own forms, you can obtain computer versions of UPS, Federal Express, and U.S. Postal Service forms.

- *Creating your own template:* If you already have your own computer forms, you can design your own on-screen template. This process isn't as difficult as it sounds. Form Filler enables you to print a grid over the computer form—the same grid you see on-screen. Looking at the printed grid, it's easy to judge where you should type the headings and data entry areas.

Having chosen Form Filler as their critical application, Ruth and Kirsten order their preprinted forms and go shopping for equipment. They equip their IBM-compatible computer with three dot-matrix printers, linked to the computer via a switch box. In the first dot-matrix printer they load the invoices; the second printer has the packing slips, and the third printer has the Federal Express airbills.

Following Form Filler's instructions, Ruth and Kirsten link the three forms—the invoice, packing list, and Federal Express airbill—so that the information typed in the Invoice template automatically is transferred to the other two forms.

Here's how Ruth takes an order. She opens Form Filler, displays the Invoice template, and types the order information (see fig. 10.6). With just one press of the key, Form Filler obtains the totals (see fig. 10.7). Ruth selects Printer 1 and prints the invoice. She then displays and prints the packing list and Federal Express airbill, which Form Filler has filled out automatically (see fig. 10.8).

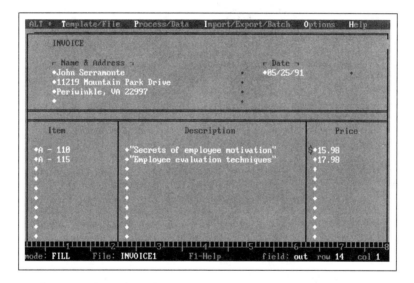

Fig. 10.6. Typing the order information (Form Filler).

What have Ruth and Kirsten gained? They've cut down the time they spend typing forms by 75 percent. And there's another benefit, too: they've cut down on waste. Before computerizing this operation, they had to throw out about one in 20 forms due to typing errors.

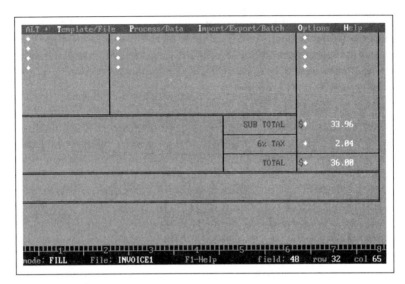

Fig. 10.7. The subtotal, tax, and totals are computed automatically (Form Filler).

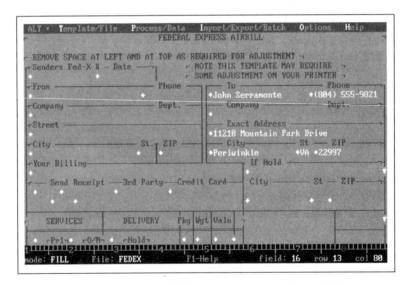

Fig. 10.8. A Federal Express airbill filled out on-screen (Form Filler).

Creating a Link with a Database Management Program

Ruth and Kirsten are pleased with their Form Filler application, but soon they realize that they're still violating one of the basic rules of small business computerization: Never type the same data twice. They're still typing the customer's name and address in their mailing list database before they type the invoice. As their knowledge of Form Filler grows, they discover how to export the name and address of every invoice they fill out to a data file, which their database manager can import.

The key to this trick is Form Filler's Quick Data Export command, which exports data from selected fields to a standard database file, readable by every database management program. Ruth and Kirsten set up Form Filler so that this command is invoked every time they fill out an invoice, so the file grows with the addition of each name and address. At the end of the week, Ruth opens their database manager, and in a few keystrokes she adds to their mailing list all the customers who have ordered this week.

TIP

Some form-filling packages offer more convenient database access. FormWorx (FormWorx Corporation) for example, includes a form-filling program that can read and write to dBASE databases directly. If database integration is important to you, you should carefully evaluate the available programs to determine whether they can work smoothly and efficiently with the database software you're planning to use.

Reviewing Guidelines for Effective Form-Design

Like many application programs, form-design software gives you many of the skills of a competent forms designer, such as the ability to lay out attractive-looking lines, grids, and boxes. But you still must exercise some judgment. Here, your judgment is needed not so much for aesthetic reasons (as it is when typesetting with the computer)—after all, nobody expects a form to be beautiful. Rather, your judgment is needed to make sure the form meets its underlying purpose: to obtain and convey information clearly.

A business form enables communication between two people: the person recording the information and the person receiving it. The headings should be comprehensible to both parties. The type should be large enough to be legible under the conditions in which both parties work. Each area to be filled in should immediately suggest the kind of response that's required: filling in a blank, checking off an item on a list, filling in a time, or filling in a date.

You use lines to create forms, and by following a few simple guidelines, you can use them effectively. Double horizontal lines (called *double rules*) signify the beginning of a section; single horizontal lines (*light rules*) indicate subsections. Group related areas in a rectangle.

Whenever possible, list the available options and use check boxes. There's no reason to burden the memory of the person filling out the form; a list of options provides reminders and speeds the task of filling out the form.

Summary

Here's a summary of this chapter's main points:

- Form-design software not only simplifies the task of creating your own custom forms, it also facilitates quick revision when the forms' limitations become apparent.

- Although you can design forms with a word processor, paint program, or desktop publishing program, form-design programs come with a library of ready-to-use forms that you can modify quickly for your purposes.

- If you find yourself typing the same data repeatedly on preprinted forms, a form-filler program may produce big efficiency gains for you. With a form-filler program, you type the data on-screen and then print on preprinted computer forms.

Software Suggestions

You can design and print forms on DOS systems, as this chapter illustrates. If you plan to create and revise many forms, you'll be wise to choose a

Macintosh or Windows form-design application, which shows all the form's elements (including fonts and font sizes) on-screen, and enables you to use a mouse to move, resize, or delete each element (such as a rectangle, line, or title) independently.

DOS Form-Design and Form-Filler Software

- *FormTool Gold (Bloc Publishing):* A best-selling form-design program. This program does not require graphics support or a mouse, and runs on virtually any PC. The program is featured in this chapter.

- *Form Filler (Bloc Publishing):* A versatile, easy-to-use program for filling out preprinted forms on-screen. The program is featured in this chapter.

- *FormWorx (FormWorx):* Combines form-design and form-filler functions in one package, and offers direct read/write access to dBASE databases. Requires no special hardware and works with virtually any PC.

Macintosh Form-Design and Form-Filling Software

- *Informed Designer (Shana Corporation):* A form-design program that takes full advantage of the Macintosh. You can use all your Macintosh fonts, and you can draw grids, tables, lines, ovals, arcs, and polygons with 1/1000-inch accuracy. Available at additional cost are Informed Mini-Manager, which adds calculation and lookup functions, and Informed AutoForm, which transforms an Informed Designer form into a stand-alone application for rapid data entry.

- *SmartForm Designer (Claris Corporation):* An exceptionally easy-to-use program that users of MacDraw, Claris's object-oriented drawing program, will find familiar. Takes full advantage of Macintosh fonts.

Windows Form-Design Software

- *PerFORM PRO (Delrina):* A versatile form-design program that takes full advantage of the Windows environment and offers the ability to read and write dBASE files directly.

11

Selling Your Ideas with Presentation Graphics

If you obtain business by making presentations to audiences, you're doubtless aware that graphics aids increase the chance that your audience will react favorably to your proposals. But today's audiences aren't satisfied with graphics alone. They want high-quality, professional-looking graphics—the sort of graphics you would expect from a big company's presentation.

Small businesses and sole proprietors are at the usual disadvantage here: lack of expert support. Large firms have their own in-house graphics departments, with experts who can turn a manager's scribblings into professional-looking, colorful slides, complete with illustrations and dynamic-looking charts. Today, however, it's possible to even the odds by equipping yourself with presentation graphics software. A presentation graphics program enables someone who lacks graphics skills to put together a professional-looking presentation. To produce output, you send the files you've created to a graphics service bureau, which produces beautiful color slides or overhead transparencies for as little as $7 per slide.

The leading programs today are easy to use. As you'll see in this chapter, most come with libraries of presentation templates, which you can open and modify for your own presentation. They also come with libraries of *clip art*, illustrations you can add to your charts and graphs. In this chapter, you see just how easy it is to develop a high-quality presentation with today's presentation graphics software.

205

Using Presentation Graphics Software

Presentation graphics programs are designed specifically to produce colorful, illustrated slides for business presentations. The best programs include the following resources for creating text charts, business graphs, image libraries, and templates.

Text Charts

Some of the most effective slides in a presentation are simple text charts, which take only a few minutes to create. Here's an overview of the text charts you can develop with all presentation graphics programs:

- *Title charts:* Opening charts that show your talk's title and your name.

- *Bullet charts:* Charts that list points set off by bullets, as shown in figure 11.1. The program adds the bullets and handles the indentations automatically.

- *Numbered charts:* Similar to text charts, except that the items are set off by numbers, which the program inserts automatically.

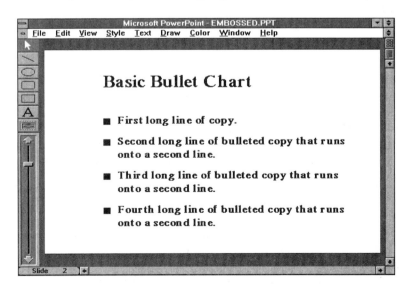

Fig. 11.1. A bullet Chart (Microsoft PowerPoint).

Business Graphs

You have two options for generating business graphs, such as line graphs and pie graphs, with most presentation graphics programs. First, you can type the data yourself, using the graphics programs' spreadsheet-like matrix of rows and columns (see fig. 11.2). Second, you can import the data from a spreadsheet program.

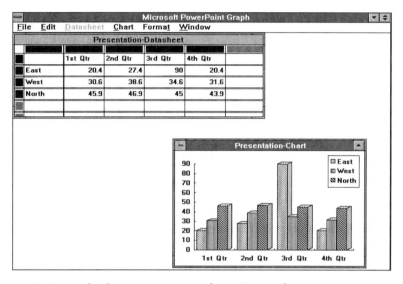

Fig. 11.2. Typing the data to generate a chart (Microsoft PowerPoint).

Most programs enable you to choose from a wide variety of graphs. Here's an overview of the graph types:

- *Column graphs:* Used to depict a *time series*, in which one or more items are shown to change over time (see fig. 11.2). You would use a column graph, for example, to show how electricity rates have increased over the past 10 years.

  Properly speaking, *column graphs* use vertical columns, while *bar graphs* use horizontal columns. You should know, however, that some popular programs (notably Lotus 1-2-3) use the term *bar graph* to refer to graphs with vertical columns.

- *Bar graphs:* Resemble column graphs, except that the bars run horizontally (see fig. 11.3). Bar graphs are used to compare items (rather than showing how an item changes over time). You would use a bar graph, for example, to show the different rates states pay for commercial electricity.

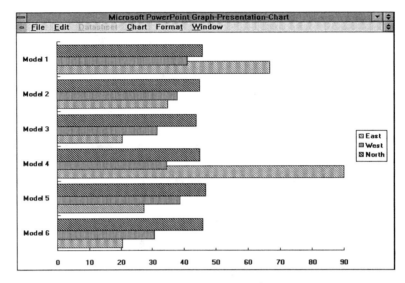

Fig. 11.3. A bar graph showing six items (Microsoft PowerPoint).

- *Line graphs:* Resemble the underlying concept of column graphs, in that they depict how one or more items change over time (see fig. 11.4). Unlike column graphs, line graphs suggest that the changes are continuous. Line graphs are better than column graphs when you have more than seven or eight data points to represent; using too many columns confuses the viewer.

- *Area graphs:* Use variables on line graphs with filled-in areas to show the relative proportions of each item being measured (see fig. 11.5).

- *Pie graphs:* Depict how a whole (such as the revenues of a corporation) is made up of parts. You would use a pie graph, for example, to explain how an electrical utility spends each dollar of revenue it collects.

Advanced business graphs combine one or more of these elements. A 100 percent column graph shows, for example, how the parts of the column make up a whole (see fig. 11.6).

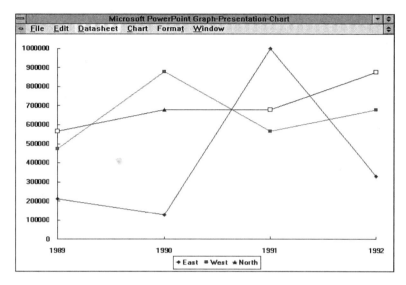

Fig. 11.4. *A line graph showing three items as they change over time (Microsoft PowerPoint).*

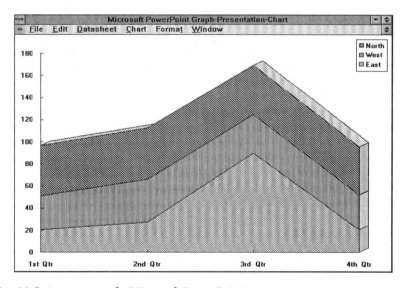

Fig. 11.5. *An area graph (Microsoft PowerPoint).*

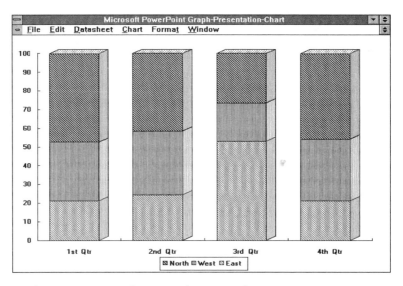

Fig. 11.6. *A 100 percent column graph (Microsoft PowerPoint).*

TIP

Presentation graphics programs differ in their emphases, and some are more versatile than others when it comes to creating business charts. Harvard Graphics, for example, can generate a huge variety of graphs, including area graphs with two measurement axes, pie graphs linked to 100 percent column graphs, and other advanced business graphs. Microsoft PowerPoint can handle the graph basics, but doesn't offer the range of graph types that Harvard Graphics and other programs do.

Image Libraries

An *image library* is a collection of *clip art* (ready-to-use illustrations), which enables you to enliven your charts and graphs—even if you don't know how to draw (see fig. 11.7). The best programs include clip art in object-oriented rather than bit-mapped graphics formats. Object-oriented graphics produce sharper images when printed or made into 35mm slides.

NOTE

If you plan to include clip art in your graphs, don't overdo it. Including many small illustrations confuses the eye. A single illustration often is sufficient to establish a theme for your graph.

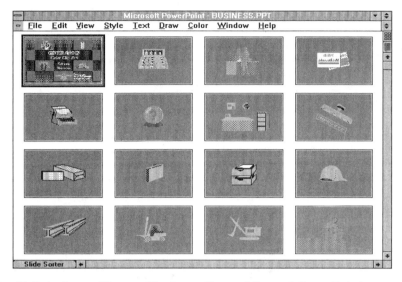

Fig. 11.7. An image library of business clip art (Microsoft PowerPoint).

There's a great deal of clip art available from public domain sources, but much of it has been scanned using optical scanners or drawn using paint programs. Scanners and paint programs produce bit-mapped graphics, which print only at the screen's resolution (which is too coarse for most business and professional purposes). If you plan to use clip art extensively, you'll be better off purchasing a commercial clip art library that includes object-oriented or PostScript clip art files. The pictures in these files will print at your printer's maximum resolution, and they will look sharp in 35mm slides.

Templates

The best programs come with preconfigured templates that are correctly formatted for a variety of presentations, including 35mm slides and over-head transparencies. Examples are included of many text charts (including bulleted lists, numbered lists, and title charts) as well as business graphs (such as bar graphs, pie graphs, and line graphs). You'll see an example of templates in action in the next section.

Developing a Presentation

Anne is an electrical engineering consultant. She's been asked by the Albemarle Valley Sanitation district to advise them on the feasibility of installing a small turbine generator at the district's central water processing plant. As she prepares for her presentation, Anne uses Microsoft PowerPoint's many resources to create a series of visually attractive slides.

Anne begins by choosing one of PowerPoint's many ready-to-use slide templates, which provide ready-to-use backgrounds as well as a variety of text charts. She displays the templates on-screen in the Slide Sorter view, which lets her see all the slides available in this template set (see fig. 11.8).

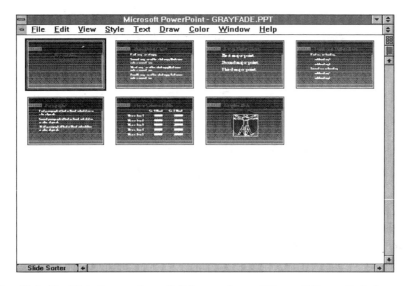

Fig. 11.8. The Slide Sorter view of slide templates (Microsoft PowerPoint).

Working quickly, Anne copies the templates she wants to use to open her presentation, and modifies the first one so that it shows the title of her talk and her name (see fig. 11.9). She modifies the second template slide, a three-item bullet chart, to indicate her three main points.

One of PowerPoint's many attractive features is the Notes Master, which gives you a way to write and print notes for each slide in your presentation. After you create the slide, you choose Notes Master and PowerPoint copies the slide to a page of notes, on which you can jot down the points you want to make while you're displaying the slide to your audience (see fig. 11.10).

After you develop your presentation, you can print the notes; PowerPoint numbers the pages and includes a copy of the slide at the top of the page, as the screen preview shows.

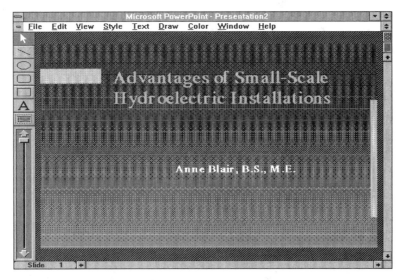

Fig. 11.9. The title slide for a presentation, using a template background (Microsoft PowerPoint).

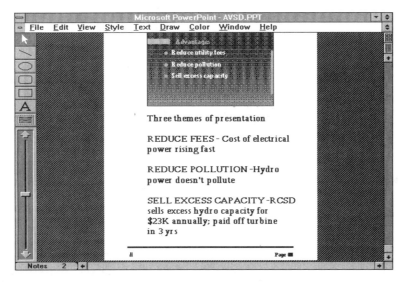

Fig. 11.10. The screen preview of notes for a slide (Microsoft PowerPoint).

Next, Anne creates a column chart to show how the district's electrical costs have increased over the past four years. She types the data in the datasheet window, which closely resembles a spreadsheet, and PowerPoint transforms the data into the column chart shown in the chart window (see fig. 11.11). Anne then adds the chart to her slide presentation, complete with a title (see fig. 11.12). To complete the slide, she dresses up the table with clip art drawn from PowerPoint's extensive image libraries (see fig. 11.13).

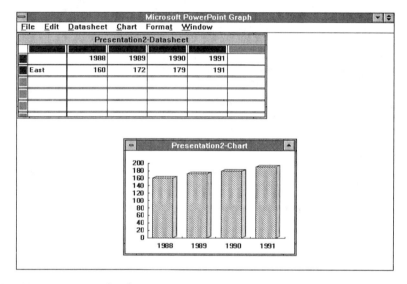

Fig. 11.11. *Creating the chart.*

This example illustrates how easy it is to use today's presentation graphics packages. If you equip your computer with a program such as Harvard Graphics or PowerPoint, your presentations will look like they're in the same league with the presentations done by bigger companies.

Obtaining Slides and Transparencies

Large firms have their own facilities for generating color slides and transparencies from presentation graphics program files, but the equipment is expensive and beyond the means of most small businesses. Chances are you'll be sending your files to *graphics service bureaus*, which transform the files into color slides or transparencies.

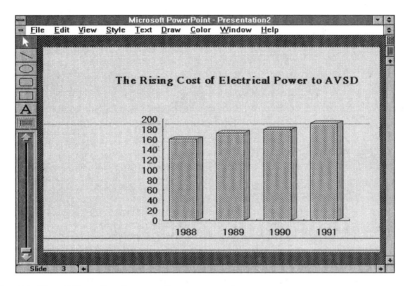

Fig. 11.12. Adding the chart to the presentation.

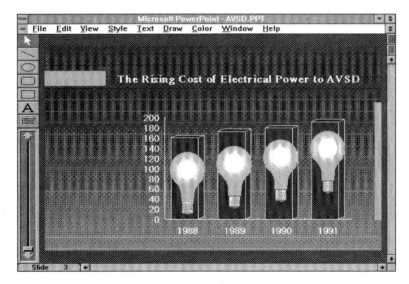

Fig. 11.13. Adding clip art.

To locate a graphics service bureau, check your local Yellow Pages under "Graphic Designers," or check the "Graphics" section in the classified advertising section in the back of personal computer magazines. To obtain your slides, you'll need to take or mail a disk containing your film to the service bureau. Some service bureaus allow you to send them files via modems, which may come in handy if you're short on time.

TIP

> When you buy a presentation graphics package, chances are it will include an information packet about a mail order graphics service bureau. Several companies offer fast (24-hour) turnaround. If you can't find a service bureau in your town, you can use one these services instead.

Printing Transparencies

If you've equipped your system with a laser printer, you can print directly on sheets of clear plastic, which you can buy at any business supplies store. You load the sheets just as you would load paper, and the printer prints a black-and-white version of the image directly on the sheet. You then use the acetate printouts as transparencies with an overhead projector.

Because they're in black and white, the transparencies you create with your laser printer lack the immediacy and impact of color slides or color transparencies. But they're suitable for less formal presentations.

Producing Desktop Slide Shows

Most presentation graphics programs include a desktop slide show mode, in which the program displays your graphics, one after another.

You can set up the slide show so that the next graphic doesn't appear until you press a key. Some programs enable you to specify an automatic display interval, such as 45 seconds, after which a new image appears. Coupled with an LCD panel designed to work with an overhead projector, this feature enables you to produce high-quality slide shows for an audience of approximately 40 or 50 people without the inconvenience, delay, or expense of making slides. You'll need a laptop computer, though, if you want to give these presentations outside your office.

Establishing Guidelines for Effective Presentations

A presentation graphics package can transfer to your computer many of the expert skills of a presentation graphics artist. Bear in mind, though, that it's still possible to create confusing and ugly slides or transparencies, even with an outstanding program such as Harvard Graphics or Microsoft PowerPoint! And there are many other things that can go wrong. Here are some suggestions that will help you create a successful presentation:

- *Don't use too many colors.* Using too many colors can force viewers to work harder to grasp the information, reflecting negatively on you and your presentation. Avoid using more than four or five colors in a chart.

- *Use colors consistently.* Establish a theme that runs through all your slides, such as yellow for major titles and blue for minor titles. If you aren't consistent in color usage, viewers may become confused.

- *Keep it simple.* No single text slide should convey more than three points; graphs and illustrations should convey a single point.

- *Make sure your slides are legible.* How big do the letters have to be so that people in the back of the room can read them?

- *Allow time for corrections.* When you get your slides back from the slide production service, you may find that the colors aren't right, and you need to have them redone.

- *Run through your presentation before the big day.* Get a friend or colleague to listen to your presentation—and be prepared to accept friendly criticism.

- *Know your equipment.* Long before your presentation, take the time you need to become thoroughly familiar with the projection equipment you'll be using. Experiment with focusing, with different sizes of the projected image, and with legibility.

- *Be prepared for equipment failure.* What do you do if the bulb blows? A very cautious person will bring *two* extra bulbs to an important presentation—after all, there's a small chance that two bulbs will blow in a single session, especially if the cooling fan isn't performing up to par.

TIP

Look for a presentation graphics program that includes a spelling checker, such as Microsoft PowerPoint or Harvard Graphics. There's nothing more embarrassing than realizing you've made a spelling mistake as you look at your slide during your presentation!

Summary

Here's a summary of this chapter's main points:

- Today's presentation graphics packages are so easy to use that almost anyone can put together a professional-looking presentation in short order.

- Presentation graphics provide tools for creating slides or transparencies for public presentation. On each slide or transparency, you can create text charts or business graphs. The best programs come with image libraries and templates, which you can use to build a professional-looking presentation quickly.

- Strive for consistency, simplicity, and legibility in your presentation. Be prepared for contingencies.

- Make full use of time-saving resources provided by your program, such as ready-to-use templates.

- Create your presentation early enough so that you have time to correct errors and have new slides made. For less formal presentations, print the output on acetate sheets using a laser printer.

Software Suggestions

You'll find high-quality software for presentation graphics in all three computing environments, although Windows and Macintosh systems will do a better job of showing you how your graphics will appear. All the programs discussed here can print transparencies on clear plastic sheets, generate output that can be transformed into 35mm color slides, and include libraries of clip art.

DOS Software for Presentation Graphics

- *Lotus Freelance Graphics (Lotus Development Corporation):* A DOS-based presentation graphics package that is especially adept at producing text charts. A library of more than 1,000 predrawn symbols and design backgrounds is included.

- *Harvard Graphics (Software Publishing Corporation):* This DOS-based presentation graphics package doesn't look as elegant on-screen as its Windows and Macintosh competition, but it's capable of producing high-quality printed output and 35mm slides. A full gallery of text chart and business graph options makes this program fully capable of professional presentation applications. The program includes a modest library of clip art images in object-oriented (vector graphics) format.

Macintosh Presentation Graphics Software

- *Persuasion (Aldus Corporation):* Designed to work with Aldus PageMaker, the leading page-layout program, Persuasion takes full advantage of the Macintosh environment's graphics capabilities. The program includes an outline mode for organizing graphics into a presentation, outstanding features for business graphics, and beautiful background color washes.

- *Microsoft PowerPoint (Microsoft Corporation):* The Macintosh version of PowerPoint takes full advantage of the Macintosh graphics environment, and is exceptionally easy to use. The program includes excellent features for text charts.

Presentation Graphics Software for Windows

- *Persuasion (Aldus Corporation):* Persuasion for Windows echoes the excellent features of its Macintosh counterpart, including an outline mode for organizing graphics into a presentation, outstanding features for business graphics, and beautiful background color washes.

- *Microsoft PowerPoint for Windows (Microsoft Corporation):* PowerPoint for Windows offers all the features of its well-regarded Macintosh counterpart, and is well designed to work in the Windows environment. The program includes an impressive library of clip art images, background textures, and ready-to-use templates for a wide variety of presentation applications.

12

Going Online

T he telephone system is one of humanity's most impressive technologi-
cal achievements. A world-wide system of awesome complexity, it
enables you to dial your choice of billions of telephone numbers and
achieve a near-instantaneous connection. Designed for the human voice,
this remarkable system is also capable of carrying computer signals—and
this fact opens up an entirely new set of possibilities for business communication. If you equip your computer with a modem and a communications program, you can easily get *online* yourself—that is, connect your
computer with a distant computer via the world telecommunications
system. And once you've done so, you can take advantage of electronic mail
and online data retrieval, which may have strategic implications for your
business.

Tom's business is a case in point. Tom's shop, located in the country, builds
custom doors for contractors who order them from building supply stores
all over town. In the past, Tom sent a courier to collect orders from the
several stores, which took the courier hours. The orders spent a lot of time
sitting at the store, and they spent more time riding in the courier's car. With
this built-in delay, the best Tom could hope to achieve was a 48-hour
turnaround. Now the offices send the orders to Tom via E-mail right after
they're received. If Tom gets the order early enough, and if there isn't a
backlog, he can sometimes finish the order the same day.

Most books that discuss electronic mail take the position that going online
is a virtual necessity for the ambitious business person. Not so. Hobbyists
can spend many happy hours exploring the resources of *computer bulletin
boards*—services set up by local computer hobbyists—as well as information services that focus on hobbyists' needs, such as CompuServe; but doing
so does not automatically give you any business advantage. You should

approach computer-based communications the way you would approach any other application discussed in this book. If an application looks as though it can help you do a better job of performing your business's primary mission, then it's worth investigating seriously. If not, it's probably a waste of time and money. In this chapter, you explore your computer-based communications options, and you learn just how—and when—going online makes business sense.

Exploring Communications Software Options

To go online, you need two essential pieces of equipment: a modem and a communications program. Modems are discussed in more detail in Chapter 16, "Designing Your System." For now, all you need to know is that the modem performs an essential (and automatic) signal-processing function: it translates (modulates) outgoing signals so that they can be transmitted via telephone lines, and untranslates (demodulates) incoming signals so that your computer can understand them. In addition, modems can open the line, dial a number, and hang up, and many can answer an incoming call. The focus here, however, is on communications software.

A communications program transforms your computer into a machine that can send and receive text through your modem. To establish a connection (an activity called *logging on*) , you choose a command that tells the modem to open the line and dial a number. Once established, the communication is a back-and-forth exchange with the computer you've contacted (called the *host computer*). When you achieve the connection, you're asked to type your password and account number; after these are verified, you see a menu listing your options. You choose an option and then proceed with whatever you want to do—searching for mail that has been left for you, writing and sending your own letter, and more.

You also may want to upload a file you've saved on disk (transmit it to the host computer) or download a file the host computer contains. You end the connection by *logging off* (instructing the host system that you're finished), and choosing the command that tells the modem to hang up the line.

The concept is simple enough—in effect, what you're doing when you go online is working interactively with a distant computer. (In most cases, you're only one of dozens, hundreds, or even thousands of telecommunicators who are using the same system, but you don't know it— as far as you know, you have complete and exclusive access to the system.)

You have a variety of options for going online. Here's a quick overview of the communications programs you can use:

- *Shareware communications programs:* Many excellent communications programs are available as shareware programs, which you obtain free and pay for only if you decide to use them. These programs were developed by computer hobbyists for their own use and amusement, and some of them are hard to use unless you're knowledgeable about the computer. Shareware programs are available from computer bulletin boards and mail-order firms that distribute shareware disks for fees as low as $2 per disk. The software is often of excellent quality from a technical standpoint, although it's often hard to use. Don't expect good documentation.

- *Commercial communications programs:* The communications programs you can buy in a computer store (or order from a software mail-order firm) may have started life as shareware programs. Having graduated, they now offer much better documentation and more features. But many of these programs still bear marks of their shareware ancestry; they're technically capable, but often cumbersome and difficult to use.

- *Communications utilities in integrated programs:* By far the best choice for computer novices (and most small business owners) is to use the communications utilities that are included in integrated programs (such as Microsoft Works) and system utilities packages (such as PC Tools). These utilities include all or most of the features you'll ever need to go online, but they're also well documented and easy to use.

- *Proprietary communications programs:* These programs run on your computer and work with your modem, but they dial only one place: the online or E-mail service that provides them. Often available free of charge or at a low cost, they're worth using because they provide menu-driven interfaces and graphics, freeing you from the necessity to memorize complicated system commands.

Communications programs vary considerably in how well they hide the complexity of telecommunications. To be sure, some of that complexity can't be hidden. Each time you dial a new online service, you must be sure to create and store a file of communication settings appropriate to that service. These settings define the *communications protocol,* or the standards by which the communication between the two computers will occur. Unfortunately, there is no single standard, so you must choose the protocol settings when you contact a communications service. Fortunately, most services use one of two combinations of settings, so it's not very difficult to get past this hurdle.

It isn't really that difficult to choose settings; there are just four settings to choose, and you can choose them without knowing what they do. (The settings have to do with such matters as how many bits of information are transmitted at a time. All that matters is that the sending and receiving computers use the same settings.) But some programs don't do a very good job of *saving* these settings under the name of a particular service. A good communications program lets you forget about these settings once you've chosen them; you just choose the service you're dialing from a menu, and the program automatically uses the settings you chose.

Personal computer communications programs include *file-transfer protocols*, which are standards that ensure error-free transmission of program and data files. The most common file transfer protocol in personal computing is called the XMODEM protocol. To upload or download a file, you choose an option that sends or receives the file using this protocol. If the program detects a transmission error, which is common due to static in telephone lines, it keeps repeating the transmission until the information is received correctly. You don't need to use a file-transfer protocol for E-mail messages or text; these are transferred as plain text.

Looking at the Benefits of Computer-Based Communications

Depending on the particular communications program you buy and the online services to which you subscribe, you should be able to perform some or all of the following tasks:

- *Storing all the information needed to dial another computer at a keystroke.* In figure 12.1, you see the opening telecommunications screen of PC Tools. For each service listed (such as CompuServe or the Central Point Software database), the program stores the communications settings, modem settings, and the log-on script.

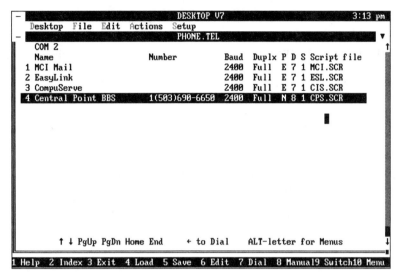

```
 ─                           DESKTOP V7                        3:13 pm
   Desktop  File  Edit  Actions  Setup
 ─                            PHONE.TEL                                ▼
   COM 2                                                               ↑
   Name                   Number       Baud  Duplx P D S  Script file
 1 MCI Mail                            2400  Full  E 7 1  MCI.SCR
 2 EasyLink                            2400  Full  E 7 1  ESL.SCR
 3 CompuServe                          2400  Full  E 7 1  CIS.SCR
 4 Central Point BBS  1(503)690-6650   2400  Full  N 8 1  CPS.SCR
                                                          █


            ↑ ↓ PgUp PgDn Home End      ← to Dial    ALT-letter for Menus    ↓
 1 Help  2 Index 3 Exit  4 Load  5 Save  6 Edit  7 Dial  8 Manual9 Switch10 Menu
```

Fig. 12.1. *Communications settings for four online services (PC Tools).*

- *Monitoring the procedure you use to log on, including typing your account number and password, and then saving all this information to an automatic procedure file called a log-on script.* This is an attractive feature of the best communications programs which greatly simplifies online communication—you don't have to memorize your account number and password, because the computer remembers them for you, and it always types them without error.

- *Addressing an electronic mail message to one or many people—as long as they're also subscribers to the E-mail service you're using.* When these people log on to the system, they'll be notified automatically that a message is waiting for them.

- *Receiving messages from others.* When you log on to the E-mail system, the host computer checks your electronic "mailbox" to see whether there's any mail for you. If so, you're notified, and you have a chance to display the message or messages. After you read each message, you have the option of holding, deleting, forwarding, or answering it.

- *Exchanging programs and data files.* You can upload a Lotus 1-2-3 spreadsheet using the XMODEM protocol, and your correspondents can receive it and open it on their computers. The XMODEM protocol ensures that the transmission will be free from errors.

- *Accessing online data resources.* Many E-mail services offer additional resources, such as news, weather reports, current stock quotes, and more. You also can subscribe to online database services, which offer huge amounts of information in databases you can search from your desktop computer. Some of these databases may contain information that is of strategic value for your business.

TIP

To minimize long-distance telephone charges, compress the files before sending them with a file compression utility such as PKZip (PKWare) or StuffIt Deluxe (Alladin Systems). Your correspondent will need a copy of the same program so that he or she can decompress the file on the other end. Some file-compression programs can produce self-extracting files, however, which automatically decompress when the user accesses them.

Using Electronic Mail

Electronic mail is a unique communication medium that may prove of value to your business. It's much faster than first-class mail (as long as your correspondent logs on). You easily can send the same message to two or more people. And your correspondent can write a reply right after reading your message. At its best, electronic mail is a fast and cost-effective alternative to telephone calls, first-class mail, faxes, or express services.

Electronic Mail Services

An electronic mail service offers what is technically known as *point-storage-point* electronic mail. Such a system employs a mainframe computer with huge amounts of storage space, in which electronic mail messages are stored until their intended recipients log on to the system.

To use a point-storage-point electronic mail service, you call the service—not your correspondent. You begin a message by *addressing* it to your correspondent (by typing his or her online name). Then you type the message. (To save online time charges, you can prepare the message in advance and upload it.) When your correspondent later logs on to the system, the system searches the message database and finds that there is a message addressed to him or her. With a simple command, the message is displayed. Having read the message, your correspondent has the following options: saving the message to read again later, deleting the message, forwarding the message to another E-mail subscriber, or answering the message.

Using an E-mail service has obvious advantages. You don't need to make an advance arrangement with your correspondent. You can address your message to more than one person. And there's no risk of *telephone tag*, in which two people try unsuccessfully to reach each other.

There are some disadvantages, too. What if your correspondent doesn't log on? There's no way he or she will know there's a message waiting. You can't communicate via E-mail with people unless you're absolutely sure they log on regularly. And then there are the costs of online communication. Most commercial E-mail services charge you a minimum monthly rate, even if you don't log on to the system. (Like health clubs, it's all the better for them if you subscribe and then don't show up.) Most also charge a per-hour fee. Even worse, these costs go up with each additional person with whom you correspond. If you want five employees to communicate on MCI Mail, you've got five monthly service bills to pay.

A new international electronic mail standard called X.400 may solve the problem of not being able to communicate with people who subscribe to some other E-mail service. An X.400-compatible message is relayed automatically via computer gateways to many other services (but not CompuServe), and quickly reaches its destination. Today, it isn't easy to use X.400 capabilities, but they're expected to become easier to use (and more popular) in the future.

A Quick Guide to E-Mail Services

If you're thinking about linking your employees (or your customers) with electronic mail, there's a variety of electronic mail services to investigate. For a bargain, pay particular attention to the hobbyist services, some of which offer unlimited E-mail usage nights and weekends for a low hourly fee.

The following telephone numbers and charges were correct at the time this book went to press, but they may have changed since then.

- *America Online (800-827-6364):* A hobbyist-oriented service, but this service provides excellent E-mail facilities for a bargain price: connect charges are only $5 per hour evenings and weekends, and the monthly service fee is only $5.95 (includes one hour of free evening and weekend usage). Included free is an outstanding, menu-driven user interface.

- *CompuServe (800-848-8199):* A widely used E-mail service with an impressive collection of online data resources for business. It is expensive, however: connect charges are $12.80 per hour, in addition to a $2 monthly user support fee. The sign-up fee is $39.95, which includes $25 of free usage.

- *GENie (800-638-9636):* A hobbyist-oriented online service, but this service provides E-mail for a bargain price: you can have unlimited electronic mail access (evenings and weekends) for a flat fee of only $4.95 per month, with no sign-up fee. Connect charges are $18 per hour business days, dropping to $6 per hour nights, weekends, and holidays.

- *MCI Mail (800-444-6245):* A professional electronic mail service that offers many features in addition to standard E-mail: for example, you can upload a message that MCI will send as a fax. There is a $35 annual fee, but no connect-time charges: You dial an 800 number to connect with MCI. Electronic mail charges vary with the length of the message: the charge for a message of up to 500 characters is 45 cents, while a message of 501 to 2,500 characters is 75 cents. A message of 2,501 to 7,500 characters is $1, and each additional 7,500 characters is $1.

E-Mail Alternatives

Electronic mail has its advantages, but there are alternatives.

If you want to link five or six employees in a local area and you are using an old, obsolete computer, you can set up your own bulletin board system (BBS). A BBS consists of bulletin board software, a personal computer equipped with a hard disk, and a modem with auto-answer capabilities. When remote callers dial the system, they are greeted with a request to state their password. If the password is correct, they see a menu showing the system's resources, which can include electronic mail, computer conferences, files to download, and databases. You'll need a hobbyist's help, a shareware bulletin board program, and an extra phone line, but for the effort you get your very own point-storage-point electronic mail system.

If you prefer to use a fax instead of electronic mail, you can equip your system with a fax board and fax software (see Chapter 16, "Designing Your System"). With this equipment, you can send and receive faxes with your computer. A disadvantage is that you have to send material that you've composed at the computer (unless you have an optical scanner), but you can receive anything and display or print it (as long as your display and printer can handle graphics).

Don't overlook traditional communications media. Most business people feel that frank or sensitive subjects are best discussed over the telephone rather than via electronic mail; E-mail just doesn't provide avenues for those subtle vocal and verbal cues that help us get our meaning across clearly. It's easier for your correspondent to misinterpret E-mail messages, particularly if an emotional or sensitive matter is being discussed.

> If you discuss highly confidential information, don't use E-mail. The courts have yet to grant electronic communication the protections normally accorded to written communications, and as a result, there is absolutely nothing illegal about someone accessing and reading your E-mail files. Moreover, some systems keep permanent records of all the messages even after you think you've deleted them, and these files could be subpoenaed successfully in a legal battle.

Using Online Data Resources

Management gurus are fond of saying that knowledge is money in today's information society, but that's only true if one of two conditions is met: first, your business involves the use of time-sensitive information; or second, you or your employees would have to spend many hours searching in the library for the information you need. In either case, it's possible that you could realize huge productivity gains by subscribing to a *database vendor*, an online service that offers access to electronic databases, of which there are more than 5,000 in existence. The largest database vendor, Dialog Information Services, offers access to hundreds of databases, all of which can be searched using the query techniques similar to those you would use with a personal computer database program.

Stacey's work in business consulting involves work with time-sensitive information. She specializes in searching U.S. Commerce Department requests for proposals (RFPs) to find contract bids of interest to the local firms she works for. "I could subscribe to *Commerce News Daily*, which contains the information I want," Stacey says, "but I'd get it two or three days after the bids are first made public. With Dialog and the Commerce Business Daily database, I can track down the RFPs within two hours after they're announced, and that gives my clients an edge."

Is online database research for you? Possibly. But it's expensive, the search software often is antiquated and exceptionally difficult to learn and use, and you could spend a lot of time without coming up with the information you want. Online database research still may be worth your while, especially if your business involves time-sensitive information or if you're spending more than two or three hours per week at the library.

Database Vendors

To access online data resources, you must contact a *database vendor*—a firm that offers online access to databases—and obtain a subscription. There are dozens of vendors, each with its own list of database offerings. For a complete list of current database vendors, see the *Datapro Directory of On-Line Services* (Datapro Research Corporation), which is available in most public libraries.

Here's just a sample of the dozens of database vendors who offer subscriptions to their services:

- *CompuServe (800-848-8199):* This service had its origins as a hobbyists' service, but has added many databases of interest to businesses. These include current and historical quotes for stocks, bonds, mutual funds, commodities, options, and currencies. Corporate and industrial information is available in databases such as Disclosure Online and Institutional Broker's Estimate System.

- *Dialog Information Services (800-334-2564):* The biggest database vendor, this service specializes in providing bibliographic information for research libraries. Many databases contain information of interest to businesses, however. You can save money by subscribing to Knowledge Index, which offers 90 of Dialog's most popular databases at reduced rates on nights and weekends.

- *Dow Jones News/Retrieval (800-522-3567):* A business-oriented online service that includes indexes and abstracts for *The Wall Street Journal*. It also includes many other resources such as Dow Jones News Service (reports on business developments as they occur) and Federal Filings (immediate news about mergers and acquisitions). This service also offers information on securities transactions by major investors such as the Dow Jones Tracking Service, which tracks 125 trend-setting companies.

- *Mead Data Central (800-227-4908):* This firm is best known for LEXIS, its massive legal database, which covers federal and state law.

Public libraries increasingly offer access to electronic databases that have been published on CD-ROM disks. Such databases include the Business and Company Index Profile, Business Index, Federal Prime Contracts, Microsoft Small Business Consultant, and many more. If your library offers patron access to its compact disk-based information sources, you can use them for free—but you'll still have to go to the library to use the CD reader.

Online Databases

Well over 4,000 online databases can be accessed via any telephone in North America. For a complete list, see the *Directory of Online Services*, a reference work published by Carlos Cuadra and Associates. You'll find this annually-updated book in the reference section of most libraries. Here's just a sample of the databases a small business may find useful:

- *American Business Lists (available on Online Information Network, 402-593-4593):* Contains the names and addresses of over 14 million U.S. businesses, 4.3 million high-income U.S. residents, and 78 million consumers. You can use this service to put together your own mailing list more cheaply than you could purchase one from a commercial bulk mail service.

- *Commerce Business Daily (available on Dialog Information Services, 800-334-2564):* Updated daily, this database contains an immensely valuable resource for any business trying to get into government contracting: the daily list of U.S. Commerce Department requests for proposals (RFPs).

- *Daily Current Exchange Rates (Available on Reuter:File, Ltd., 800-387-1588):* Gives current exchange rates for 14 major currencies and provides historical data for over two decades of currency transactions.

- *Disclosure Online (Dialog Information Services, 800-334-2564):* Indexes the publicly disclosed facts about more than 12,000 publicly owned companies that are required to file such disclosures with the Securities and Exchange Commission (SEC). Contains more than 250 facts for each firm.

- *Dun's Market Identifiers (available on Dialog Information Services, 800-334-2564):* A directory of all U.S. firms with five or more employees and more than $1 million in sales. Included is a profile of each firm with more than 40 facts.

- *National Newspaper Index (Dialog Information Services, 800-334-2564):* Front to back indexing of the *New York Times*, *Washington Post*, *Wall Street Journal*, *Christian Science Monitor*, and *Los Angeles Times*.

- *Thomas New Industrial Products (Dialog Information Services, 800-334-2564):* A database including technical descriptions of thousands of new industrial tools, machines, processes, and materials.

- *TRW Business Profiles (CompuServe, 800-848-8199):* Lists the credit rating of public and private companies, and provides a confidence rating that the firm will succeed in paying its bills within 30 days.

For more information on online database resources, see *Online Access*, a quarterly magazine published by Chicago Fine Print, Inc., 2271 North Lincoln Avenue, Chicago, Illinois 60614 (312-935-1400). This high-quality publication offers in-depth articles and reviews, as well as extensive lists of online database vendors and databases.

Summary

Here's a summary of this chapter's main points:

- A telecommunications program isn't a good thing in itself. You should get involved in telecommunications only if you see an application that makes good strategic sense for your business.

- Communications programs transform your computer into a device for communicating with a distant computer. You also need a modem.

- Many communications programs are difficult to use. Easiest to use, and adequate for most small business purposes, are the communications modules found in integrated programs such as Works or utility packages such as PC Tools.

- Electronic mail services store your messages until your correspondents log on. Both parties must subscribe to the service. To save money, investigate budget nighttime and weekend service rates.

- A wealth of business-related data is available through online database vendors, but it's of interest to you only if your business involves the use of time-sensitive information or if you're spending too much time in the library.

Software Suggestions

You can find easy-to-use or professional-quality telecommunications programs in all three computing environments—DOS, Macintosh, and Windows.

DOS Software for Telecommunications

- *Microsoft Works (Microsoft Corporation):* Includes an easy-to-use telecommunications module that is highly recommended for light E-mail use.

- *PC Tools (Central Point Software):* Besides offering an easy-to-use telecommunications utility with log-on scripting, PC Tools includes an electronic mail manager specifically designed to work with MCI Mail, CompuServe, and EasyLink. You can send and receive mail in the background while working with other applications.

- *PKZIP/PKUNZIP (PKWare):* The file compression/decompression software of choice for DOS.

- *PROCOMM Plus (Datastorm Technologies, Inc.):* A popular and full-featured DOS telecommunications program that can handle professional applications.

- *Smartcom Exec (Hayes Microcomputer Products, Inc.):* Another popular and full-featured DOS telecommunications program, suitable for professional applications.

Macintosh Software for Telecommunications

- *Microphone II (Software Ventures):* An easy-to-use communications program that also includes a powerful scripting language. Includes predesigned scripts for MCI Mail, CompuServe, Dow Jones News/ Retrieval Service, and other leading services.

- *Microsoft Works (Microsoft Corporation):* The Macintosh version of Works contains a communications module that's even easier to use than its DOS counterpart.

- *StuffIt Deluxe (Alladin Systems):* The leading Macintosh file compression/decompression program.

Windows Software for Telecommunications

- *Crosstalk for Windows (DCA):* A Windows version of a popular, full-featured communications program; capable of handling professional E-mail applications.

- *Terminal (Microsoft Corporation):* An accessory program provided with Windows, Terminal is a simple, easy-to-use program that provides all functionality needed for electronic mail. You can't create a log-on script, however.

Part IV

Keeping Business Records

Includes

Billing for Time and Expenses

Keeping the Books

13

Billing for Time and Expenses

Many businesses charge by the hour, and in an increasingly service-oriented society, their numbers are growing daily. Included in this category are the legal, medical, and psychiatric practices that you would expect, but there's a huge variety of additional businesses that charge their customers per hour: desktop publishers, child care centers, landscape architects, pet groomers, private investigators, building contractors, chiropractors, physical therapists, dieticians, free-lance typists, educational consultants, and more. And they're all facing the same problem: how to keep track of the time their employees expend on each account, and how to bill their clients correctly.

Standard accounting systems just aren't up to the task, and an enormous development effort would be required to customize single-purpose programs such as dBASE or Lotus 1-2-3 for time-billing purposes. This is a job for special-purpose programs such as Timeslips III (the market-leading special-purpose program) and a host of vertical-market applications, which are customized for the specific needs of medical, psychiatric, dental, accounting, and legal practices.

If you're involved in a business that bills clients or customers by the hour, this chapter contains valuable information for you. You'll learn how many time-billing businesses (ranging in size from one to dozens of employees) can develop excellent applications with Timeslips, while others—particularly firms in medical areas, where insurance billing complicates the picture—will be better off with a vertical-market program.

237

Looking At Software Options for Time and Expense Billing

If you're shopping for time-billing software, you'll be looking at two categories:

- *Special-purpose programs:* The market leader is Timeslips III, available for DOS and Macintosh systems, and it's virtually in a class by itself. Just about any business that bills for time can use Timeslips III, with the exception of health-related businesses, which have special insurance billing needs that Timeslips III can't handle.

- *Vertical-market programs:* A medical practice must deal with two additional problems besides billing for time: tracking patient information and creating health insurance forms. Vertical-market programs include the features that are needed by practitioners of a specific profession. Time-billing programs for medical practices therefore include features for tracking patient information and dealing with health insurance forms—a feature that special-purpose programs usually do not offer.

As you will quickly discover if you research the market, vertical market time-billing software can get expensive quickly: many legal and medical packages sell for five figures. The rationale underlying this often rather extravagant pricing is that these programs embody substantial experience in a narrowly defined line of work, such as psychotherapy or dentistry, and therefore offer sufficient value to justify a high price. If you're running a more modest time-billing operation, however, a more generic program such as Timeslips III may very well suffice for you.

One of the purposes of this chapter is to show what Timeslips III can do; you can decide whether the program really meets your time-billing needs.

Examining the Benefits of Time-Billing Software

Today's special-purpose time-billing programs can perform the following actions:

- Record each billable event as it occurs or later, showing who performed what for whom, and for how long. You can bill by the person, by the client, or by the activity.

- Sort, organize, and search records about specific time-related events (indicating who did what for whom, and when).

- Record expenses (such as mileage, FAX charges, or copying) as well as timed activities. You can set the rates, as well as charge sales or service tax, if applicable.

- Time activities as they occur by using an optional terminate-and-stay-resident (TSR) mode, which enables you to access the program even if you're using another DOS application. This feature is very useful for professionals who bill for telephone advice: when someone calls, you press the key that displays your time-billing program, which automatically and accurately times the call.

- Bill at a fixed rate (for example, $125 for a specific job) or at a timed rate ($38 per hour). Most businesses need this flexibility. Some customers will not agree to a job unless you bill at a flat rate.

- Record descriptive notes that identify and explain the activity. These notes appear optionally on bills, helping to explain the charges to the customer.

- Add new clients, employees, and activities on the fly. You easily can expand the scope of the application, even after you add data.

- Compile all records at the end of a billing cycle and print itemized bills. These programs also include facilities for keeping a mailing list of clients and printing mailing labels, so billing goes quickly.

- Maintain a client's account and post payments and other transactions to it. When you receive a payment, you record it, and the client's balance is reduced. You also can handle credits and refunds.

- Generate reports (data printouts) that show which clients haven't paid their bills on time. More than a few businesses have closed their doors because they didn't track overdue accounts. This feature alone is well worth the cost of developing a time-billing system.

By automating time billing, programs such as Timeslips produce major time savings. But there's an additional benefit that shouldn't be underestimated: these programs also put information about your business at your fingertips. As you'll see in the next section, which examines a Timeslips application in detail, one of the dividends of a computerized time-billing system is your ability to answer a series of important questions, such as: Which of your employees is generating the most hours? The least? Which of your clients is generating the most income for your firm? Is your firm spending its time on its most profitable activities? And last but not least, who owes you money?

Developing a Time-Billing Application

Teresa runs a thriving tutoring business, specializing in the areas of English as a Second Language (ESL) and learning disabilities. She works with more than a dozen freelance tutors, who visit the clients in their homes. Every week, each tutor turns in a timesheet for as much as 15 or 20 hours of tutoring in the field, as well as mileage charges for each field session. Once a month, Teresa must spend as much as two days on billing tasks: assembling all the charges for a particular client, typing a bill, computing sales and service taxes, and addressing the envelope.

Sometimes Teresa puts off doing the billing for a couple of weeks, and even worse, she has developed no system at all to deal with unpaid or late bills. Some clients don't pay for months before Teresa discovers what's going on. But in the meantime, Teresa has paid the field tutors like clockwork, every two weeks.

In thinking about how to computerize her business, Teresa wisely decides to focus on two problem areas that are critical to the business: getting bills out on time and figuring out who has paid (and who hasn't). She finds exactly what she's looking for in Timeslips III.

Defining Names

Teresa finds that it takes only a few minutes to develop a Timeslips III application. Just four steps are required:

1. Define nicknames for employees and clients. These names don't appear on bills; they're used for Timeslips III's internal record-keeping purposes and for helping you fill out timeslips quickly.

2. Change Timeslips III's default terminology. A legal business employs attorneys, who perform services for clients; a medical practice employs physicians, who perform services for patients. Teresa employ tutors, who perform services for clients. Timeslips III enables her to define the default terminology so that the terms *tutor* and *client* appear on all on-screen menus.

3. Type the client's full names and addresses. Timeslips III needs this information to print the bills and mailing labels.

4. Tell Timeslips III whether to charge service tax on time services, sales tax on expense charges, and interest on overdue accounts. Some states require that service businesses charge tax, and Timeslips III gives you the option of charging interest on overdue accounts.

It takes Teresa only a couple of hours to set up her Timeslips III application. When the next batch of timesheets comes in, she's ready.

Creating Timeslips

When the tutors bring in their timesheets each week, Teresa sits down at the computer and enters each transaction on a timeslip. The timeslip shows the name of the employee (the tutor), the client (normally the parent of the tutored child), and the activity (learning disability tutoring, ESL tutoring, diagnostic testing, and expense-related activities such as mileage or photocopying).

Here's how Teresa handles Karina's timesheet. Karina tutored Daniel Hopkins twice last week. In addition to his regular Tuesday session, Karina also tutored Daniel for an additional hour on Thursday. She logged 13.5 miles driving to Daniel's house each time. Teresa will enter four timeslips, making use of Timeslips III's ability to copy information quickly from one record to the next.

To enter the first timeslip, Teresa chooses the Make Slips option, which displays a blank timeslip. Teresa chooses the tutor, client, and activity names from on-screen menus that appear at the touch of a key. Figure 13.1 shows how Teresa chooses the tutor's name (Karina) from the menu at the bottom of the screen. Figure 13.2 shows how Teresa chooses the activity (Tutoring, at a rate of $28 per hour). Figure 13.3 shows the completed timeslip.

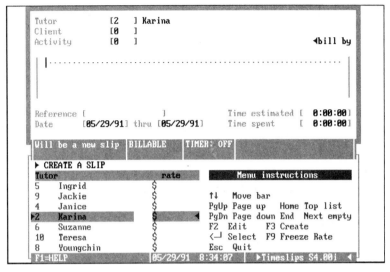

Fig. 13.1. Choosing the tutor's name.

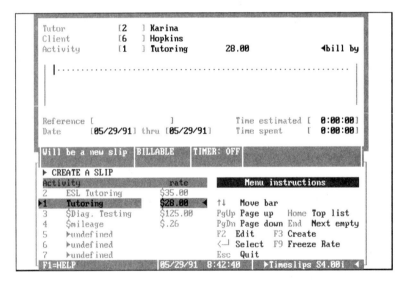

Fig. 13.2. Choosing the activity.

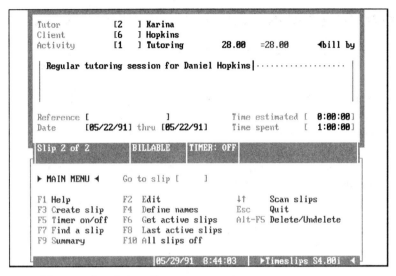

Fig. 13.3. *The completed timeslip.*

Now that one of the timeslips is completed, Teresa copies the current information to the next record, so that all that's required is a few changes to complete the next slip. Figure 13.4 shows an expense slip: a slip that charges the client for Karina's mileage driving to and from Daniel's house.

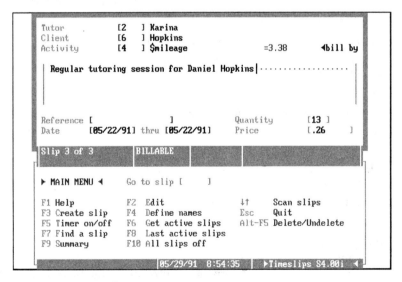

Fig. 13.4. *An expense slip.*

Printing Bills and Posting Transactions

At the end of the month, Teresa prints bills with Timeslips III. Instead of taking two days, however, the job takes only a couple of hours, and that includes the time spent checking a draft of the bills to make sure that all the charges are correct. Figure 13.5 shows the first page of the bill that Timeslips III prepares for Daniel's mother, Janice Hopkins. The bill is printed so that, when Teresa folds it, the address and return address are positioned in the envelope's window.

Teresa's example shows how easy it is to create bills with a time-billing program such as Timeslips. If the program has done its job, your customers will respond with payments, which you post to their accounts using a Timeslips screen. What happens if they don't pay? You can set up Timeslips to charge interest on overdue accounts.

Getting Timely Information

One of the chief benefits of using a computer for storing and retrieving information is that this information becomes available to you for analysis. You can produce the following reports with Timeslips III—and you can use them to answer the following questions:

- *Detail report:* A detailed summary of all time and expense activity. Are all the entries correct?

- *Client budget worksheet:* If you've established a budget with your client, have you exceeded any of the spending limits that have been established?

- *User report:* A report (including a graphics display option) showing how many hours each employee spent on billable activities during the previous billing period. Which of your employees is the most productive?

- *Client report:* A report (including a graphics display option) showing how many hours was spent on the behalf of each client during the recent billing period. Which clients are making the most use of your services?

- *Activity report:* A report (including a graphics display option) showing the activities your employees performed. Is your firm spending its time on the activities that produce the biggest payoffs?

```
        The Reading and Learning Center
        127 Martin Way
        Palo Alto, CA 94388


        Invoice submitted to:
        Janice Hopkins
        1387 Mountain View Rd.
        Los Altos, CA 94798


        May 29, 1991


                                                Hours        Amount

                Professional services

        05/01/91 Regular tutoring session        1.00         28.00

        05/07/91 Regular tutoring session        1.00         28.00

        05/15/91 Regular tutoring session        1.00         28.00

        05/22/91 Regular tutoring session        1.00         28.00

        05/24/91 Special tutoring session        2.00         56.00

        05/29/91 Regular tutoring session        1.00         28.00


                For professional services rendered 7.00      $196.00

                Additional charges:

        05/01/91 Tutor's mileage ($.26/mile)                   3.38

        05/03/91 Diagnostic test for Daniel Hopkins (processing 125.00
                 and analysis)

        05/08/91 Tutor's mileage ($.26/mile)                   3.38

        05/15/91 Tutor's mileage ($.26/mile)                   3.38

        05/22/91 Tutor's mileage ($.26/mile)                   3.38
```

Fig. 13.5. A bill printed by Timeslips III.

- *Accounts receivable:* A report that lists some very important people: those who owe you money. Who's late paying? Who owes you money? How much?

Bear in mind that one of the best reasons for doing your own billing or accounting is your increased ability to answer questions such as these. Chapter 14, which examines personal computer approaches to small business accounting, repeats this point.

With a modest amount of development effort, Timeslips III can serve as a time-billing application for a surprisingly large firm. The program is available in networked versions, and is being used in legal practices with a dozen or more practicing attorneys. But Timeslips doesn't include insurance billing capabilities that would be needed to apply the program to medical, dental, and psychotherapeutic practices. And as you'll see in the next section, time-billing programs, including vertical-market programs, cannot take on all the responsibilities of a computerized accounting system.

Using an Accounting Program

Although time-billing programs such as Timeslips III offer many of the features of accounting programs, such as tracking late payments and keeping client balances, they're not intended for accounting purposes and lack many of the features needed to keep your firm's books. If you're planning to computerize your bookkeeping, as discussed in the next chapter, you should choose a time-billing and accounting program that are compatible with each other. MedPac, for example, a medical time-billing system, is designed to work with ACCPAC Plus, a popular accounting program that runs in the DOS environment.

If you're planning to use Timeslips III, you can take advantage of an add-on program called Timeslips III Accounting Link (TAL), which exports Timeslips III data to the accounting packages that follow.

Accounting Packages Compatible with Timeslips Accounting Link

ABM Platinum General Ledger
ACCPAC Bedford (U.S. and Canadian versions)
ACCPAC BPI Accounting 3.0
Computer Associates ACCPAC Plus 6.0a
ACCPAC Plus 5.0/4.2
ACT 1 Cougar Mountain
Books

Business Works Advanced Accounting
Champion III Business Accounting
Cyma Professional Accounting
DacEasy Accounting 4.1
Great Plains Series Version 5
IBM Platinum
Lake Avenue Software Version 6
Macola Accounting Software 4.0
Manusoft Ready to Run
One Write Plus Master Version 2.05
One Write Plus Master Version 2.06
Open Systems
Peachtree Complete III
Versa Professional Business Series

Summary

Here's a summary of this chapter's main points:

- Time-billing programs combine database management with event timing, billing, accounts receivable tracking, and other features tailored to businesses that bill by the hour.

- The market-leading special-purpose program, Timeslips III, is versatile and well conceived, but it isn't the best choice for fields that have to file insurance claim forms.

- The two biggest benefits of a time-billing system are the time saved in billing clients and the increased access to fundamental information about your firm's performance.

- A time-billing program isn't an accounting program. If you plan to computerize your firm's books, you should choose a time-billing package and an accounting package that can work together.

Software Suggestions

At this writing, Timeslips III is available in equally good DOS and Macintosh versions. Time-billing software probably will appear soon for Windows systems. If you're looking for a vertical-market application, you're looking at a DOS system.

DOS Time-Billing Programs

- *MedPac (Syscon Computers):* A complete time-billing program for a medical practice, this program exports data to ACCPAC Plus and supports electronic claims submissions. The program tracks patient records and works with a wide variety of insurance forms.

- *DentPac (Syscon Computers):* A version of MedPac developed for dentistry practices, DentPac exports data to ACCPAC Plus, tracks patients' dental records, and works with a wide variety of insurance forms.

- *Threshold (Physicians Practice Management):* A complete accounts receivable program for patient billing. Supports electronic claims submissions. Tracks patient records. Creates a wide variety of reports (aged trial balances, appointment listings, and so on).

- *Shrink Direct, Shrink 3.0, Shrink Plus (Multi-Health System):* A family of products for large and small psychotherapy practices that is highly regarded by practitioners in the profession. All versions support time billing, track patient records, and include appointment scheduling.

- *TimePiece Legal (Impact Software Productions):* A time-billing program devised for legal practices, this program includes export links to a popular accounting package and is fully integrated with WordPerfect, the law profession's word processing program of choice.

- *Timeslips III (Timeslips):* The DOS version of the time-billing program featured in this chapter.

Macintosh Time-Billing Programs

- *Timeslips III (Timeslips):* The Macintosh version of the time-billing program featured in this chapter.

14

Keeping the Books

Accounting programs have an unenviable reputation for difficulty of use. But there's a new breed of computer bookkeeping programs developed with the ordinary user in mind. These programs are much easier to use than the previous generation of accounting software—and as you'll see, some aren't much more difficult to use than an ordinary checkbook! Should you try to keep your books on your computer?

Increasingly, small business owners are answering "Yes!" to this question. They're learning they can save hundreds of dollars yearly by performing their own accounting and tax preparation. But there's an even bigger payoff than saving money. Accounting isn't just a matter of keeping records; a good computerized accounting system gives you an almost instantaneous assessment of how well your business is doing. You can ask questions such as, "Is business better now than it was at the same time last year? Who haven't paid their bills? Who's taking too long to send me shipments? What's not moving in my inventory?" and many, many more. Getting timely answers to these questions may make the difference in the game of business survival.

This chapter surveys a range of accounting software options and shows how they're appropriate for a range of businesses. Whether you're running a part-time home business or a thriving firm with many employees, there is a computerized accounting solution that may be right for you. At the most modest level, a home or other modest-sized business can use a checkwriting program to track a business and get ready for tax preparation. Larger businesses, especially businesses with more than one or two employees, can benefit from using an accounting package.

Even if you don't have any accounting background, you can learn to use these programs, and you can benefit from having information about your business at your fingertips. But bear in mind that you'll need some accounting background, or (even better) the assistance of a professional accountant, to *design* your computerized accounting system and to make sure that it conforms to the highest accounting standards. After you set up your accounting system properly, the remaining tasks—day-to-day data entry and report generation—are easy and could even be handled by a computer-literate clerical worker.

Deciding Whether To Computerize Your Books

Bear in mind that computerizing your books may not be the wisest decision for you. Just in itself, keeping your own books isn't necessarily a good idea: in fact, an accounting service probably can do the job for a very reasonable price, and you get all the firm's experience in the bargain. Crucial to your decision is whether you need the information an accounting system can give you. If there's a critical area of your business that's giving you no end of trouble—such as collecting past due accounts, dealing with payroll paperwork, keeping control of your inventory, or tracking cash flow—a computerized accounting system could become a strategic investment in your firm's future.

> Before you embark on an effort to computerize your accounts, you'll be wise to explain your plans to a professional accountant and ask for advice. The money you'll pay for an hour or two of consultation time will be well worth it.

To answer the question "Should you computerize?" it's helpful to know that accounting isn't just keeping records of transactions. That's a big part of the job, of course, but there's more. An accountant also categorizes transactions—for example, some transactions are tax-related, while others aren't. And finally, an accountant summarizes information, providing answers to questions such as "Am I making money?" Accounting, then, is a three-step process: recording, categorizing, and summarizing.

Now here's the point. Chances are pretty good that you're already doing a lot of the recording right now—and if you're not, you should be.

Perhaps you or your clerical staff is painstakingly writing down every transaction in a general ledger. Or perhaps you're just recording checks and deposits in a business checking account. Either way, you're already doing a lot of the work that goes into a computerized accounting system: you're recording transactions in a *journal*, which records each transaction on a chronological, blow-by-blow basis. *But you're not getting the benefits of this work.* Your bookkeeper or accountant categorizes and summarizes this information for payroll tax computation, Schedule C business taxes, and business financial statements. You don't have the answers to questions about how your business is performing, however.

Perhaps you're not categorizing or summarizing this information at all, waiting until the last moment before taxes are due to wade through months of records with meanings you've forgotten.

The big benefit of computerizing your books is that you just keep on recording transactions, as you do now (or *should* be doing now). The program automatically categorizes and summarizes the information you record. As long as your approach is well-conceived, the program does a lot of the mundane work that you're paying a bookkeeper or an accountant to do. But you get answers immediately. And you can ask the kind of questions that were mentioned in this chapter's introduction, such as the all-important, "Who owes me money?"

There's another major benefit to computerizing your books. If you're jotting down every transaction on paper, chances are you're writing every transaction twice. Suppose that you're using your computer to create an invoice for a customer. At the end of the day, you still have to write down the transaction in the ledger. With the correct computerized accounting solution, you type a transaction just once. You fill out and print an invoice, and the program updates the books automatically. You fill out and print a check, and the program updates the books automatically. Not only does this save time; it also reduces the chance that you'll make a mistake, and it eliminates the chance that you'll put off updating your books. By entering all transaction information into the computer directly and letting the computer categorize it, you eliminate one of the major sources of errors in business accounting.

Looking at Accounting Software Options

If you think your business could benefit from computerizing your books, you'll need to decide which software best meets your needs. Here's a quick overview of the bookkeeping software options open to small businesses: checkwriting programs, accounting programs, and point-of-sale programs.

Checkwriting Programs

Originally designed for home use, checkwriting programs present an on-screen simulation of an ordinary checking account register. You can buy checks that work with these programs. When you write a check, the program posts the transaction to the register. But here's the biggest attraction of these programs for small businesses (and particularly sole proprietors): you can categorize each check or deposit and produce on-screen or printed reports and summaries.

For example, you can use codes that duplicate the categories you'll find in Schedule C—the form on which you report business-related expenses. At the end of the year, you can quickly produce a report that totals all your expenses for one of these categories—such as Advertising or Office Expense—and the program quickly generates an itemized list, showing each check you coded with this category.

Who should use a checkwriting program? If you can check off two or three of the following boxes, chances are a checkwriting program will meet your needs.

- ❑ You have no employees, or at most only a few, so you don't need much help with payroll-related tasks such as filling out W-2 forms and computing taxes.

- ❑ You seldom write invoices or purchase orders, and you don't need to send statements. Your customers don't need fancy invoices—at the most you just write out a simple receipt—and when you buy something, you just write a check.

- ❑ The only classification system you need is one that tracks tax-related income and expenses. You need a running record of income and expenses, and you need to categorize the expenses so you can fill out IRS Schedule C quickly and easily.

What are the limitations of checkwriting programs for small business accounting? Here's an example. If you have just a few employees, you can use a program such as Quicken (Intuit) to handle your payroll tasks, but you run into a shortcoming when it comes time to print W-2 forms: Quicken can produce summaries of what you've paid an employee, but it can't print W-2 forms directly. You have to get the numbers and type them yourself. That's no problem for two or three employees, but it's a major problem if you have 20 or 30 employees. Most accounting packages can print W-2s automatically.

Despite this and other drawbacks of checkwriting programs for accounting purposes, bear in mind that a checkwriting program is exceptionally easy to use, and using one requires no accounting knowledge. For a modest business, a checkwriting program can provide an excellent solution for record-keeping and tax preparation.

Most checkwriting programs cannot handle payroll tasks, such as computing withholding or printing W-2 forms. However, Intuit (the maker of Quicken, the leading checkwriting program) now offers a payroll add-in program that adds all the necessary payroll capabilities to the IBM version of Quicken.

Accounting Programs

Does your firm need more bookkeeping power than a checkwriting program can provide? If you need to perform such operations as printing invoices, calculating employee withholding, tracking inventories, and producing a balance sheet for banks or investors, investigate personal computer accounting packages. You'll find that there are bargains in today's market. Pacioli 2000 (M-USA), a highly-rated package that includes virtually everything needed for small business accounting purposes, sells for just $49.95—and the price includes full network capabilities.

Today's accounting programs are easier to use than previous ones, but you'll need a solid grasp of accounting concepts—or the help of a professional accountant—to set up your chart of accounts (a necessary step in implementing your computerized accounting system). You probably can find an accountant who would be willing to help you select a program, design your chart of accounts, and set up standard day-to-day data entry and reporting procedures. The money you spend will be well worth the cost.

The Ideal Package

Small businesses should look for an accounting package that enables them to do the following:

- *Obtain balances and print forms before posting takes place.* In professional accounting firms, the daily journal is checked and scrutinized for accuracy before the transactions are transferred to the general ledger, where they are categorized. This transferring operation is called *posting*.

Small businesses need programs that enable them to print checks and other forms, as well as obtain current account balances, without waiting for the daily posting. They can achieve this goal in two ways. The first is *online processing* (also called *real-time processing*), in which every transaction is posted immediately and automatically to the general ledger and categorized, so that invoices, checks, and statements can be printed immediately.

The second is a modified batch-posting procedure, in which the program maintains working account balances and enables you to print forms; you finalize these "working" balances and documents when the posting takes place.

- *Create new accounts on the fly.* A professional accountant's expertise lies in predicting all the ways that transactions should be categorized and tracked. At the minimum, a firm needs a checking account, an owner's equity account, an inventory account, an accounts payable account, an accounts receivable account, and an expenses account. The complete list of such accounts is called a *chart of accounts*.

  Because small business users will need to fine-tune their charts of accounts after they've added data, the ability to add accounts on the fly is essential.

  - *Enter all transactions using on-screen versions of familiar forms, and view the document that generated a transaction when tracking it.*

All the programs listed in the "Software Suggestions" section at the end of this chapter meet these three fundamental criteria.

Accounting Program Modules

Accounting programs are divided into components, or modules, which reflect standard accounting practices. In some accounting packages these modules are actually separate programs designed to work together; in other packages these modules are distinct parts of one seamless, integrated package. The components of an accounting program follow:

- *General ledger:* Keeps a running record of all transactions, categorized by account. A good program handles at least 500 accounts—

the minimum considered necessary for a full-scale small business application.

- *Accounts receivable:* Prepares invoices, tracks customer balances, applies cash received against the balance, and charges interest on overdue accounts. Many programs limit the number of customer accounts you can create; be sure to choose a program that is adequate for your needs.

- *Accounts payable:* Prepares purchase orders, tracks amounts owed, prepares checks, and reconciles checking accounts. Many programs limit the number of vendor accounts you can create; be sure to choose a program that is adequate for your needs.

- *Inventory control:* Adjusts stock levels as transactions occur, warns of low stock levels, provides reorder forms, and looks up inventory status.

- *Payroll:* Prints payroll checks, computes withholding and other deductions, prints W-2 and 1099 forms, and tracks employee information (hire dates, sick leaves, and vacations). Usually available as an add-on module.

Point-of-Sale Programs

Because today's personal computer accounting packages display an on-screen invoice and enable you to enter transactions directly, you can use many of them as point-of-sale programs. A *point-of-sale program* runs in a computer stationed where the sale is made, such as a sales counter. But accounting packages have many drawbacks for point-of-sale use. They aren't really designed for this application. They don't include features such as automatic control of cash drawers, interfaces to bar code readers, and automatic price lookup.

If you're running a retail business, a point-of-sale program can provide these and other benefits. For more information, see the following section, "Accounting Software Benefits."

A point-of-sale program isn't designed to replace an accounting package. To avoid duplicate data entry, it's essential to find a point-of-sale and accounting program that work together. The point-of-sale program must be able to export data to the accounting program in a format the accounting program can recognize. Retail Store Controller, Jr. (MicroBiz), for example, can export data to ACCPAC Plus and ACCPAC BPI (Computer Associates), the checkwriting program Quicken, and One Write Plus (Great American Software).

If you want to use a point-of-sale program, you narrow your accounting package options considerably—and you completely rule out some programs. Pacioli 2000, commendable in almost every other respect, is a poor choice if you want to use a point-of-sale program; the program does not enable you to import data of any kind.

TIP

If you're running a small retail business, but you don't want to get into an accounting package, the combination of Retail Store Controller, Jr. and Quicken is hard to beat. Retail Store Controller, Jr. adds complete point-of-sale functionality to Quicken, including invoicing, inventory control, and accounts receivable.

Examining Accounting Software Benefits

With a checkwriting package, you can perform the following tasks, which meet the minimal record-keeping requirements of a modest business:

- Creating a timely, accurate record of income and expenses. The failure to keep such records could deprive you of the privilege of deducting your business expenses from your business income.

- Writing checks to employees and suppliers by filling out an on-screen simulation of an actual check. The benefit here is that you don't have to write the same data twice, as you would if you wrote a check by hand and then typed in the data later.

- Setting up recurring transactions, so that you don't have to type in the same information at every billing or payment cycle. Remember the rule: Try to avoid typing the same data twice.

- Categorizing your expenses so that they're summed at the end of the year using IRS Schedule C income tax categories. This feature alone makes these programs worth the effort; tax preparation becomes a breeze. Most checkwriting programs can export these figures directly to tax preparation programs.

- Establishing expense and spending budgets and having the computer inform you when you've exceeded them. It's easy to set up such a budget and view a day-to-day, ongoing display—often in graphic form—of where you stand in your spending.

- Reconciling your account with the bank statement quickly and easily. You can get the accounts to square to the penny.

An accounting package can perform all of the tasks in the preceding list. In addition, you should be able to tackle some or all of the following additional tasks:

- Entering data by filling out on-screen versions of familiar forms, such as checks, invoices, and purchase orders. The program records these transactions in the journal and categorizes them appropriately.

- Creating and printing bills, purchase orders, statements, and checks. You'll have to buy forms from the software publisher. Some programs enable you to use standard forms or to create your own forms.

- Tracking a customer's balance against payments and credits, and assessing interest on overdue accounts. The better programs enable you to set up credit terms for individual customers.

- Detecting overdue accounts and generating dunning notices. The better programs come with form-letter capabilities, including mailing lists and mailing label printing.

- Generating all basic accounting reports, such as balance sheets, receivable/payable reports, account activity reports, cash flow (aging) reports, price lists, inventory reports, and others. Obtaining this information in a timely fashion is one of the major benefits of computerizing your accounting.

With a point-of-sale program, you can perform these tasks with the aid of a computer:

- Using a bar code reader to scan product-information codes and look up prices automatically. You'll need to equip your system with a bar code reader.

- Updating inventory automatically. These programs take over the inventory-tracking functions of your accounting program. You can check the status of the inventory even while you're in the midst of a transaction.

- Handling a variety of transactions, including cash, credit card, charge account, layaway, split tender (combination of cash and charge), returns, and exchanges.

- Producing a variety of sales, customer, and inventory reports, including reorders, inventory activity, and product movement.

To sum up, many one-person businesses will find checkwriting programs to be sufficient. You'll need an accounting package if you have more than a few employees, you need to print bills and track customer accounts, or you need timely reports (such as accounts receivables). If you're running a retail business, you can avoid duplicate data entry by using a point-of-sale program.

Choosing a Computerized Accounting Approach

If you're still wondering whether the checkwriting or accounting program approach is right for you, here's another way to think of this question. The choice boils down to whether you want to use single-entry or double-entry accounting in your business.

Most of the accounting programs available for personal computers use double-entry accounting methods, which are often said to be far too difficult for laypeople to grasp. But that's not strictly true. In a single-entry system, like a checkbook register (or a checkwriting program), you just write down your income and expense in an ongoing, chronological order. It's called a *single-entry* system because you record just one fact about each transaction: where it came from and where it went to. This approach has a big limitation: it can't produce a balance sheet.

To produce a balance sheet, you have to record two facts about each transaction: you have to record where the money came from (a *credit*) and where it's going to (a *debit*). A system that records both of these facts about every transaction is called a *double-entry system*.

Double-Entry Accounting

Here's a brief example that explains the merits of a double-entry system. Suppose that Susan is turning her pottery hobby into a business. She puts $1,000 into a new checking account. In a single entry system, all you know is that $1,000 was deposited. Here's what a double entry looks like:

	Debit (*going TO*)	*Credit* (*coming FROM*)
Checking account		1,000
Owner's capital	1,000	

Now it's a recorded fact that the money in the checking account comes from the owner's capital. In figure 14.1, you see how this transaction looks in Pacioli 2000's transaction entry screen.

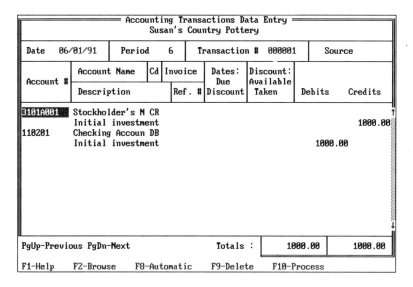

Fig. 14.1. *A double-entry transaction (Pacioli 2000).*

Suppose that Susan takes $187.50 from her checking account to buy supplies (this amount goes to Inventory). She takes another $100 to buy an advertisement for her pottery sale (this amount goes to Expense—Advertising). The next weekend, she cleans out her whole inventory and takes in $350 at her pottery sale (this money comes from Sales Revenue and goes to the checking account). Her checking account balance is now $1,062.50

Now Susan prepares a trial balance. A trial balance quickly tells her whether she's made any mistakes in typing in these figures, because the debit and the credit columns have to match exactly.

	Debit (going TO)	Credit (coming FROM)
Checking Account	1,062.50	
Owner's Equity		1,000.00
Inventory	187.50	
Expense—Advertising	100.00	
Sales Revenue		350.00
TOTALS:	1,350.00	1,350.00

Susan can now prepare an income statement:

Total Revenues	350.00
Cost of Goods Sold	−187.50
Expenses	−100.00
Profit	62.50

After computing her profit, Susan can prepare a balance sheet:

	Assets	Liabilities
Checking	1,062.50	
Owner's equity		1,000.00
Inventory		-0-
Profit		62.50
Totals	1,062.50	1,062.50

In summary, double-entry accounting always shows where money comes from (as well as where it goes). With this information, you can keep track of how much capital you've tied up in your business, and you can tell in an instant—just by seeing whether the asset and liability figures are identical— if you've made a data-entry error.

The Single-Entry Alternative

As you can see, it isn't difficult to understand the basic concepts of double-entry accounting. But this example is simplified—and unrealistically so. It takes quite a lot of initial setup work with Pacioli or any other accounting package to design a chart of accounts that works for your business, and to learn how to carry out transactions so that the money comes from (and goes to) the right places.

Worse, the procedures you must follow may be more complicated than you want to get into. You can't debit your inventory, for example, unless you fill out purchase orders, which is a tedious job if you're in the habit of just dashing down to the hardware store and picking up a few items.

If an accounting program seems like overkill, a checkwriting program such as Quicken may offer an attractive alternative, even though checkwriting programs use single-entry techniques. You should understand the major limitation of checkwriting programs, however: they are designed to help you balance a checkbook—not for accounting.

In figure 14.2, you see how Susan can track her business using Quicken. But in figure 14.3, you see how single-entry accounting can produce erroneous or misleading results: the program can't distinguish between an owner's investment of equity and ordinary income, so it overstates the business's income by $1,000.

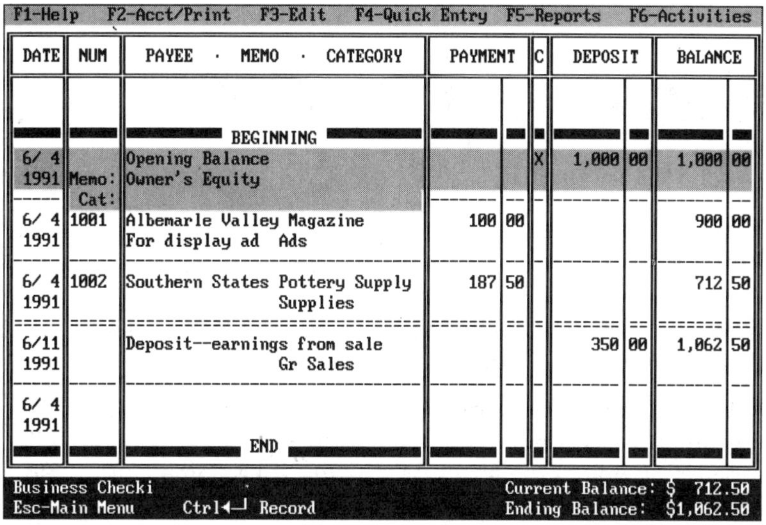

Fig. 14.2. Tracking a business with a checkwriting program (Quicken).

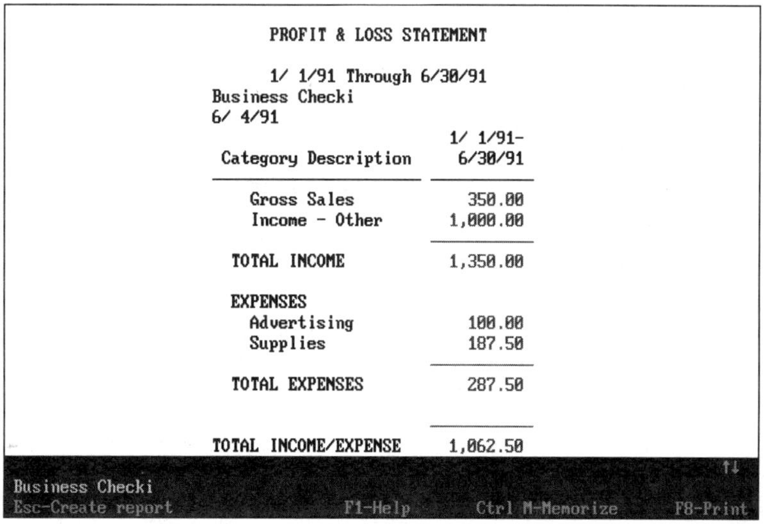

Fig. 14.3. A summary report of income vs. expenses (Quicken).

Is Quicken's overstatement of Susan's income a serious problem? Only if she forgets that the $1,000 is her investment, rather than sales, and pays tax on it! As you can see, a checkwriting program's first duty is to maintain a correct checking account balance, rather than to perform accounting functions. You can use a checkwriting program for some accounting-related purposes, though, if you keep its limitations in mind.

Using Tax Preparation Software

If you've set up your checkwriting or accounting application correctly, filling out tax forms should be a breeze. You've been categorizing those transactions all year, so the year-end summary should produce a printout that precisely parallels all those entries you make in Schedule C. So what's the advantage of tax-preparation software? Here are two huge benefits:

- *Automatic recalculation:* Have you ever filled out an entire tax return, only to find out that you forgot to include a deductible expense on one of the forms or schedules? Like an electronic spreadsheet program, a good tax preparation program keeps all the forms in memory. When you discover that you've entered a number incorrectly or forgotten to enter a number, the program automatically updates all the linked parts of the tax return. This feature can save hours and hours of work.

- *Error prevention:* Most tax preparation programs have at least some built-in safeguards against common errors, such as neglecting to fill in Social Security numbers, entering the same data twice, and—most of all—making calculation errors. A tax preparation program can't prevent you from making errors on your returns, but it can help.

A tax preparation program isn't a substitute for good tax advice, even though some programs—such as Andrew Tobias' Tax Cut (MECA)—claim to be able to offer on-screen advice for tough tax questions. Even after you've prepared your return with a tax preparation program, it's a good idea to show your return to a competent tax accountant.

Summary

Here's a summary of this chapter's main points:

- The best reason for computerizing your books is to get better information about your business—who owes you money, which products are moving, and how much money you need to cover employee withholding. You should choose a computer solution that directly addresses a critical problem area in your business.

- You're already keeping records of income and expenses—and if you're not, you should be. At the minimum, typing these records into the computer gives you the ability to categorize income and expenses. A simple system that categorizes income and expenses using IRS Schedule C categories can save you huge amounts of time as April 15th comes around.

- If you want to computerize your books, you choose between two basic computer approaches: checkwriting programs and accounting programs. Checkwriting programs are easy to use, but accounting programs offer much more functionality. If you have a retail business, you may want to add a point-of-sale program.

- If you select an accounting program, choose one that enables you to obtain balances and print forms before posting, create new accounts on the fly, and enter all transactions using on-screen versions of familiar business forms (such as checks, invoices, and purchase orders).

- The double-entry accounting approach offered in most accounting programs is in line with established accounting principles. But single-entry programs are much easier to use. Checkwriting programs are single-entry programs, but some accounting programs (such as One Write Plus) use single-entry techniques.

- The two main benefits of tax preparation software are automatic recalculation and error prevention. Both make tax preparation software worth having, even if you later take your return to a tax accountant for further scrutiny.

Software Suggestions

Quicken, by far the best checkwriting program, is available for DOS (the Macintosh version isn't as good), and DOS is also the environment of choice if you want to develop a point-of-sale system complete with bar code reader and cash drawer. However, there's a very good case for Macintosh or Windows systems when it comes to accounting and tax preparation packages. Mind Your Own Business (Teleware), a full-featured accounting package, takes full advantage of the Macintosh and Windows user interfaces to offer the first reasonably user-friendly accounting package on the market. MacInTax, from Softview (Macintosh and Windows versions), is arguably the best tax preparation software available.

DOS Checkwriting and Accounting Programs

- *Andrew Tobias' Tax Cut (MECA):* A popular tax-preparation program that imports data directly from Checkwrite Plus. Tax Cut prints forms that the IRS will accept.

- *Checkwrite Plus (MECA):* A check-writing program similar to Quicken with many attractive features for small business accounting, including accounts payable, accounts receivable, and invoicing capabilities. An added plus: Checkwrite Plus exports directly to Andrew Tobias' Tax Cut.

- *Quicken (Intuit):* This market-leading checkwriting program offers much more business functionality in its DOS version than its Macintosh counterpart. Quicken can track cash, credit cards, investments, capital equipment, and liabilities as well as checking accounts. With a modest amount of development work, you can use Quicken to develop a complete single-entry accounting system for a small business (including accounts receivable and accounts payable). A payroll add-in package is available. Because Quicken can't track inventory, however, this approach would be best suited to a service business.

- *Pacioli 2000 (M-USA):* An impressive bargain, Pacioli 2000 offers general ledger, accounts receivable, accounts payable, and inventory capabilities; a payroll module is also available. Pacioli 2000 is network-ready. Easier to user than DacEasy Accounting, Pacioli 2000 offers a host of excellent features. Keeping track of all the five- and six-digit account numbers makes the program somewhat tedious to use, however. Pacioli 2000 uses double-entry accounting techniques and offers modified batch processing (you can get trial balances and print checks before posting transactions).

- *One-Write Plus (Great American Software):* An accounting program aimed at first-time, small business users, this single-entry program is easy to use but doesn't offer much of an upgrade path should your business grow.

- *Peachtree Complete III (Peachtree):* Highly regarded by accountants and users alike, Peachtree accounting programs are in use by over 400,000 small businesses. Peachtree offers an excellent upgrade path to a full-scale, professional accounting system, should your needs increase. Peachtree Complete III features online processing and comes with nine modules (General Ledger, Accounts Payable, Accounts Receivable, Payroll, Inventory, Invoicing, Purchase Order, Fixed Assets, and Job Cost).

- *Retail Controller (MicroBiz):* A point-of-sale program with many attractive features for a small retail business. Versions are available for video stores, liquor stores, and auto repair shops. Compatible bar code readers and cash drawers with receipt printers are also available. Retail Controller exports to One Write Plus.

Macintosh Checkwriting and Accounting Programs

- *MacInTax (Softview):* A highly regarded tax-preparation program with on-screen simulations of IRS forms that is exceptionally well developed; this program is highly recommended. MacInTax accepts data from Quicken.

- *Mind Your Own Business (Teleware):* An impressive, full-featured, double entry accounting system that makes full use of the Macintosh user interface. A general ledger and a checkbook with reconciliation, accounts receivable, accounts payable, and inventory capabilities are included. An unusual feature is a complete time-management and contact-management system.

- *Quicken (Intuit):* The Macintosh version of this popular DOS checkwriting program is not as well developed as its DOS counterpart, and lacks many of the features that make the DOS version so attractive for small business accounting. The Macintosh version would be suitable only for a modest home business. One plus for small home and service businesses is that Quicken exports directly to MacInTax, an outstanding tax preparation program.

Windows Accounting Programs

- *Crystal Accounting (Peachtree):* A Windows entry from the respected publisher of DOS accounting software, Crystal Accounting includes general ledger, accounts receivable, accounts payable, and payroll modules.

- *MacInTax for Windows (Softview):* A Windows version of the acclaimed Macintosh tax preparation software; highly recommended.

- *Mind Your Own Business (Teleware):* A Windows version of the acclaimed Macintosh accounting program, MYOB offers an impressive collection of accounting functions with an intuitive user interface. Graphics are used extensively to simulate checks, invoices, purchase orders, and other forms on-screen. Best of all, entries are linked so that when you click on an item in the journal the check or invoice is displayed. A general ledger and a checkbook with reconciliation, accounts receivables, accounts payables, and inventory capabilities are included. An unusual feature is a complete time-management and contact-management system.

Part V

Selecting and Using Your System

Includes

Identifying Your Primary Application Area

Designing Your System

Buying and Installing Your System

Maintaining Your System

15

Identifying Your Primary Application Area

By now, you've explored a variety of small business application areas. Chances are you've developed a working list of the application areas you want to tackle, and you may have already identified some specific programs you want to try. But it's time for some realism. You will be wise to tackle just one, or at the most, two applications during the first year you computerize your business. It takes time to learn application software, apply it to your business, enter the initial data, work out the problems, and train yourself and your staff to use the program intelligently and productively on a day-to-day basis. Prudence alone dictates that you narrow your list down to just one or two applications, with a list of additional applications that you want to add later.

There's another reason for narrowing the list—a reason that has to do with this book's main theme. Your reason for getting involved in small business computing is practical: you're doing it because you need computer solutions to problems in a critical area of your business—an area in which you must perform tasks efficiently and well if you hope to make money and keep your customers. So choosing a computer is really a very simple matter: you choose the system that's optimal for your *primary* application—the one that addresses a crucial problem that you need to solve if your business is to remain profitable or continue to grow.

How do you identify a primary application? Out of all the application areas that this book has discussed (such as time billing or electronic mail), your primary application area is the one that holds the most promise for helping you address a problem you're having in a *critical* area of your business. This is the area in which you're failing to provide an adequate level of service or efficiency. You've run up against the limits of manual paper-shuffling systems, and your business can't grow or remain profitable unless you improve your performance in this area. This isn't something that would be *nice* to do; it's something you've *got* to do. This is the application area around which you should design your computer system.

This chapter helps you identify your primary application, and Chapter 16 discusses the specifics of choosing hardware that is optimally suited to running that application.

Choosing Primary Applications

Now for your list-making exercise. Your task: identify your primary application areas, choosing from the list that follows. As you think about the chapters you've read in this book, you've surely found some that seem more likely candidates than others. Use this list to work out a ranking of these areas. When you've identified #1, you've found your primary application area.

Small Business Application Areas

> Accounting
>
> Business form design
>
> Contact management
>
> Database management
>
> Desktop publishing
>
> Electronic mail
>
> Mailing lists/mailing labels
>
> Mailing lists/personalized form letters
>
> Number crunching
>
> Personal information management
>
> Point-of-sale system

Presentation graphics

Project management

Reports and proposals

Routine business correspondence

If you found it difficult to choose between #1 and #2, it could be that you've identified a secondary application area that's important for your business. And that's OK—but don't try to tackle three or four applications just now, unless you have a lot of previous experience in personal computing.

The following scenarios illustrate how small business owners may choose primary and secondary application areas. In some cases, they've identified particular programs they want to use:

- *Sales:* John sells high-end marine craft and needs to keep in contact with his customers. He needs help getting his contact list organized, and he wants to do a better job of staying in touch with his customers. For his primary application, he selects the contact management software that seems to meet his needs (Current). For his secondary application, he selects desktop publishing for the newsletter he hopes to create.

- *Business consulting:* Sarah makes presentations to businesses on a wide variety of current legal questions. She wants to bill her clients professionally and do a better job with visual aids in her presentations. For her primary application, she chooses time-billing software (Timeslips III). For her secondary application, she chooses a presentation graphics package. Additional applications include word processing and mailing list management.

- *Retail:* Dave and Joan run a shop that sells gifts and gourmet items. They want to serve their customers faster at checkout and keep better tabs on their inventory. For their primary application, they select a point-of-sale system (Retail Controller, Jr.) with a bar code reader and cash drawer. For their secondary application, they choose a desktop accounting program that imports the data that the point-of-sale system creates (One-Write Plus).

- *Restaurant and catering:* Shannon is paying too much money to have her menus printed, and she needs to design forms that help her do a better job of meeting the needs of her catering clients. For her primary application, she chooses a desktop publishing program that will print her menus beautifully. For her secondary application, she chooses a form design program.

- *Professional practice:* Barbara and Ted run a small, specialized legal practice that often involves writing extensive reports. They need to do a better job billing for time, and they need all the help they can get with lengthy documents. For their primary application, they select a time-billing program (Timeslips III). For their secondary application, they choose a DOS word processing program (WordPerfect) that is exceptionally well-suited to the legal profession.

- *Service:* Vick runs a carpentry business that specializes in decks. He needs to calculate his costs and get proposals to prospective clients quickly after he gives them an estimate. He chooses the integrated program Works, which contains his primary application (a spreadsheet for job costing), his secondary application (the word processor for writing a nice-looking proposal), and additional applications (mailing list and mailing labels).

Choosing Software

After you identify application areas, it's time to choose software. But how? It's hard to get information that's relevant to a small business point of view. Salespeople, quite frankly, may not know what they're talking about. And some computer stores give salespeople commissions if they succeed in moving high-margin items: *caveat emptor*. So what to do?

Develop a list of specific software requirements. You're not just looking for "good software," whatever that is. You may be looking for a package that can handle 800 accounts, print laser labels, sort by ZIP code, print PostNet bar codes, and so on. The more specifically you state your software requirements, the more likely it is that you'll find the right program for your business. This also arms you against salespeople; when you get the big pitch for WonderCalc, you can just ask, "Well, that sounds great, but does it have a built-in summation function?"

Visit computer stores, tell the salespeople your needs, and listen to what they have to say. Don't buy anything on the spot, but be open to the possibility that you'll run into an outstanding and knowledgeable person who has some very good advice to offer. But bear in mind that the advice may not be impartial.

Check for reviews in respected personal computer magazines (*InfoWorld, PC World, PC Magazine, MacWorld, MacUser,* and *PC Computing*), especially the featured comparative reviews, where the magazine examines as many as two or three dozen programs in an application area (such as relational database management). But bear in mind that the ranking may not have much meaning for you if you're looking for a special feature—one that's critical to your business. The feature may mean little or nothing to others, and in consequence, the program gets a lackadaisical review. Also, watch out for reviews in some computer magazines that are nothing more than glorified press releases, written by public relations people at software companies.

Ask people who are working in your line of work what they're using, what they've heard, and what they prefer. Go to trade association conventions or professional association conventions, and ask away.

Check trade journals or magazines in your line of work for ads concerning vertical applications. Software stores usually don't stock these programs because they are so specialized; mass-market personal computer magazines rarely review them for the same reason.

Ask for demo disks. Some software publishers offer demo disks that are often "working models" of the actual program; you can explore almost all program features, and even create and save limited amounts of work.

Evaluating Programs

As you identify programs that appear to meet your needs, you should be thinking about these issues:

- *Accommodating growth:* What if your business grows? You need to handle a mailing list of only 500 right now. But what if you find yourself on the right end of a marketing phenomenon, and 7,500 people want your catalog? Be sure to pick a program that provides ample room to accommodate your business's growth.

- *Technical support:* How long does free technical support last after you register the program? Can you buy additional support? For how much? Is there an 800 number? Will you be placed on hold all day when you call? Ask current users of this program how they fared when they called for technical support.

- *Documentation:* Does the documentation include a "Getting Started" book or brochure for novices, or is there just a reference manual? Is there an on-screen tutorial on disk? A videotape that you can obtain cheaply? Are there many books on this program at your bookstore? Do you have to train any of your employees to use the program? If so, then tutorial resources may be indispensable.

- *Upgrades:* How much does it cost to upgrade to a new version of the program, when an upgrade becomes available? Will you be notified automatically?

Developing a Custom Program

If you have trouble finding a program that meets your needs, you may be tempted to have a custom program developed for your business. But be forewarned. Although many small businesses have benefitted enormously from custom software, there are pitfalls, such as delays, cost overruns, inadequate documentation, and lack of after-sale support.

Given these drawbacks, it might be better to settle for an off-the-shelf application that lacks one or two minor features. If you decide to hire a programmer to develop custom software for your firm, be sure to obtain the programmer's signature on a contract that precisely specifies what you expect. The contract should clearly specify what is to be done, by whom, and for how much. It should detail the remedies, or grounds for termination of the agreement, if the software fails to perform satisfactorily or if the programmer fails to finish the project in a timely fashion. Don't forget to include provisions for your ownership of the resulting source code, for staff training, and for technical and user documentation. Have your attorney review the contract before you sign it.

Choosing the Environment

Read this section after you choose specific software—your primary application program (and perhaps a secondary application program). Chances are you fit into one of these categories:

- The program you've chosen for your primary application area is available in only one environment, so your decision is made for you. Once Dave and Joan choose a point-of-sale system as their primary application, they've all but restricted themselves to the DOS environment. John's choice of Current means that he'll be looking for a Windows desktop publishing program.

- The program you've chosen for your primary application area is available in two or more environments, so your choice will be shaped by your secondary application. Sarah's primary application is time billing, but she wants to use a desktop publishing program.

The time-billing program she wants, Timeslips III, is available for Macintosh as well as Windows systems. Sarah likes the presentation software available for the Macintosh, so she decides on the Mac environment.

- Both your primary and secondary applications are available for two or more environments. You've got more latitude. But be careful! Just because a program is available for both DOS and the Macintosh doesn't mean they're identical! The Mac version of Quicken, for example, isn't as feature-rich as the DOS version.

If you've gotten to this point, you're almost ready to buy a system! What's it going to be—DOS, Windows, or Macintosh?

Here's a way to reduce the confusion a bit: Even if you're planning to run nothing but DOS programs, there's still a very good rationale for buying a system that's capable of running Windows. As you'll learn elsewhere in this chapter, you can use Windows to run more than one DOS program at a time. What's more, there's a very good chance that the DOS application you're using right now will become available in a Windows version, which will have enhanced capabilities. You will almost surely want to upgrade. So your choice really boils down to a Windows-capable system or a Macintosh system.

Buying Software

After you choose the environment and settle on the programs you want, you can begin the shopping process. After looking at local prices, you'll probably decide to order by mail—and why not? In general, it's a much better idea to buy mail order software than it is to buy mail order hardware. (Chapter 16 discusses the limitations of buying mail order hardware.)

Responsibly-run computer magazines (such as *MacWorld* and *PC World*) feature ads from well-established software mail order firms such as the venerable MacConnection and PC Connection, and won't accept ads from firms known to be experiencing problems. These well-established firms don't offer the best prices (more about that in a moment), but they make up for it with truly impressive service; one firm will have the program on your doorstep the next morning if you order it by midnight! The best software mail order firms offer a no-questions-asked, 30-day refund policy. Don't settle for less.

Be cautious when ordering software by mail. You occasionally can find a software mail order firm that offers markedly lower prices than the established firms. Be wary of such firms, however, because they may be running on so slim a margin that a slight business downturn could cause them to topple. When you order, make sure that you're receiving the latest version of the programs.

Summary

Here's a quick review of this chapter's main points:

- Identify the primary and secondary application areas you want to computerize, and choose the software that suits your needs. Don't try to tackle more than two applications unless you have a great deal of computer experience.

- Develop a list of specific software requirements. Then visit stores, read reviews, talk to colleagues, find trade journals, and obtain demo disks.

- Before deciding, consider how well the programs you've selected accommodate growth. Check out technical support, documentation, and upgrade prices.

- It's better to live without a few nice (but dispensable) features than it is to go through the ordeal of having custom software developed for your business.

- Choose the environment in which you must run your primary application (DOS, Macintosh, or Windows).

- Consider mail order to buy your software, but beware of the firms offering the lowest prices. Look for ads in respected magazines, and order from a well-established mail order firm.

16

Designing Your System

O nce you've chosen the computer environment you need to run your primary application (DOS, Macintosh, or Windows), your task is now simple: You're going to design and purchase a system that's optimal for running this application. In this chapter, you learn how to chart your way through the forest of hardware options and how to buy a system that meets your needs.

A complete computer system includes the computer *system unit* (which includes the computer's processing circuitry, its memory, and its disk drives), the *display*, the *keyboard*, a *printer*, and—if you're planning on going online—a *modem* (see fig. 16.1). The term *system* implies that all these components should be matched so they perform optimally with each other.

Defining an Optimal System

You're hunting for an optimal system for your primary application. Fine, but what does *optimal* mean? That's actually a very easy matter, if you adhere to these suggestions:

- Your computer system should be able to run your applications speedily, without forcing you to wait unnecessarily while the program performs a computation or retrieves data from a disk. Don't settle for a slow, "bargain" computer; don't let anyone talk you out of the minimum system configurations this chapter recommends.

277

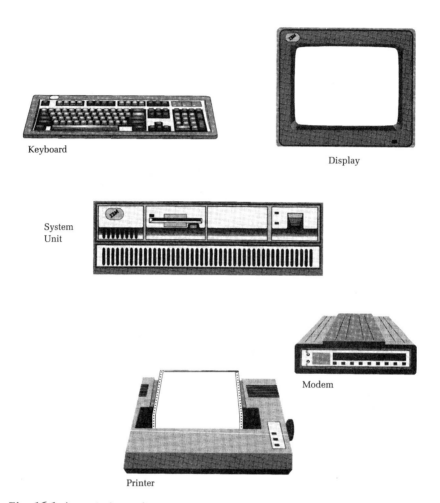

Keyboard

Display

System Unit

Modem

Printer

Fig. 16.1. *A computer system.*

- Your computer system should have enough disk storage space and memory to accommodate your applications, and in particular, it should not force you to take extraordinary and tedious steps to conserve memory space. You will be amazed at how fast you can fill up disk space and memory. You may need more than you think you need—much more.

- You have a right to run more than one program at a time, without the programs invading each other's memory space and causing the system to crash. This isn't easy to pull off under DOS. Windows and the Macintosh do a much better job. With the right equipment, you can successfully run more than one DOS application at a time under Microsoft Windows.

- Your computer application should display text and graphics with clarity and beauty. Your eyes matter—and the sharper the display, the less chance of error.

- Your printed output should send a clear message about your professionalism and commitment to quality. You shouldn't use low-resolution dot-matrix output, unless you need to produce backup printouts inexpensively and quickly.

So what does all this mean, in practical terms? For small business applications, you need the minimal system configurations recommended in table 16.1. The sections that follow discuss each of the categories mentioned in the table (such as microprocessors and disk drives) in more detail.

Table 16.1
Recommended System Configurations for Small Businesses

Component	Minimum System Recommendation
DOS or Windows Systems	
Microprocessor	Intel 80386 or 80386SX
Clock speed	At least 16MHz
Memory	At least 2M; 4M recommended for Windows
Ports	At least 1 parallel, 2 serial
Floppy disk	Two drives: 1.2M (5 1/4 inch) and 1.44M (3 1/2 inch) or 2.88M (3 1/2-inch disk)
Hard disk	At least 40M
Display	At least VGA color
Printer	Hewlett-Packard or compatible laser printer or 24-pin dot-matrix printer
Macintosh Systems	
Microprocessor	Motorola 68030
Clock speed	At least 16MHz
Memory	At least 2M; 4M recommended for System 7

continues

Table 16.1 *(continued)*

Macintosh Systems	
Ports	Standard Macintosh ports OK
Floppy disk	1.4M SuperDrive (reads DOS data disks)
Hard disk	At least 40M
Display	Full page mono or 14-inch color
Printer	Non-PostScript laser printer

The sections that follow explain the rationale for meeting these minimal system requirements.

Your primary and secondary applications may have more specific, additional needs, such as requiring a mouse, a bar code reader, expanded memory, or a PostScript laser printer. You learn more about these system features in this chapter. The minimal system configuration listed in table 16.1 is only a starting point for designing your system.

Microprocessors

More than any single factor, the limits of a computer's capabilities are determined by its microprocessor. A microprocessor is a tiny chip of silicon that contains the equivalent of hundreds of thousands of transistors. These chips can be mass-produced by the millions at exceptionally low costs, which is why the personal computer is possible. The rest of the computer is built around the microprocessor.

Here's a brief survey of the microprocessors commonly found in today's PCs:

- *Intel 8088, 8086 (IBM PC, XT, and compatibles, including so-called "Turbo" compatibles.):* You can buy an 8088-based system for as little as $300, but it's a waste of money. These chips can't run many of today's leading applications effectively; rightly or wrongly, programmers now assume at least an 80286 as a standard environment, and software runs at an appallingly sluggish pace on these systems.

- *Intel 80286 (IBM AT and AT-compatibles):* Avoid these unless you can buy an 80286-based system very cheaply; acceptable for a secondary system. The major problem with 80286-based computers is that they restrict the functionality of Microsoft Windows. Windows requires an 80386 to reach its optimum level of performance (80386 Enhanced Mode).

- *Intel 80386SX:* A version of the Intel 80386 microprocessor that can use inexpensive support chips created for 80286-based computers. 80386SX-based machines are an excellent bargain for small business use. They're inexpensive and reasonably fast, and they're capable of running Windows in its 80386 Enhanced Mode. Ideal for all the DOS applications discussed in this book; acceptable for Windows.

- *Intel 80386 and 80386DX:* These microprocessors require more expensive support chips and other devices, but deliver better performance than 80386SX-based machines. Overkill for DOS applications, but ideal for Windows.

- *Intel 80486SX:* A version of Intel's state-of-the-art microprocessor that lacks the numeric coprocessor. Overkill for most of the applications discussed in this book.

- *Intel 80486:* Intel's state-of-the-art microprocessor; includes a numeric coprocessor that speeds mathematical computations. Overkill for most of the applications discussed in this book.

- *Motorola 68000 (Macintosh Classic):* Avoid this sluggish and obsolete microprocessor, which is too slow to run many of the Macintosh business applications discussed in this book.

- *Motorola 68020 (Macintosh LC):* An improvement over the 68000 microprocessor; however, this should be avoided because it cannot take advantage of System 7's advanced memory-management capabilities.

- *Motorola 68030 (most current Macintosh II models):* The minimal microprocessor for Macintosh applications.

Clock Speed

A given microprocessor's performance is rated by its clock speed, which is measured in megahertz (MHz). The faster the clock speed, the more the computer costs. Faster clock speeds require faster computer support chips, which dramatically increase the cost of the system.

How fast is enough? For 80386 and 80386SX systems, as well as 68030 Macintosh systems, this book recommends a minimum clock speed of 16MHz. Even at 16MHz, some of the applications discussed in this book—particularly Windows applications—perform sluggishly. If you can afford a 20MHz or 25MHz system, you'll notice significant performance gains. There are faster systems still (more than 25 MHz), but these are overkill for small business applications. Note, however, that clock speed cannot be compared among different processors. (For example, you cannot say that a 25 MHz 80486 is twice as fast as a 33 MHz 80386.)

Memory

Memory is measured using a basic unit of measurement called a *byte*, which is equivalent to approximately one character (a letter or number). A kilobyte (K) is approximately 1,000 bytes, while a megabyte (M) is approximately 1 million bytes. (The *approximately* qualifier is necessary because computers are constructed on binary principles; a kilobyte is actually 1,024 bytes.) These measurements are applied to your computer's internal memory (often called *random-access memory* or *RAM* as well as to its external memory (hard disk drives, floppy disks, and CD-ROM drives).

Memory considerations vary greatly among the three environments discussed in this book: DOS, Macintosh, and Windows.

TIP

To get the full benefit of your computer's memory with DOS or Windows, be sure to equip your system with DOS 5.0, which offers greatly improved memory management. To learn how to get the most out of DOS 5.0, see Que's *MS-DOS 5 QuickStart*.

DOS Memory Considerations

If you're running DOS, you have a memory problem: owing to design decisions made long ago, DOS is restricted to just 640K of internal memory (RAM). The Intel 8088 and 8086 microprocessors, the only ones available when DOS was designed, could use only 1M of RAM at the most, so the designers used 640K for programs and set aside the rest for internal, system uses. At one time, 640K was considered an awesome, even extravagant figure. Today, however, there are many popular applications that just barely squeeze into this 640K of memory, which is called *conventional memory*.

To get beyond the 640K limit of conventional memory, engineers came up with *expanded memory*. Expanded memory uses a trick called bank-switching, in which a bank of conventional memory is used to swap in units of additional memory—up to 8M worth. (It's as if you could hold only one page of text at a time, but there are hundreds of pages on the desk. You can read a whole book if someone swaps the pages out of your hands, even though there is only one page in front of your eyes at once.)

Expanded memory isn't as fast as real memory, but it does give programs more room. The only problem is that programs have to be specially adapted before they can use expanded memory. Many of the DOS programs in this book can use expanded memory, but not all programs can.

When the Intel 80286 (and later still, the 80386) microprocessors came along, new memory opportunities presented themselves, because these microprocessors can use 16M or more of RAM directly. But they can't do so under DOS. DOS applications are limited to 640K, even if the microprocessor can use more RAM. If you buy an 80386 computer with 5M of RAM, you can only use 640K of RAM if you're running DOS applications. (There are ways around this problem, as you'll see in a moment.) The memory beyond the old 1M limitation of 8088s and 8086s is called *extended memory*. A few DOS applications, such as Lotus 1-2-3 Release 3.1, know how to use extended memory, but most don't.

If you're planning to run DOS applications under DOS, you're probably wondering why this book recommends a minimum configuration of 2M of RAM. There are two reasons for this recommendation:

- Sooner or later, you'll run Windows. As you'll see in the next section, there's a good reason to run Windows even if you're only running DOS applications: in Windows' 80386 Enhanced mode, you can run more than one DOS application at a time.

- If you're running DOS applications that can use expanded memory, you can use a system configuration trick that configures your computer's extended memory (the memory above 1M) so that the applications think they're using old-fashioned expanded memory.

As you contemplate memory, just remember an old (and wise) computing adage: There's no such thing as too much memory. You'll be wise to configure your system with as much memory as you can afford.

Windows Memory Considerations

Microsoft Windows can run on 80286 or 80386 systems with a minimum of 1M of RAM, but to get the program's full benefit, you need a minimum of 2M—and 4M or 5M is better. With 2M or more of RAM and an 80386, you can run Windows in its 80386 Enhanced mode, which is an attractive mode for users of DOS applications.

Many computer users have purchased Windows—not to run Windows applications, but to run DOS applications in the 80386 Enhanced mode. The Windows 80386 Enhanced mode takes full advantage of a rather bizarre capability of the Intel 80386, 80386SX, and later microprocessors: the ability to simulate a virtually unlimited number of 8086 microprocessors. This may sound strange, but it has a wonderfully practical meaning: Windows knows how to take advantage of this feature so that you can run more than one DOS program at a time. It gives each DOS program its very own, 640K 8086 "computer." Running in their isolated "computers," these programs can't interfere with each other. So you can run Timeslips III at the same time you're running WordPerfect or Lotus 1-2-3; and what's more, a simple keyboard command lets you switch instantly from one program to the other. Windows applications are designed so that you can open more than one application at a time and switch among them quickly.

Whether you're running Windows or DOS applications, Windows gobbles up huge amounts of memory. If the program runs out, it knows how to use some of the space on your hard disk to store information that won't fit in RAM. (This capability is called *virtual memory*.) Virtual memory is great in a pinch, but it's much slower than RAM. If you're planning to run Windows, you can get by with 2M, but this book recommends 4M or more.

Macintosh Memory Considerations

Apple Computer's answer to Microsoft Windows is System 7, a sophisticated new operating system for all its Macintosh computers. The ability to open more than one program and switch among them quickly is built into System 7, and it's available on all Macintosh computers. To take full advantage of this capability, however, you'll need an absolute minimum of 2M of RAM—but you'll find that 4M or more gives you the room you really need to run two or three Macintosh applications at a time (with a full complement of desk accessories and fonts).

Just as Windows doesn't really shine unless you're using an 80386, so too does System 7 perform at its peak only on 68030-based systems. On these systems, System 7 becomes capable of virtual memory; if you run out of

RAM, the operating system makes room on the disk to store the information that won't fit. As with Windows, though, this storage technique is slower than RAM. You can run System 7 with 2M of RAM, but this book recommends 4M or more.

Hard Disks

No business computer system is complete without a hard disk: a mass-storage medium that employs a number of rapidly-spinning, magnetically encoded platters within a sealed chamber (see fig. 16.2). With a hard disk, the operating system loads automatically at the start of an operating session, and all your software and data are available without any disk-shuffling. It isn't impossible to use certain applications on a dual-floppy system, but it isn't worth the trouble.

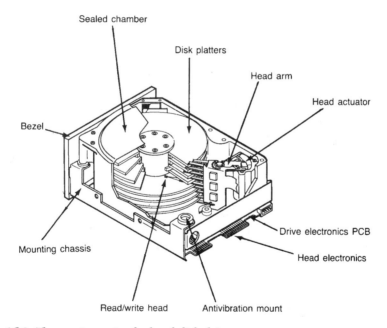

Sealed chamber

Disk platters

Head arm

Head actuator

Bezel

Drive electronics PCB

Mounting chassis

Head electronics

Read/write head   Antivibration mount

Fig. 16.2. The components of a hard disk drive.

Size

For business purposes, 40M is the minimum disk capacity that this book recommends—but you'll be wise to shoot for an 80M disk or an even bigger one. 40M may seem bigger than Montana right now, but you'll be amazed at how fast it fills up. Many of the applications discussed in this book require 6M or 7M of disk space, and that's just for the program, not to mention the data. Windows applications, in particular, consume enormous amounts of disk space. If you're running Windows, a 40M disk drive will seem very short on storage space.

Speed

Hard disks are rated by *access time*—the time it takes the disk's magnetic read/write head to locate a unit of data after it receives the instruction to do so. Access time is measured in microseconds (ms). For small business applications, don't settle for a drive with an access time slower than 28ms. A 19ms drive is considered fast, and some drives are even faster. 28ms will suffice, though.

Type

As you're shopping for a DOS or Windows system, you'll find that hard disks are associated with strange, undefined acronyms such as ESDI, IDE, MFM, and SSCI. These acronyms refer to the design of the electronic interface that connects the drive to the computer. For small business computing, your best bet is an IDE (intelligent drive electronics) drive, which is reasonably fast and fully compatible with the most widely-used standards in the IBM-compatible world.

TIP

Watch out for "bargain" 80386 systems that don't mention the hard disk's access time in the ad; chances are you're getting stuck with a slow drive.

Floppy Disks

There's a profusion of available disk sizes and drives, but for small business applications, you can narrow down the choices considerably.

Disks come in two sizes: 5 1/4-inch and 3-1/2 inch (*microfloppy* disks), as shown in figure 16.3. Of the two, 3 1/2-inch drives are by far the best, because their hard plastic cases protect the disk surface from contaminants such as dust and fingerprints. Both kinds of disks are available in two *densities*, a term that refers to the fineness of the magnetic particles that make up the disk's surface. The finer the particles, the more information the disk can store. Double density 5 1/4-inch disks can store 360K; high density 5 1/4-inch disks can store 1.2M. Double density 3 1/2-inch disks store 720K (800K on Macintosh systems); high density 3 1/2-inch disks store 1.44M (1.4M on Macintosh systems). High density disks cost more per unit, but they offer a price advantage when you consider their increased storage capacity.

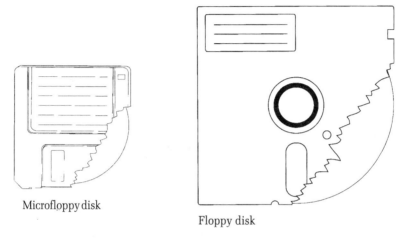

Microfloppy disk

Floppy disk

Fig. 16.3. *The two most popular disk sizes.*

For DOS systems, you can choose among the following drives:

- *360K, 5 1/4 inches:* An outmoded, low capacity format that should be avoided for small business computing.

- *1.2M, 5 1/4 inches:* This drive can read the 360K disks on which a lot of application software is still distributed, and it also can use 1.2M, high-capacity disks.

- *1.44M, 3 1/2 inches:* This drive can read the 720K disks on which application software often is distributed, and it can also use 1.44M disks that are ideal for backup purposes.

- *2.88M, 3 1/2 inches:* The latest disk drive technology, capable of reading and writing to 720K and 1.44M disks.

- *720K, 3 1/2 inches:* The lowest capacity format for 3 1/2-inch disks, this drive uses inexpensive 720K disks and is common in laptop computers.

For DOS or Windows systems, you'll be wise to equip your computer with two drives: 5 1/4-inch and 3 1/2-inch.

Why both drives? If you get a computer with just one drive, you're locked out of one of the disk sizes. Sooner or later, you'll find yourself at a computer store asking them to copy a bunch of 3 1/2-inch disks to the 5 1/4-inch disks your computer can use. These stores probably will charge you a fee for this service.

TIP

> Don't settle for a 360K 5 1/4-inch drive or a 720K 3 1/2-inch drive. The higher-capacity models cost only a few dollars more.

For the Macintosh, the rule is very simple: don't settle for anything other than Apple's SuperDrive—a 1.4M drive that accepts 800K and 1.4M 3 1/2-inch disks. What's extraordinary about this drive is its ability to read and write on 720K or 1.44M DOS disks. With this drive, you can exchange data files between IBM and Macintosh computers. If someone creates an Excel spreadsheet on a Windows system and gives it to you, for example, you can transfer this disk to your Macintosh and use the spreadsheet with the Macintosh version of Excel.

Keyboards and Mice

Most computers come equipped with keyboards, but some machines require you to select among two or three alternatives. If you must choose, look for a keyboard with a full numeric keypad, which often has uses beyond typing numbers (see fig. 16.4). (The Macintosh version of Microsoft Word, for example, enables you to use the numeric keypad to guide the cursor, which is a real boon for good touch-typists who dislike taking their fingers away from the keyboard to use the mouse.)

If possible, try out the keyboard before buying the system; some keyboards have a "mushy" feel that makes it hard to tell when you've entered the character.

All Macintoshes come with a mouse, and increasingly, IBM-compatible systems come with a mouse (see fig. 16.5). If you haven't tried a mouse already, by all means do so. Remember, too, that a mouse doesn't remove input functionality from your system; it adds input functionality. You don't need to use a mouse for all operations; there are usually many other options for performing operations, such as choosing commands. If you do any writing, you'll soon become addicted to the mouse for text-selecting and editing operations, which you can emulate at the keyboard only by pressing dozens and dozens of keys.

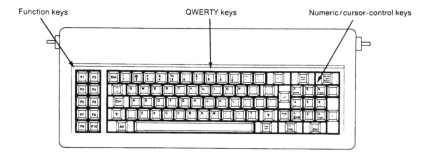

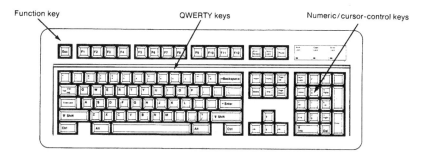

Fig. 16.4. Standard and extended keyboards.

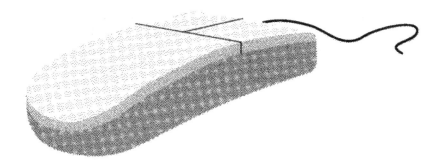

Fig. 16.5. A typical mouse.

TIP

For a DOS or Windows system, look for a Microsoft-compatible mouse. In these systems, you must load special software before you can use the mouse, and if the program doesn't recognize the software, you can't use the mouse. All programs that use mice recognize Microsoft or Microsoft-compatible mice; it's an unstoppable standard. To be on the safe side, it's smart to buy a genuine Microsoft mouse; Microsoft is constantly changing the assumptions that underlie mouse usage at the system level, and if you've got a Microsoft mouse, the mouse software will be automatically upgraded when you install new versions of DOS or Windows. If you use a non-Microsoft mouse, you'll have to go back to the company that made the mouse to obtain the software, giving you yet another headache at upgrade time.

Displays

For business applications, you need a sharp, clear display—one that won't bother your eyes or raise the possibility of error. Color displays help differentiate the various areas of the screen; data entry areas stand out vividly. The sharpness of the screen display depends on the *resolution* (sharpness and density of the on-screen image) of which the display adapter and monitor are capable. Resolution is measured in linear dots per inch, such as 800 horizontally by 600 vertically. The higher the resolution, the sharper the display. For business computing, you'll need a system with a resolution of at least 720 by 320 for monochrome (black and white) monitors, or 640 by 350 for color monitors.

When you choose your system, you may not need to select a video adapter; increasingly, the video adapter circuitry is included on the computer's *motherboard*—its main circuit board. If you want to use a monitor with a higher resolution, you may need to purchase an add-on adapter, which will be installed in one of the computer's expansion slots.

DOS and Windows Systems

For DOS and Windows systems, choose a Video Graphics Array (VGA) color monitor and a VGA color adapter, if one isn't included on the motherboard. Hold out for a 16-bit VGA adapter with at least 512K of video memory; don't settle for an 8-bit VGA adapter, which is considerably slower, or for less than 512K, which dooms you to the use of the lowest-resolution VGA modes.

Here's a brief overview of the display adapter/video monitor standards available in the DOS environment:

- *Monochrome Display Adapter (MDA) in a monochrome monitor:* An outmoded, text-only display format that can't display graphics other than those constructed with the built-in graphics characters in the IBM PC's character set.

   Text is displayed in green or yellow characters against a black background, with a resolution of 720 dots horizontally and 350 dots vertically.

- *Hercules or Hercules-compatible adapter and monochrome monitor:* This combination of adapter and monitor displays both text and graphics on monochrome monitors with reasonably good resolution (720 by 320).

- *Color Graphics Adapter (CGA) and monitor:* A low-resolution (640 by 200) color display system designed for games and educational use; not recommended for business use.

- *Enhanced Graphics Array (EGA) adapter and monitor:* This combination offers up to 16 colors on-screen simultaneously with a resolution of 640 by 350, but it's technically inferior to the popular VGA standard (which is usually available for only a small increased cost).

- *Video Graphics Array (VGA) and VGA monitor:* The contemporary standard for color monitors, VGA adapters and monitors display as many as 256 colors simultaneously with a resolution of 640 by 480. An enhanced VGA mode displays your work with a resolution of 800 by 600, and you can also obtain high-end VGA adapters and monitors that display your work with a resolution of 1,024 by 768.

Macintosh Systems

For the Macintosh, the display options are less numerous. Built into the Classic is a nine-inch monochrome monitor that displays text and graphics with reasonably high resolution. You choose your own monitor with Mac II models: an inexpensive choice is Apple's 12-inch monochrome monitor, although a full-page monochrome monitor is highly recommended for word processing and desktop publishing applications. Apple's standard color video circuitry supports 16 simultaneous colors; you can purchase video adapters and monitors that support 256 or as much as 16 million colors simultaneously. Also available for Macintoshes are gray-scale adapters and monitors, which are useful for certain specialized applications, such as photographic retouching.

Ports and Slots

If you scan computer ads, you probably notice that most computers come equipped with parallel and/or serial ports, and some have expansion slots into which you can press add-on adapter boards. Here's a brief explanation of what ports and slots do, and what you should look for.

Ports

A *port* is a channel through which the computer can communicate with peripheral devices, such as printers, external modems, and mice. Every Macintosh comes with a good selection of ports, but DOS and Windows machines vary considerably in what the system assembler decides to give you. Look for an IBM or IBM-compatible computer equipped with a minimum of one parallel port (used for printers) and one serial port (used for mice and modems). If you're planning to equip your system with a mouse and a modem, you should look for a system with two serial ports. Increasingly, you find systems equipped with an IBM PS/2-standard mouse port; for such systems, one serial port is adequate.

Expansion Slots

Expansion slots are receptacles that enable you to add press-in adapter boards, which add features to your system (see fig. 16.6). The more expansion slots that come with your computer, the more easily you can add adapters that expand your computer's functionality. Just as there's no such thing as too much memory, there's no such thing as too many expansion slots.

Here's a brief survey of the adapters you can add:

- *Video adapters:* As just mentioned, some computers include the video circuitry on the computer's motherboard, but others require you to use a slot for an add-on board.

- *Internal modems:* You learn more about modems, which are needed for telecommunications, in the section called "Modems," later in this chapter.

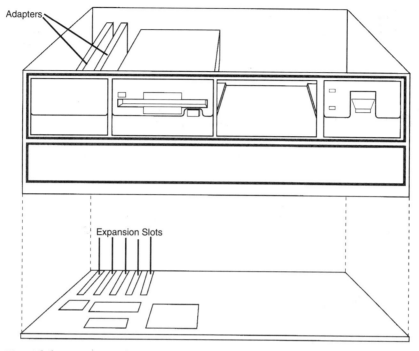

Fig. 16.6. Expansion slots.

- *Fax boards:* You learn more about fax boards in the "Fax Boards" section, later in this chapter.

- *Voice-mail cards:* You can add an adapter—such as The Complete Answering Machine (The Complete PC)—that turns your computer into a voice mail answering system that is capable of storing messages for many different people.

- *Bus mouse:* A mouse that comes with an adapter and requires a slot; needed if your system lacks a serial port (or enough serial ports).

- *Hard cards:* These adapter boards press into your computer's expansion slots like any other adapter, but they contain hard disks. If your main hard disk turns out to be too small, you can quickly upgrade your system—if you have an additional slot.

- *Network adapter boards:* Necessary if you want to connect two or more computers to a high-speed local area network (LAN). (Macintoshes come with low-speed network circuitry and a network port as standard equipment.)

- *Scanners:* You can equip your system with optical scanners that can digitize photographs or drawings so that you can view, store, and print these images with your computer. Scanners often require an expansion slot.

Selecting a Printer

Just a few years ago, offices were the scenes of noise pollution caused by a variety of *impact printers*—printers that form an image by physically striking the paper. Most commonly used with personal computers were *letter-quality printers*, which created fully-formed characters by using an electronic typewriter's mechanism, and *dot-matrix printers*, which formed an image by extruding a pattern made up of little rods and hammering the page with them.

With high-quality laser printers now available for less than $1,000, they're the best bet for most small businesses. But laser printers can't print carbons. If you're working with an application that requires multipart forms, such as the accounting program Pacioli 2000, you must equip your system with an impact printer. This fact doesn't prevent you from adding a laser printer to your system for other uses, but for the sake of convenience, you'll need a printer switch box that enables you to connect two printers to one computer. Here's another reason you may prefer a dot-matrix printer: laser printers cannot print in color. Many dot-matrix printers can print in color.

Understanding the Benefits of a Laser Printer

For most readers of this book, a single printer—a laser printer—will suffice. Laser printers have many advantages for business:

- Because laser printers are designed to work with cut sheets (rather than tractor-fed, continuous paper), you can use your firm's letterhead. Your letters will have an attractive, professional appearance.

- Even the cheapest laser printers can print faster than high-quality dot-matrix printers. For text, speeds range from four to eight pages per minute.

- Laser printers can print graphics, although some of the cheapest laser printers don't have enough memory to print a full page of graphics. If you need to make presentations, you can print charts and graphs directly on the clear plastic sheets to make transparencies.

- Many laser printers come with a built-in selection of fonts, and you can add additional fonts as you want.

- Text output is readable and clear. Printing at a resolution (density) of approximately 300 dots per inch (dpi), the text printed by laser printers isn't as good as that produced by professional typesetting equipment, which prints with resolutions of up to 1,200 dpi. However, it takes a trained eye to see the difference.

After 3,000 to 4,000 pages of output, you'll have to replace the toner cartridge, at a cost of about $80 to $100; you're paying about two to three cents per page for every page you print, not including the price of paper.

You can cut down the cost of laser printing by having your toner cartridges refilled. Most cartridges can be refilled a few times, and the cost is about half of what you would pay for a new toner cartridge.

Choosing a Laser Printer

There are dozens of laser printers available, but they boil down to four basic price categories. As you'll see, you pay more for printers that can interpret printer commands phrased in the PostScript page description language, as discussed in Chapter 9, "Getting into Desktop Publishing." PostScript capabilities are needed only if your computing plans include printing typeset-quality brochures, annual reports, menus, price lists, or newsletters. (You can print attractive documents using non-PostScript laser printers, too, but PostScript is the best-supported printer control language for professional desktop publishing applications.)

- *Inexpensive printers with no scalable fonts ($750 to $1,000):* The market leader in this category is the Hewlett-Packard IIP. The least expensive laser printers for DOS and Windows systems generally lack any built-in fonts other than the default Courier (typewriter) font. To equip these printers with additional fonts, you must download them from disk (*soft fonts*) or insert an optional font cartridge

(*cartridge fonts*). Printer speeds average about four pages per minute, and paper trays may accommodate as few as 75 sheets. Memory may be inadequate for desktop publishing applications. Suitable for light office applications only.

- *Low-priced printers with non-PostScript scalable fonts ($1,000 to $1,500):* This category includes printers such as the Hewlett-Packard IIIp for DOS and Windows systems, and the Apple Personal LaserWriter. Printer speeds average around four pages per minute, and paper trays may accommodate as few as 75 sheets. Suitable for light office applications only.

- *Medium-priced printers with non-PostScript scalable fonts ($1,500 to $2,500):* This category includes printers such as the Hewlett-Packard LaserJet III and the Apple LaserWriter SC. You get faster print speeds (up to eight pages per minute), more durable mechanisms, and larger paper trays. An excellent choice for small business applications, these printers are capable of cranking out moderate workloads.

- *High-priced printers with PostScript scalable fonts ($2,500 and up):* This category includes printers such as the Apple LaserWriter NT and LaserWriter NTX. Needed only if you're very serious about desktop publishing or for heavy workloads. These printers are much more expensive because they require their own microprocessing circuitry to decode and process the PostScript instructions.

If you're equipping a DOS or Windows system with a laser printer, choose a Hewlett-Packard or HP-compatible laser printer. Hewlett-Packard's laser printer control language (HPPCL) and scalable font technology have become solid standards in the world of IBM-compatible computing, and are fully supported by most applications.

TIP

If you're planning to equip your office with two or more computers, you can save money by having them share a laser printer. Apple's LaserWriter SC and higher models work with Apple's built-in LocalTalk network; it's a very easy and inexpensive matter to connect four or five Macintoshes to a single LaserWriter. To connect two or more PCs (up to a maximum of 12) to an HP LaserJet inexpensively, install a SimpLAN ServerJet network (ASP Computer Products, Inc.).

Using an Inkjet Printer

If you can't come up with the money for a laser printer, the next best choice isn't necessarily a dot-matrix printer. Get an inkjet printer instead. Hewlett-Packard's DeskJet and Apple's StyleWriter printers offer many of the benefits of low-end laser printers (including high-quality printouts and a choice of fonts), but for a fraction of the cost. You'll see ads that claim the output of inkjet printers is indistinguishable from that of laser printers, which is almost true. Inkjet printer speeds are lower but still acceptable for light office use, and the ink cartridges are cheaper (about one cent per page, not including the cost of paper).

One drawback to inkjet printers is that they use water-soluble ink, which means that your letters and reports—which otherwise resemble laser printer output—can be smeared if someone rubs a damp finger over them.

Like a laser printer's toner cartridge, inkjet cartridges are refillable. You can save money by doing it yourself: buy a kit that refills three cartridges.

TIP

Adding Modems and Fax Boards

If you've decided to go online, you'll need a modem, and if you want to send and receive faxes from your computer, you'll need a fax board. The sections that follow briefly explain your options.

Modems

The term *modem* is short for modulator-demodulator, and that's exactly what a modem does. A modem takes the digital signals coming from your computer and converts them into sounds that can be transmitted over the telephone system. A modem also demodulates the sounds coming in from another computer.

All this modulation and demodulation translates into transmission speeds much slower than the speeds your computer can muster. For business computing, don't settle for less than a modem capable of transmitting and receiving communications at the pace of 2400 bits per second (bps). (Such modems often are called *2400-baud modems*, although the use of the term *baud* in this context is inaccurate.) A 2400-baud modem transmits text at a rate that's faster than you can read on-screen, but the faster the modem, the lower your telephone bill.

Reasonably-priced modems that can operate at transmission rates of 4800 and 9600 bits per second are increasingly available, although they bring the risk of higher error rates. An occasional transmission error in text isn't much more than an annoyance. But do you need the speed? If you're using your modem to transmit occasional letters or memos, 2400 baud will do. If your business is dependent on the frequent exchange of lengthy reports with clients in the field, you'll be wise to spend the extra money for a 9600-baud modem.

Modems do much more than modulate and demodulate signals; they also dial the number (using touch-tone or pulse signals), and they can even receive calls if you want to set up your computer to receive point-to-point electronic mail from someone (see Chapter 12, "Going Online").

Modems are of two kinds: external modems and internal modems. An *external modem* comes in its own case and requires its own power cord. An *internal modem* presses into one of your computer's expansions slots, if a slot is available. Internal modems are preferable; they're housed within your computer's case, so they don't clutter up your desk. But external modems usually have lights to tell you what's going on and a speaker—major shortcomings of most internal modems.

If you're thinking about buying a modem, be sure to read the next section on fax boards. Some fax boards include modems, giving you a two-for-one deal.

Fax Boards

As you learned in Chapter 12, "Going Online," a send/receive fax board can give your computer much of the functionality of a fax machine, and for a fraction of the price. Here are some pointers if you're looking for a fax board:

- Be wary of send-only fax boards: For just a little more money, you can get full send-receive capabilities.

- If you're shopping for a modem as well as a fax board, you may be able to save some money by buying a combination fax/modem board.

- Remember that you'll need software to support the fax board, and when you buy the board, the vendor probably will try to sell you some. But you get excellent fax software as well as a full panoply of utility programs when you buy PC Tools (Central Point Software), discussed in Chapter 17. Note, however, that PC Tools supports only a limited number of fax boards—and if the program doesn't fully support your board you can't use PC Tools to send and receive faxes.

- If your fax board shares your phone line, look for a fax that can tell the difference between an incoming fax signal and a voice call. One board for IBM PCs and compatibles that can perform this trick is Trecom's 1-Liner, an advanced version of the firm's popular and highly-rated Fax96 board.

Adding Other Peripherals

You can equip a computer with an amazing variety of peripheral equipment. Here's just a quick survey:

- *Hand-held scanners:* These scanners "read" a portion of a page (usually about 4 inches wide) and construct a graphics file that many programs can read. Suggestion: use a hand-held scanner to add a picture (of an employee or product, for example) to a Windows or Macintosh database. Hand-held scanners are available in both monochrome and color models. A hand-held scanner is a good bet for light desktop publishing use or other light applications where you need to scan pictures and store them in the computer.

- *Flatbed scanners:* These scanners "read" a full page of text at a time, and are used frequently in professional desktop publishing firms. Advanced scanners offer optical character recognition (OCR) capabilities, which can scan printed or typed text and convert it into text that you can display, edit, and print with your word processing program.

- *Trackball:* An alternative to the mouse, the trackball stays put, and you twirl the ball that is on top.

- *Bar code readers:* A bar code reader scans a computer-readable bar code, such as the Uniform Product Code (UPC)—codes you see on almost all retail items—and transforms the code into what appears to your computer as ordinary numbers, just as if you typed them at the keyboard. The readers attach to your computer by a serial port or expansion slot.

- *Cash drawers and receipt printers:* Designed to work with point-of-sale software, these peripherals enable you to turn a PC into a complete cash register system for a retail operation.

- *Tape Drives:* If you're using your computer as a point-of-sale terminal for a busy retail operation, or if you're doing any other work that produces a lot of data every day, floppy disks may not be sufficient for backup purposes. You can add a tape drive to your system that backs up your entire hard disk quickly to a tape cartridge. With backup software such as PC Tools, you can even schedule a tape backup to take place automatically while you're away from your office.

Networking

With its philosophy that you should approach small business computing one step at a time, this book has assumed that you'll be buying and installing just one computer in your business—and that's a wise move, especially when you're just getting started. But bear in mind that it's becoming increasingly easier to install and use local area networks (LANs). A *LAN* provides the adapter circuits and cables that can connect as few as two or three, or as many as dozens or hundreds, of personal computers (see fig. 16.7).

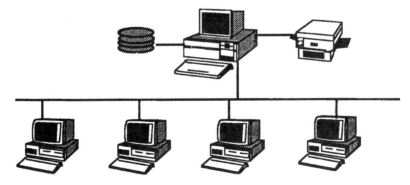

***Fig. 16.7.** A personal computer local area network.*

LAN-linked personal computers can perform some or all of the following tasks:

- Sharing expensive peripherals, such as laser printers.

- Providing internal E-mail, linking everyone who has a computer that is connected to the system.

- Enabling users of different computers to contribute to, and benefit from, a common database. In an attorney's office, for example, each attorney can track his or her time and add it to the common, shared Timeslips III database.

A LAN may sound like a very good idea, and it is, but there are some drawbacks. First, you'll probably have to set aside one of your computers to serve as the network's file server. A file server's only functions are to run the network's operating system—the software that integrates the network and controls communication—and to serve as a repository for network software and data resources.

Second, you'll need network versions of most programs, and the network version is usually a lot more expensive.

Third, it's often a hassle to get a network working correctly, and somebody has to take care of backing up the system regularly and attending to technical crises, which still occur frequently.

If you just want to share a laser printer and provide E-mail, consider a low-speed, low-cost LAN. Low-speed networking capabilities (suitable for printer-sharing and E-mail) are built into Macintoshes, and you can create a simple Macintosh network quite cheaply. Similar inexpensive networks can be achieved by connecting a few IBM PCs or compatibles via their service ports.

Summary

Here's a quick review of this chapter's main points:

- You have chosen the computer environment you need for your primary application; now you're going to design an optimal system for it.

- An optimal system runs your application speedily, accommodates the application with memory to spare, runs more than one application without crashing, displays text and graphics clearly and colorfully, and prints attractive output.

- For small business computing, a minimal DOS system employs an 80386 microprocessor running at 16 MHz with at least 2M of RAM; equip the system with 1.2M and 1.44M floppy drives. Make sure that you're getting at least one parallel port and two serial ports. You'll need at least a 40M hard disk, a VGA color monitor, and an HP or compatible laser printer. For Windows, get another 2M of RAM for a total of 4M.

- For small business computing, a minimal Macintosh system employs a 68030 microprocessor running at a minimum of 16MHz with at least 2M of RAM (4M if you're running System 7). You'll need at least a 40M hard disk, and you will prefer a system with the SuperDrive that reads DOS disks. Choose a full-page monochrome monitor for word processing or desktop publishing applications; choose a 14-inch color monitor otherwise. Equip your system with a non-PostScript laser printer.

- Networks enhance personal computing when you have two or more systems in an area, but networks can be expensive to buy, difficult to set up, and a hassle to administer. You can set up a simple, easy network for exchanging mail and sharing a printer if you choose the Macintosh environment.

17

Buying and Installing Your System

You've made all your decisions at this point: you've selected your primary application, you've settled on a computer system configuration and printer, and you're ready to move. Here's some guidance on two essential steps: shopping for your system and installing it once you've got your hands on all those big boxes.

TIP

Should you consider leasing instead of buying? As a small business owner, you're well aware that it's best not to tie up your capital unnecessarily. One of the advantages of today's personal computers is that you don't need to spend all that much to get a very nice system. A minimal system, such as the ones recommended in Chapter 16, shouldn't cost much more than $5,000, and it may cost less. And that includes the computer itself, a high-quality display monitor, a laser printer, a modem, and a mouse! But there are some advantages to leasing, including tax advantages in some cases (you would be wise to discuss this matter with an accountant).

Buying Your System

Before you buy your system, think about some last-minute issues. If you've decided on DOS or Windows, do you want to buy a genuine IBM system, or will an IBM-compatible (sometimes called a *clone*) suffice? What can you expect from warranties? Where is it best to buy your system? What should

303

you ask the dealer? Should you buy a used computer? You'll find guidance on all these questions in the section that follows.

Buying an IBM or Clone

If you've decided on a DOS or Windows system, you'll be faced with a choice between a genuine IBM computer (one of its PS/1 or PS/2 models) or an IBM-compatible (a *clone*). You can find high-quality IBM compatibles; IBM's much-touted Micro Channel Bus architecture does not offer decisive technical advantages for the applications discussed in this book. Consider IBM machines along with IBM compatibles as you shop, but make your decision on the basis of features, support, warranties, and service.

Examining Warranties

Be sure to carefully investigate the firm's guarantee and the equipment manufacturer's warranty before signing on the dotted line, regardless of where you buy your system. If your computer isn't working, who fixes it? This question takes on an extra significance if you're buying from a mail-order firm. If you order by mail, by all means investigate the warranty with special care—and be sure to read the following section, "Deciding Where To Buy Your System."

Increasingly, you can find stores and especially mail order firms that will refund the full price of a computer system if you return it in 30 days, no questions asked. If you can find a firm that will give you these terms, you're protected in the unlikely event you get stuck with a computer that doesn't run well and doesn't meet your needs.

Beware of 90-day warranties; they're all too common. Hold out, if possible, for a one-year warranty, at the minimum, on all the equipment you buy.

In some cases, you may be invited to purchase an extended warranty, and it isn't a bad idea. A recent survey disclosed what many personal computer owners have long suspected: over 60 percent of PC repairs occur after the warranties have expired (the most frequent culprits are disk drives), with an average repair cost of $257. So it may be worthwhile to spend $100 or $200 for an additional year of warranty protection. The best extended warranties are those offered by the equipment manufacturer, who is less likely to disappear from the scene overnight. Computer retailers come and go. One local fly-by-night store offers a two-year warranty with on-site service, but will it be there in six months?

If you have a credit card, call the vendor to determine whether using the card to buy the system will give you any additional protection. Some credit card firms automatically add one year of warranty protection for some items. But note that some mail-order vendors charge extra for using credit cards—as much as 3 percent of the total purchase price.

Deciding Where To Buy Your System

If you're buying a Macintosh, you're limited to authorized Apple dealers—and until quite recently, that meant that you couldn't shop around for the lowest prices. Recently, however, Apple has agreed to sell its low-end products through computer superstore chains (see the following section, "Computer Stores"). A few mail order firms offer Apple hardware at competitive pricing. If you're still in college, buy your Macintosh system now before you graduate—chances are you can qualify for hefty educational discounts.

If you're buying a DOS or Windows system, you have more choices. You can buy from computer stores, independent system integrators, or mail order firms.

Computer Stores

If you're a complete beginner in personal computing and you don't know anyone who can help you get your system up and running, it may be worth your while to buy a complete system—including a printer—from a local computer store. You'll pay more—perhaps much more—but you should be able to extract a commitment that the store will help you get the system up and running. That includes installing DOS (and Windows, if you're using Windows), configuring your system optimally for the applications you're running, getting your fonts to work with your printer, and other tasks that are very challenging for novice users.

TIP

Before you buy a system, beware: many stores rationalize their high prices with vague promises of service, but don't deliver. Get a specific agreement in writing about just what service you can expect, and when. It's unreasonable to ask the store personnel to teach you how to use the applications, but they should be willing to make sure the computer is installed properly, runs the programs you've purchased, and prints correctly.

Readers who live in urban areas should visit computer and electronics superstores (if there are any in the area) such as Fry's Electronics (Mountain View, California), Computer Factory (Elmsford, New York), CompuAdd (Austin and San Antonio, Texas), Micro Center (Columbus, Ohio), Soft Warehouse (Dallas, Texas), and The Computer Store (Louisville, Kentucky). These stores are opening branches very rapidly in cities such as Boston, Portland, New Orleans, Milwaukee, and Washington, D.C. You'll find yourself in a most appealing wonderland of over 20,000 square feet of floor space devoted to computer goodies—PC compatibles, peripherals, books, software, and office furniture, all at prices from 30 percent to 80 percent off retail. Just don't expect to get a lot of advice! Other places to hunt for bargains include department store sales and wholesale clubs.

Independent System Integrators

The name *independent system integrators* (ISI) sounds fancy, but sometimes an ISI is little more than a 19-year old kid operating out of a garage. Just about anyone with a little technical knowledge can order the parts and create a PC compatible. What you get for your money is a "No-Name" clone at bargain prices. Will it be any good? Actually, it may be. Many of the big mail order firms are playing exactly the same game, and with a few exceptions, they're using the same parts. It's a gamble buying from an ISI, but you can't beat the price, and some of the people in this system are genuine computer wizards. Just be sure you get an agreement in writing— and hold out for a 30-day, no-questions-asked return guarantee. Insist that the dealer install the system at your site—and that includes formatting the hard disk, configuring the system so that it *boots* (starts) automatically from the hard disk, and getting your printer to work.

If you buy a system from an independent system integrator, make sure that it is FCC-certified against radio interference. It is illegal to sell computers without FCC certification, but some small-time ISIs try to get away with it. For more information on FCC certification, see the section "Asking Questions Before You Buy," later in this chapter.

Value-Added Resellers (VAR)

Fancier than independent system integrators are *value-added resellers* (VAR), who frequently specialize in a particular line of work, such as setting up complete desktop publishing or desktop accounting systems. Working with one of these firms may be an excellent idea, particularly because the staff tends to be knowledgeable and technically skilled. You may pay more, but it probably will be worth it.

Mail Order

Buying a complete computer system by mail is more risky than buying software. Several spectacular mail-order firm failures have cost consumers millions, the advertised systems sometimes lack crucial features or components, and—despite offers of "on-site service"—you may find that you can't get quick service if the system breaks down. Generally, it is much more risky to order hardware by mail than it is to order software—and it's often unnecessary if you live anywhere near a city where you can find computer electronic superstores, department stores, and other sources for hardware bargains.

To protect yourself, know your legal rights before you order. Don't pay by check or money order; use a credit card, which gives you some protection should the firm fail to deliver your computer. And most of all, order from a reputable firm. At this writing, firms considered reputable were Austin Computer Systems (800-752-1577), CompuAdd (800-456-3660), Dell Computer Corporation (800-627-1470), Gateway 2000 (800-523-2000), Northgate Computer Systems (800-828-6125), PC Brand (800-722-7263), and Zeos International (800-423-5891). All of these firms have been in business for several years and produce computers that have won high marks from reputable magazine reviewers. But be aware that businesses' fortunes change, and a firm that is reputable now may experience difficulties down the road. Before ordering any hardware by mail, call the Better Business Bureau in the vendor's area and ask whether it has received complaints.

If you read computer mail order ads carefully, you'll see many signs of price competition. In an effort to offer the lowest possible price, some firms cut back certain features that they believe consumers don't pay much attention to, such as hard disk access time, RAM, ports, and DOS. Don't settle for anything less than the minimum system configurations listed in Chapter 16; you may find that the true price of the system you want is several hundred dollars higher than the price you see in the ads.

Many mail order firms offer "on-site service" through major national service firms operated by GTE, TRW, and other service contractors. This service may not live up to your expectations, however. Find out whether the service contractor has an office nearby; if it doesn't, you may find that you're asked to ship your computer elsewhere for servicing! The service contractor may not be of much help, too, if the firm doesn't stock parts.

Asking Questions Before You Buy

No matter where you've decided to buy, there's a long list of questions you should ask before you commit yourself:

- *Is the computer FCC Class B Certified?* Class B certification means the system meets the FCC's radio frequency (RF) emission and protection requirements for home use, which are more stringent than the Class A (business use) requirements. Class B certification means that your system will be less likely to interfere with televisions and radios in the workplace, and less likely to be disturbed by RF interference (which can distort the video image or even cause data loss). Don't buy a system that isn't FCC-certified, because if an uncertified system causes interference, you may be forced to stop using it.

- *Is DOS included? Windows?* If not, you'll have to pay as much as $150 to buy both locally. Don't settle for less than DOS 5.0, which is now the minimal DOS version for future application development. Are all the manuals included?

- *Is the hard disk formatted with both a low-level (physical) format and a high-level (logical) format?* Both are necessary before you can use the system, and both are tedious procedures.

- *Is DOS installed on the hard disk and will the system boot when I turn it on?* Unless you're confident you can format the disk and install DOS yourself, insist that this be done.

- *Is there a service contractor in my city? Does the contractor stock parts for this computer?* These questions are particularly important if you are ordering by mail.

- *Is the merchandise in stock?* You may not be told if it's not, and you may have to wait as much as a month before your computer is shipped. (By law, the vendor must inform you of a shipping delay of one month or more.)

- *When will my credit card be charged?* This is an important question. If the firm is in financial trouble, it will try (illegally) to charge your card right away, before your computer is shipped. This may mean that the firm is using your money to buy the parts to build someone else's computer. Who's going to pay for *your* computer? If you're told that your card is charged immediately, order from another firm.

- *Is there an extra charge for using credit cards?* Get a complete, realistic price quote before ordering.

- *Is there a restocking fee for the no-questions-asked 30-day return?* This fee may come to as much as 20 percent of the purchase price. If so, the firm isn't really offering a full 30-day refund. On the other hand, it's reasonable that you pay the return shipping fees. Shop elsewhere, though, if it turns out there is a restocking fee on 30-day returns.

- *Is there a toll-free technical support line? When is it available? How long is the average wait for help?*

- *If you're buying a printer or modem, does it include the cable needed to connect it to your computer?* If not, be sure that you order the correct cable.

Buying a Used Computer

If you're an experienced computer user and you know what you're looking for, you sometimes can find great bargains in the used computer market. Companies get rid of perfectly good systems because they are fully depreciated for tax purposes. Hobbyists get rid of even better systems, much more lightly used, because they want the latest and greatest. If you're new to personal computing, however, you would be well advised to leave the auctions, Sunday classifieds, and computer flea markets to more knowledgeable shoppers.

Setting Up Your System

The big day's here, and your computer system has arrived. Save the boxes! You'll need them if you decide to return the computer or printer to the dealer.

In the sections that follow, you receive guidance on locating your computer, supplying glitch-free power, ensuring physical security, avoiding water damage, performing setup tasks, and equipping yourself with essential supplies.

Locating Your Computer

Computers draw a surprising amount of electricity (as much as a portable hair dryer, in some cases), and a fully grounded outlet is absolutely required. If the outlet isn't grounded, your computer's memory may be insufficiently protected against static electricity, which can cause system failure and increase the risk of electrical shock. If there isn't a three-pronged outlet near the computer, hire an electrician to install one. Don't try to use an extension cord, which is unsafe and could cause serious data losses if somebody trips on it.

Situate the computer's display screen so that it doesn't catch glare from windows or lights. If you can't keep the monitor away from glare, you can buy a glare filter that improves the screen's readability.

Surge Protectors and Uninterruptible Power Supplies

Don't install your computer without a *surge protector*—a device that stops current surges before they can harm your computer. Surges are common in electrical lines; they're caused by the intermittent operation of power-hungry equipment such as cooling units, elevators, and heaters, as well as by switching operations conducted by the power company itself. Another cause of surges, and a particularly dangerous one, is lightning, which can send surges of millions of volts headed straight for your computer. Insist on a surge protector that conforms to Underwriter's Laboratory (UL) listing No. 1449.

If your area is subject to severe voltage fluctuations and brownouts, you may need a *voltage regulator*, which ensures that a steady voltage is delivered to your computer.

In some areas, power outages are common, and they can play havoc with a business computer system. If your business has experienced even one power outage during the past year, invest in an *uninterruptible power supply* (UPS). A UPS switches automatically to backup battery power in the event of a power failure, giving you time to back up important business records. When the power comes back on, the battery charges automatically.

Physical Security

Professional thieves don't often steal computers—they don't understand them and neither do most fences—but an amateur may decide that your computer or printer would make an enchanting addition to his or her own system. You can purchase an inexpensive cable-lock security system for as little as $20. Such a system won't stop the pros, but it will send the amateurs hunting elsewhere. If they see the security constraints during the day, they won't bother coming back when they think no one's around.

Water Damage

According to a *Wall Street Journal* article, by far the most common cause of data loss is water—water from leaking roofs, condensed water dripping from overhead pipes, rain water streaming through open windows, water spewing over computers from humidifiers left on high, and a huge variety of spilled drinks. Don't install your computer anywhere near dripping, leaking, or condensing water, and be very careful to avoid spilling coffee when you're working.

Performing Setup Tasks

If you buy your computer locally, you're in luck: you probably can get the dealer to deliver it and set it up for you. This procedure should involve at least the following:

- Formatting the hard disk

- Installing the operating system on the hard disk so that the computer starts automatically

- Connecting all peripherals (including mouse, modem, and printer) to the computer and making sure all of them are working correctly

- Making sure the printer prints all the fonts that you've purchased (if any)

- Running diagnostic tests to make sure the computer is working correctly

If you've purchased a mail order computer, get some help from a local computer whiz, if at all possible; the manuals provided with mail-order systems vary considerably in quality. Somebody who knows what he or she is doing can connect everything in 15 minutes, but it may take *you* five hours of pure frustration, as you plow through an incomprehensible, poorly written reference manual. You probably know two or three people who use computers successfully and seem to enjoy talking about them—one of them may be able to save you a lot of time.

TIP

When you ask for help, be sure to offer to pay for it. People with computer smarts are constantly besieged by acquaintances who call at all hours and expect them to drop everything and spend hours resolving a problem only to be rewarded with a Pepsi or two.

Getting Supplies

To get started with your computer, you'll need the following:

- *Floppy disks:* Buy several boxes of high-density disks. If possible, buy *preformatted disks*—but make sure that they are formatted for the correct type of disk drive. These disks already have the magnetic pattern that must be encoded on the disk's surface before your computer can store and retrieve data on it. If you buy unformatted disks, you'll have to format them yourself, and it's a tedious, time-consuming job.

- *Printer paper:* If you're using a laser printer, you can use ordinary xerographic bond paper for test printing.

- *Disk storage boxes:* Spend some money on a sturdy, lockable disk storage cabinet that's capable of storing up to 100 disks. You'll use this cabinet to store your original program disks as well as backup disks, both of which are valuable items; they deserve good protection.

Learning To Use Your Computer

Now that you've set up your system, you're ready to get started. Don't expect to learn everything in a few days; this is going to take time. Start by learning the operating system. Then install and learn your primary application.

Learning the Operating System

Start by learning the operating system. Read the manuals that came with your computer. If they're incomprehensible, go to your local bookstore and get a book that's specifically aimed at novice users. Que Corporation has a number of useful beginners' books for DOS, Windows, and the Macintosh, including the following:

- *MS-DOS 5 Quick Start*, *MS-DOS 5 Quick Reference*, *Using MS-DOS 5*, *MS-DOS PC Tutor*

- *Windows 3.1 Quick Start*, *Windows 3.1 Quick Reference*

- *The Little Mac Book*

You may also want to read Que's *Introduction to Personal Computers*, 2nd Edition, or *Que's Computer User's Dictionary*, 2nd Edition.

Before you attempt to use your application software, you should master all of the following operations:

- Starting your computer and displaying the main directory of files

- Checking the time and date, and resetting them if necessary

- Changing the current or default drive

- Navigating the disks' directory structure (DOS and Windows) or folders (Macintosh)

- Copying files to a floppy disk

- Naming files in accordance with your computer's file name constraints and limitations

- Renaming files

- Deleting unwanted files

- Opening, sizing, moving, and scrolling windows (Windows and Macintosh systems)

Installing Your Primary Application

Once you've learned the basics, you can install your primary application program. (If you've purchased other programs, leave them alone for now.) You install a program by transferring the software from the distribution disks to your hard disk, as well as preparing the program for operation. Before you start, make a list of the following:

- Name and model of your printer

- Port through which your printer is connected (DOS systems only)

- Type of video adapter and display you're using (DOS systems only)

You probably will need this information in order to respond to the installation utility's on-screen questions.

Open the package and read the installation instructions carefully. Almost all of today's programs include an *installation utility*, which guides you through the installation process step by step and makes any necessary modifications to your computer's system files. Find out how to start the installation utility and follow the on-screen instructions to install the program on your computer's hard disk.

Learning Your Primary Application

After you install your primary application, you need some time to learn the program. Trying to learn it yourself may not be the best option. Your local community college or computer store may offer a class on the program. To learn the program yourself, follow these steps:

1. Read the computer's manuals to find out whether the program comes with an on-screen tutorial. If so, use it.

2. If there's no on-screen tutorial, check the manuals to see whether there's a keystroke-by-keystroke "getting started" tutorial. If all you find is a reference manual, look for a book that includes a keystroke-by-keystroke tutorial.

3. Create a test application using fictitious data that resembles the real data you'll enter, and try all the operations that you're planning to perform once the system becomes part of your business. Continue working with the test application until you're confident you understand what you're doing and how the program works.

If your employees will use the system, now's the time to train them, too. Use the test application, and give your employees plenty of time to become comfortable with the system. Be open to their suggestions: they may have some very good ideas for improving your application design. You may want to hire someone to provide in-house training aimed at the business's specific needs.

Once you've learned your computer's operating system and thoroughly explored your primary application, you're ready to install and learn additional programs. You'll be amazed at how much easier it is the second time around—especially if you took the time to learn the first program well before proceeding.

Looking At Computers and Your Health

You've installed your system successfully, and it has become part of your daily business routine. Is it a threat to your health or that of your employees? Here's a brief discussion of the two most widely-discussed health issues of computer use: repetitive strain injuries (RSI) and extremely low frequency (ELF) radiation.

Repetitive Strain Injuries (RSI)

RSI is a serious and potentially debilitating occupational illness caused by prolonged repetitive hand and arm movements, which may damage, inflame, or kill nerves in the hands, arms, shoulders, or neck. Also known as *cumulative trauma disorder* (CTD), RSI occurs when constantly-repeated motions stress tendons and ligaments, resulting in scar tissue that squeezes and may eventually kill nerves.

RSI has long been experienced by meat packers, musicians, and assembly-line workers who repeatedly perform the same hand movements. With the proliferation of computer keyboards, RSI is increasingly noted among white-collar office workers and poses a genuine threat to personal computer users who work long hours at the keyboard.

Specific RSI disorders include carpal tunnel syndrome (CTS), which causes burning, tingling, or numbness in the hands, as well as a loss of muscle control and dexterity. Potentially incapacitating to full-time writers, secretaries, and journalists, CTS and other RSI injuries are estimated to cost United States corporations $27 billion per year in medical bills and lost workdays.

RSI can be prevented. Adjust your chair height to eliminate any unnecessary extension or flexing of the wrist. Take frequent breaks, use good posture, and vary your daily activities so that you perform a variety of actions with your wrists.

> Avoid glare filters that claim to reduce radiation. These filters are designed to suppress x-rays, which today's monitors don't emit in measurable quantities, but do nothing to stop ELF—despite vaguely-worded claims to the contrary.

Extremely Low Frequency (ELF) Radiation

An extremely low frequency magnetic field is generated by commonly used electrical appliances such as electric blankets, hair dryers, food mixers, and computer display monitors. This frequency extends one to two meters from its source. ELF fields are known to cause tissue changes and fetal abnormalities in laboratory test animals and may be related to reproductive anomalies and cancers among frequent users of computer displays.

Although a link between computer display usage and cancer has not been proven beyond doubt, there is sufficient evidence to suggest that computer users should take steps to reduce their exposure to ELF fields. Contrary to what you may suppose, a computer display's ELF emissions are weakest in front of the screen; emissions from the back and sides are stronger. If your desk is positioned back to back with another, so that you are close to the side or back of another computer display, you should move your desk away. To reduce exposure to the emissions coming from the display's screen, remain an arm's length away from the screen.

Here's an excellent argument for investing in a Windows or Macintosh system, preferably with a large, full-page or two-page display. Because these systems can display font sizes on-screen, you can define a 14- or 18-point font size as the normal font for writing and editing purposes. You easily can read such a font from a distance of two or three feet. When it's time to print the document, switch to 12-point or 10-point type.

Another strategy: Sweden has instituted tough new emissions standards for computer displays, and displays now are available on the U.S. market that meet or exceed these standards. You may be able to replace your current display with a low-emissions model that meets the Swedish standards.

Yet another alternative: use a laptop or notebook computer with an LCD or gas-plasma display. LCD and gas-plasma screens use technologies other than the cathode ray gun that ordinary monitors use, and neither emits an ELF field.

Summary

Here's a quick summary of this chapter's main points:

- Don't turn your nose up at so-called "clones" (IBM-compatibles). Many offer superb design, excellent reliability, and good value.

- Look for bargains locally; use mail order as a last resort.

- Before you buy, ask about FCC certification, DOS, hard disk formatting, warranty service, credit card charges, "restocking fees," technical support, and cables.

- Keep your computer away from moisture, install a surge protector, and install a cable-lock security system. Get some help from a local computer whiz when you set up your system, but offer to pay for this help.

- Learn to use your computer one step at a time, beginning with the operating system. When you or your employees use your computer, try to avoid prolonged, repetitive data entry and don't get too close to the screen.

18

Maintaining Your System

To keep your computer system and applications running smoothly, you must back up your work regularly, detect and eliminate viruses, cope with inadvertent file deletions, and defragment your hard disk. To perform these tasks, you will need to buy and use system utility programs, the subject of the sections that follow.

Backing Up Your Work

Serious business use of a computer requires daily backup procedures. Power outages, erased files, catastrophic hard disk failures, or burst pipes could wipe out your firm's valuable accounts, mailing lists, presentations, and contact lists. Part of using the computer for business involves backing up your work on a regular basis; if you're not willing to back up your work, you shouldn't use the computer.

It's not sufficient just to use the operating system's file-copying utility to copy files to floppy disks. For one thing, you'll almost surely create a data file that's larger than a single disk can accommodate. What's worse is that you can't tell which files to back up. Will you remember all the files that changed today, and the ones that didn't? If you forget to back up an important file that was altered and your system fails, you could lose important work. Rather than relying on the copy command, you need a backup utility.

A *backup utility* is a utility program specifically designed to back up your hard disk to floppy disks or, if you have one, a tape drive. Backup utilities offer the following advantages over manual backup methods:

- They automatically detect which files have changed, and back up only the files that have changed since the last backup. This is a significant advantage, because the backup operation goes much more rapidly.

- They copy files faster. Backup programs use special file-copying techniques that are substantially faster than the operating system's file copy command.

- They can handle large files. If a data file is larger than the capacity of the floppies to which you're backing up, the backup utility divides up the file over several disks.

- If a valuable file is lost, or if your entire disk is wiped out, restoring your data is easy; you just select the files you want to restore, and the backup utility tells you which disks to insert.

TIP

Most accounting programs come with their own backup utilities. However, you probably will prefer to forego using these utilities, which only back up the accounting program's files, in favor of a backup utility such as Norton Utilities, Central Backup, or FastBack Plus, which back up all the files on your disk.

Developing a Backup Routine

Today's backup utilities call for a simplified version of the classic backup strategy. The classic strategy called for the creation and rotation of three or more sets of backup disks. The two-week cycle recommended here is adequate for most users; it creates only two backup diskettes:

1. Begin with a complete backup of all the directories on your hard disk that contain data. (You don't need to back up your programs—if your hard disk fails, you can restore the program files from the original distribution disks.) Follow the on-screen instructions and label the disks carefully.

2. Perform a daily incremental backup. An *incremental backup* backs up only the files that have been altered or created during the day's work. Continue to perform daily incremental backups for two weeks.

3. After two weeks, store the backup disks in a secure location. Call this *Archival Set #1*.

4. Perform a new backup of all the files in the directories containing data, and perform daily incremental backups for another two-week period. At the end of two weeks, label these disks *Archival Set #2* and store them.

5. After two more weeks, take out the Archival Set #1 disks and reuse them for a new, complete backup of all the files in your data directories.

6. Continue rotating Archival Sets #1 and #2 in this way, every two weeks.

Why create two disk sets? The first set you create stays near your computer, where an accident or spillage could wipe it out. But after two weeks of incremental backups, you put the disk set away in a safe place and start a new disk set. Now imagine that the ultimate disaster has occurred: your hard disk crashes and, when you get your backup disks, you discover that a part-time employee left them next to an open window during a thunderstorm, and they're ruined. But, thank heavens, you've still got the other disk set squirreled safely away! Of course, this disk set will be from one day to two weeks out of date, but that's better than nothing.

Using a Tape Drive

Tape drives use removable cartridges that are capable of storing up to 100M or more of data. Do you need a tape drive? You'll find out quickly enough. If you only have to insert two or three floppy disks to perform an incremental backup, you probably don't need a tape drive. But if you find yourself spending 15 minutes inserting 10 or more disks every day, you can save time by adding a tape drive to your system.

Some backup programs include scheduling utilities that perform backups to tape drives automatically. You can set up the scheduler to perform the incremental backup at 5:15 p.m. every day, for example, recording the whole day's transactions. The backup takes only about five minutes, and when it's done, you turn off the computer and you're out the door.

There has been a price break on tape drives, so you can buy one for less than $300. At such prices, no small business should be without a tape drive.

TIP

Safeguarding Your System Against Computer Viruses and Trojan Horses

Computer viruses are hidden, self-replicating programs that attach themselves to other programs. When you start an infected program, the virus infects other programs on your computer.

Most computer viruses are little more than computer versions of pranks; some cause letters to fall from the screen, while others make your mouse pointer go in the wrong direction. But some viruses are more destructive. Many are unstable and cause your computer to crash, wiping out all your unsaved work. And some are deliberately destructive. A common virus tries to erase your entire hard disk. Whether the intent is merely to play a prank or cause damage, you should take steps to keep viruses off your system.

Less common than viruses are *Trojan horses*—programs that pretend to be one thing while actually doing something else (usually very destructive). A common Macintosh Trojan horse is a HyperCard stack known as Sexy Ladies. While you ogle the erotic pictures, the program erases your hard disk.

A common source of viruses is pirated software. Many pirated programs originate from university campuses, where software piracy and public access computer systems are often infected. You can avoid one very common source of infection by refusing to place any disks containing pirated software on your computer's disk drives.

Another common source of infected programs and Trojan horses is computer bulletin boards. Don't download software from BBS systems to your business computer. Bulletin boards are fun and contain many resources for computer hobbyists, but you should stay away from software downloading if you want to make sure your business computer is virus-free.

A prudent computer user avoids pirated software and doesn't download software from bulletin boards. But even these steps won't completely safeguard your system. There have been several celebrated cases in which commercial software has been infected by unseen viruses in the software publisher's computer systems. Sometimes a brand-new computer comes to you with viruses unknowingly added by infected diagnostic programs, which the computer seller ran on your behalf.

To protect yourself fully from viruses, purchase and use a virus-detection-and-elimination program, such as Central Point Anti-Virus. A virus-protection program scans your disk for known viruses and alerts you if you try to open an infected file. This program also scans the floppy disks you insert to see whether they contain infected files. If an infected file is detected, the anti-virus program has the ability to remove the virus code, making it possible to use the program safely.

To eliminate the virus, you need a virus-elimination program, which is capable of removing these viruses from infected files so that you can continue to use them. Because new viruses are being developed all the time, these programs usually include a subscription to a quarterly update program. Each quarter you receive a disk containing detectors for new viruses.

TIP

All too many computer users are affected by virus paranoia, interpreting every little computer system glitch as a sign of an unseen, rapidly proliferating virus. Viruses unfortunately do exist, but most minor computer malfunctions have nothing to do with viruses. The best way to avoid virus paranoia is to purchase and run a good virus-detection program. If these programs report that your system is clean, you have a high degree of confidence that the problems you're experiencing have nothing to do with computer viruses.

Recovering from Disasters

What happens if disaster strikes? Let's say you inadvertently erase your entire inventory database, and when you try to restore the database from backup disks, you find that someone has spilled coffee all over the disks and ruined them. Are you sunk?

Not if you've equipped your system with a good set of disaster-relief utilities. See to it that you've equipped yourself with all of the following:

- *File undelete utility:* When the operating system deletes a file, it doesn't actually erase the data; it just removes the file's name from the directory list. As long as you haven't written any more data to the file, you can undelete it with a file undelete utility. With Version 5.0 of DOS, this utility is finally part of this widely used operating system and need not be purchased separately.

- *Automatic file archiving utility:* The problem with a file undelete utility is that it won't work if the operating system has overwritten the file with a newly created or expanded file. An automatic file archiving utility stores all deleted files in a special, hidden directory. If you use this utility, you will always be able to recover deleted files. The only problem is you can't free up any space on your disk unless you override the utility.

- *Automatic safe format and unformat:* One of the worst computer-related disasters is an accidental format of a hard disk. An automatic safe format program replaces the operating system's normal format command with one that performs a *safe format*—a format operation that doesn't wipe out all the data. If you perform a safe format by accident, you easily can restore the whole disk. Safe format and unformat utilities are now included with DOS, starting with Version 5.0.

- A *disk-repair utility that extracts data from corrupted disks:* A serious problem arises when a disk's *hidden file table*—the table that tells the operating system exactly where the parts of each file are stored—becomes corrupted. To get the data from such a disk, you need a disk-repair utility that's capable of repairing the damaged table.

TIP

Central Point Software's PC Tools Version 7 offers by far the most comprehensive set of utilities for DOS and Windows systems. The package includes a complete, high-quality backup program, an undelete utility, automatic file archiving, safe format and unformat, a disk repair utility, and much more.

Optimizing Your Hard Disk

Your computer's operating system doesn't necessarily store a program or data file in a nice, contiguous unit, like a song on a cassette tape. On the contrary: it hunts down bits and pieces of free space, which may be here and there on the disk—and probably is, if you've created and deleted many files. This phenomenon, which is called *file fragmentation*, slows down your hard disk's data-retrieval speed: the read/write head has to travel all over the disk to retrieve all the pieces of a file. Worse, if you delete a fragmented file accidentally, you'll find that it is much more difficult—and perhaps impossible—to undelete the file.

If your disk becomes fragmented, you can significantly improve your disk's performance by running a *file defragmentation* utility such as Compress, a utility included in PC Tools Version 7. A file defragmentation utility rewrites your entire disk, and in so doing, accomplishes what all the king's men couldn't do for Humpty Dumpty: it puts all the parts of every file back together. The result is a significant improvement in your disk's retrieval speed.

Using a Disk-Expansion Utility

The hard disk that seemed so spacious when you bought it will quickly become stuffed with programs and data files. Do you have to buy a new disk? Not necessarily. A new alternative is a *disk expansion utility*. A disk expansion utility such as Stacker or Disk Doubler doesn't really expand your hard disk's size physically. It works by compressing the program and data files you're not using. When you want to use these files, the program quickly decompresses the files. It takes a little longer for programs to start and for files to open, but you get an apparent expansion of the amount of storage space available on your disk—you can store up to 70M or 80M of data and software on a 40M disk.

Securing Your System

You've already learned how to secure your system physically. This section focuses on preventing unauthorized access to vital or sensitive company information, such as payroll records, performance evaluations, and the company's books. You can protect these files from unauthorized access by requiring the user to type a password before the files appear on-screen. To provide even more protection, you can encrypt (code) the files so that it becomes impossible for even an expert hacker to access the data.

You can secure these files in two ways:

- *At the program level:* Almost all accounting programs, and some others, include password-protection features. By all means use these features, but don't forget the password! Bear in mind, though, that a knowledgeable and determined hacker will be able to access these files. Password protection is sufficient for most small businesses, however—as long as you don't write the password on a post-it note you stick on the monitor!

- *At the system level:* You can buy system utilities that encrypt sensitive files so that even the most talented hacker can't access them. An example is PC Secure, a utility included in PC Tools Version 7's amazing repertoire of system utilities. Encryption is needed only if you are working with highly sensitive or secret data, your computer installation is accessible to people whose loyalty you have reason to doubt, or the encryption is required as a prerequisite for contract work with a governmental or defense-related organization.

TIP

As you've already learned, an "erased file" isn't really erased; hackers know this and may scan your disk for sensitive files that you've copied to a floppy and erased from your hard disk. To erase a file completely so that there's no chance of recovering the data, you need a *file wipe* utility, which overwrites the file with random data.

Considering Other Utilities

Here's a sampling of some additional utilities you may find helpful:

- *Laptop file transfer:* If you use a laptop computer when you go to the field or on trips, you can buy a utility program that enables you to exchange files between your laptop and your desktop computers. An example is Commute, a utility included with PC Tools Version 7.

- *File switchers:* These utilities enable you to load two or more programs under DOS and switch among them at a keystroke. Task Swapper, a utility provided with MS-DOS Version 5.0, performs this function for DOS systems, while MultiFinder, which is built into Apple's System 7 operating system, performs this function for Macintoshes.

- *Disk caching utility:* This utility speeds your computer's operation significantly by setting aside a portion of the internal memory (RAM) for the most frequently accessed disk information. The utility runs automatically in the background; all you know is that your computer runs noticeably faster. Examples are SMARTDRIVE, a utility included with DOS Version 5.0, and PC-Cache, which is included with PC Tools System 7. The Macintosh's operating system includes a disk-caching utility that is activated through the control panel (a Finder utility).

- *Remote computer operation:* If you ever continue working in a home office after you close your business's doors for the day, you may find a remote computer operation utility (such as Carbon Copy) useful. It enables you to control a remote computer to which a computer is linked via telecommunications. You see on your screen what you would see on the remote computer's screen, as if you were actually sitting in front of the remote computer. You can use this utility, for example, to look up a transaction that occurred during the day or to add data that you didn't have time to type at work. The big disadvantage of these utilities is that you have to leave your office computer on all night. If you do, be sure to turn off the monitor when you leave.

- *System information:* This utility tells you all about your computer system: which ports are connected, how fast your microprocessor is running, how much memory you have and how it's allocated, and much more. A system information utility is included with PC Tools Version 7.

Summary

Here's an overview of this chapter's main points:

- Backing up regularly is required for serious business use of the computer. Purchase a backup utility and develop regular backup procedures.

- You can avoid most viruses by refusing pirated and bulletin board software, but a virus utility will assure that your system is free from virus codes.

- Purchase a good utility package such as PC Tools Version 7 or Norton Utilities. Although some system utilities are included with the new DOS and Macintosh operating systems, these other packages give you more utilities and a higher level of protection.

Software Suggestions

You'll find excellent system utilities for all three computing environments.

DOS Utility Programs

- *Central Point Anti-Virus (Central Point Software):* Detects and "cures" more than 400 common viruses. Free updates are available from an Oregon bulletin board.

- *Central Point Backup (Central Point Software):* The backup utility from PC Tools; works with a variety of tape drives.

- *Disk Optimizer (SoftLogic Solutions):* A file defragmentation program.

- *Fast! (Future Soft Engineering Inc.):* A disk-caching utility that can noticeably increase your computer's apparent speed.

- *Fastback Plus (Fifth Generation Systems, Inc.):* A backup program that's noted for speed and ease of use; not compatible with tape drives.

- *PC Tools (Central Point Software, Inc.):* An amazing variety of system utilities and desktop accessories, including a DOS file manager; DOS and Windows backup; DOS and Windows undelete utilities; disk defragmentation; disk surface analysis; virus detection; telecommunications; a mini-word processor; an appointment scheduler with to-do list; FAX support software; remote computer operation; laptop file transfer; and system-level security, including file encryption, disk caching, and much more. The backup utility works with a variety of tape drives.

- *QEMM-386 (Quarterdeck Office Systems):* A memory manager that takes full advantage of memory that DOS and Windows may not fully utilize, such as the upper memory area between 640K and 1M. Note, however, that MS-DOS 5.0 includes HIMEM.SYS and EMM 386.EXE, which provide the same capabilities.

- *Stacker (Stac Electronics):* A disk expansion program that automatically compresses files and applications when you're not using them, and decompresses files when you want to use them.

- *SuperStor (AddStor):* A disk expansion program that automatically compresses files and applications when you're not using them, and decompresses files when you want to use them. Includes disk defragmentation.

- *The Norton Anti-Virus (Symantec Corporation):* A respected anti-virus package with frequent updates.

- *The Norton Utilities (Symantec Corporation):* An outstanding backup utility that's fast, capable, and tolerant of errors. Works with a variety of tape drives. Also includes many other utilities, such as disk defragmentation and undelete.

Macintosh Utility Programs

- *Carbon Copy Mac (Microcom Software Division):* A remote computer utility for the Macintosh.

- *DiskDoubler (Salient):* A Macintosh disk expansion program that appears to double hard disk capacity by automatically compressing unused files and decompressing them when they're needed.

- *DiskFit (SuperMac Technology):* A fast file-backup and restore utility that performs incremental backups at high speed.

- *FastBack II for the Macintosh (Fifth Generation Systems, Inc.):* A Macintosh version of the popular DOS file-backup program.

- *FileGuard (ASD):* A complete security system for Macintosh computers, including file encryption and password protection.

- *The Norton Utilities for the Macintosh (Symantec Corporation):* A respected package of utilities, including disk defragmentation, accidental format recovery, and file undeletion.

- *The Norton Anti-Virus (Symantec Corporation):* A highly-regarded virus-detection-and-elimination program.

Glossary

3 1/2-inch disk A floppy disk originally developed by Sony Corporation and used as a secondary storage medium for personal computers. The magnetic disk is enclosed in a hard plastic case.

5 1/4-inch disk A floppy disk enclosed in a flexible plastic envelope and used as a secondary storage medium for personal computers. Synonymous with *minifloppy*.

a

abandon To clear a document, spreadsheet, or other work from the computer's memory without saving it to disk. The work is irretrievably lost.

absolute cell reference A spreadsheet cell reference that does not adjust when you copy a formula. Use an absolute cell reference to keep the reference the same when being copied.

access To retrieve data or program instructions from a secondary storage device or some other on-line computer device.

access time The time that elapses between the time the operating system issues an order for data retrieval and the time the data is ready for transfer from the disk.

adapter A circuit board that plugs into a computer's expansion bus and gives the computer additional capabilities.

add-in program An accessory or utility program designed to work with and extend the capabilities of an application program.

alignment 1. The adjustment of tolerances within a disk drive's mechanism so that read/write operations occur without error. 2. In word processing, the horizontal arrangement of lines on the page with respect to the left and right margins (flush left, centered, flush right, or justified).

American Standard Code for Information Interchange (ASCII) Pronounced "ask´-ee." A standard computer character set devised in 1968 to enable efficient data communication and achieve compatibility among different computer devices.

analytical graphics The preparation of charts and graphs to aid a professional in the interpretation of data.

anchored graphic A graph or picture that is fixed in an absolute position on the page so that text flows around it.

application The use of a computer for a specific purpose, such as writing a novel, printing payroll checks, or laying out the text and graphics of a newsletter. This term also is used to refer to a software program that accomplishes a specific task.

application program interface (API) System software that provides resources on which programmers can draw to create user interface features, such as pull-down menus and windows, and to route programs or data to local area networks (LANs).

application software Programs that perform specific tasks, such as word processing or database management; unlike system software that maintains and organizes the computer system and utilities that assist you in maintaining and organizing the system. Synonymous with *read-only memory* (ROM).

area graph In presentation graphics, a line graph in which the area below the line is filled in to emphasize the change in volume from one time period to the next. The x-axis (categories axis) is the horizontal axis, and the y-axis (values axis) is the vertical axis.

ASCII character set Pronounced "ask´-kee." A character set consisting only of the characters included in the original 128-character ASCII standard.

ASCII file Pronounced "ask´-kee." A file that contains only characters drawn from the ASCII character set.

automatic backup An application program feature that saves a document automatically at an interval the user specifies, such as every five or ten minutes. After a power outage or system crash, you see your work on-screen (up to the last time it was backed up) when you restart the application. This feature can help you avoid catastrophic work losses.

automatic font downloading The transmission of disk-based, downloadable printer fonts to the printer, done by an application program as the fonts are needed to complete a printing job.

b

background printing The printing of a document in the background while a program is active in the foreground.

bad page break In word processing and desktop publishing, an inappropriate or unattractive soft page break that has been inserted by the word processing or page layout program.

bad sector An area of a floppy or hard disk that will not reliably record data.

bank switching A way of expanding memory beyond an operating system's or microprocessor's limitations by switching rapidly between two banks of memory chips.

bar code A printed pattern of wide and narrow vertical bars used to represent numerical codes in machine-readable form.

bar code reader An input device equipped with a stylus that scans bar codes; the device then converts the bar code into a number displayed on-screen.

bar graph In presentation graphics, a graph with horizontal bars, commonly used to show the values of independent items. The x-axis (categories axis) is the vertical axis, and the y-axis (values axis) is the horizontal axis.

base font The default font a word processing program uses for a document unless you specifically instruct the program otherwise. You can choose a default base font for all documents or for just the document you are currently editing.

batch file A file containing a series of DOS commands executed one after the other, as if you typed them. Batch files are useful when you repeatedly need to type the same series of DOS commands. Almost all hard disk users have an AUTOEXEC.BAT file, a batch file that DOS loads at the start of every operating session.

baud Pronounced "bawd." A measure of the number of times per second that switching can occur in a communications channel.

baud rate The transmission speed of an asynchronous communications channel.

bit The basic unit of information in a binary numbering system (BInary digiT).

bit map The representation of a video image stored in a computer's memory. Each picture element (pixel) is represented by bits stored in the memory.

bit-mapped font A screen or printer font in which each character is composed of a pattern of dots. Bit-mapped fonts represent characters with a matrix of dots. To display or print bit-mapped fonts, the computer or printer must keep a full representation of each character in memory.

bit-mapped graphic A graphic image formed by a pattern of pixels (screen dots) and limited in resolution to the maximum screen resolution of the device being used. Bit-mapped graphics are produced by paint programs, such as MacPaint, SuperPaint, GEM Paint, PC Paintbrush, and some scanners.

bits per second (bps) In asynchronous communications, a measurement of data transmission speed.

block move A fundamental editing technique in word processing in which a marked block of text is cut from one location and inserted in another.

body type The font (normally 8- to 12-point) used to set the paragraphs of the text (distinguished from the typefaces used to set headings, subheadings, captions, and other typographical elements).

boilerplate A standard passage of text used over and over in letters, memos, or reports.

boot To initiate an automatic routine that clears the memory, loads the operating system, and prepares the computer for use.

browse mode In a database management program, a program mode in which data records are displayed in a columnar format for quick on-screen review. Synonymous with *list view* or *table view* in some programs.

bug A programming error that causes a program or a computer system to perform erratically, produce incorrect results, or crash.

built-in font A printer font encoded permanently in the printer's read-only memory (ROM).

built-in function In a spreadsheet program, a ready-to-use formula that performs mathematical, statistical, trigonometric, financial, calendrical, logical, and other calculations.

bulleted list chart In presentation graphics, a text chart used to communicate a series of ideas or to enumerate items of equal weight.

bulletin board system (BBS) A private telecommunications utility, usually set up by a personal computer hobbyist for the enjoyment of other hobbyists.

byte Pronounced "bite." Eight contiguous bits, the fundamental data word of personal computers.

C

calculated field In a database management program, a data field that contains the results of calculations performed on other fields.

cartridge font A printer font supplied in the form of a read-only memory (ROM) cartridge that plugs into a receptacle on Hewlett-Packard LaserJet printers and clones.

case-sensitive Responsive to the difference between upper- and lowercase letters. DOS is not case-sensitive; you can type DOS commands in upper- or lowercase letters.

case-sensitive search A search in which the program attempts to match the exact pattern of upper- and lowercase letters in the search string. A case-sensitive search for Porter, for example, matches Porter but not PORTER, porter, or pOrter.

cell In a spreadsheet, the rectangle formed by the intersection of a row and column. You can place constants, labels, or formulas in cells.

cell format In a spreadsheet, the way the program displays values and labels on-screen.

cell protection In a spreadsheet program, a format applied to a cell, a range of cells, or an entire file. The format prevents you from altering the contents of protected cells.

cell reference In a spreadsheet formula, a cell address that specifies the location of a value to be used to solve the formula. Cell references are the keys to a spreadsheet program's power and usefulness. A spreadsheet program would not be very useful if you had to write formulas with constants, such as $2+2$. Because formulas are not visible on the worksheet, you would have to edit the formula to perform the exploratory what-if recalculations that make spreadsheets useful. Using cell references instead of values, you write the formula as B1+B2. B1 and B2 are cell addresses. When used in a formula, they instruct the program to go to the named cell (such as B1) and to use the value appearing in that cell. If you want to change the constants, you don't have to edit the formula; you type a new constant in cell B1 or cell B2.

central processing unit (CPU) The computer's internal storage, processing, and control circuitry, including the arithmetic-logic unit (ALU), the control unit, and the primary storage.

character-based program In IBM PC-compatible computing, a program that relies on the IBM PC's built-in character set and block graphics rather than taking advantage of a windowing environment to display on-screen fonts and bit-mapped graphics.

character mode In IBM and IBM-compatible computers, a display adapter mode in which the computer displays only those characters contained in its built-in character set. Synonymous with *text mode*.

character set The fixed set of keyboard codes that a particular computer system uses.

checkwriting program A program designed to help individuals and small business owners to keep track of checking accounts, credit card accounts, tax records, and budgets. The industry leader is Quicken (Intuit).

chip A miniaturized electronic circuit mass-produced on a tiny chip or wafer of silicon.

Class A certification A Federal Communications Commission (FCC) certification that a given brand and model of a computer meets the FCC's Class A limits for radio frequency emissions, which are designed for commercial and industrial environments.

Class B certification A Federal Communications Commission (FCC) certification that a given brand and model of a computer meets the FCC's Class A limits for radio frequency emissions, which are designed for homes and home offices. Class B standards are tougher than Class A and are designed to protect radio and television reception in residential neighborhoods from excessive radio frequency interference (RFI) generated by computer usage. Class B computers are also shielded more efficiently from external interference.

clip art A collection of graphics images, stored on disk and available for use in a page layout or presentation graphics program.

clipboard In a windowing environment such as Microsoft Windows or the Macintosh Finder, a temporary storage area in memory where text and graphics are stored as you copy or move them.

clock/calendar board An adapter that includes a battery-powered clock for tracking the system time and date and is used in computers that lack such facilities on their motherboards.

clock speed The speed of the internal clock of a microprocessor that sets the pace (measured in megahertz [MHz]) at which operations proceed within the computer's internal processing circuitry.

clone A functional copy of a hardware device, such as a non-IBM PC-compatible computer that runs software and uses peripherals intended for an IBM PC-compatible computer, or of a program, such as a spreadsheet program that reads Lotus 1-2-3 files and recognizes most or all of the commands.

command-line operating system A command-driven operating system, such as DOS, that requires you to type commands at the keyboard.

communications parameters In telecommunications and serial printing, the settings (parameters) that customize serial communications for the hardware you are contacting.

communications program An application program that turns your computer into a terminal for transmitting data to and receiving data from distant computers through the telephone system.

compatibility The capability of a peripheral, a program, or an adapter to function with or substitute for a given make and model of computer. Also, the capability of one computer to run the software of another company's computer.

configuration The choices made in setting up a computer system or an application program so that it meets the user's needs.

constant In a spreadsheet program, a number you type directly into a cell or place in a formula.

conventional memory In any personal computer employing an Intel 8086, 8088, 80286, 80386, or 80486 microprocessor, the first 640K of the computer's random-access memory (RAM) that is accessible to programs running under DOS.

cost-benefit analysis A projection of the costs and benefits of installing a computer system. The analysis compares the costs of operating an enterprise with and without the computer system and calculates the return (if any) on the original investment.

crash An abnormal termination of program execution, usually (but not always) resulting in a frozen keyboard or an unstable state. In most cases, you must reboot the computer to recover from a crash.

d

data Factual information stored on magnetic media that can be used to generate calculations or to make decisions.

data deletion In a database management program, an operation that deletes records according to specified criteria.

data-entry form In a database management program, an on-screen form that makes entering and editing data easier by displaying only one data record on-screen at a time.

data field In a database management program, a space for a specified piece of information in a data record. In a table-oriented database management program, in which all retrieval operations produce a table with rows and columns, data fields are displayed as vertical columns.

data file A disk file containing the work you create with a program, unlike a program file that contains instructions for the computer.

data insertion In a database management program, an operation that appends new records to the database.

data integrity The accuracy, completeness, and internal consistency of the information stored in a database.

data modification In database management, an operation that updates one or more records according to specified criteria.

data record In a database management program, a complete unit of related data items expressed in named data fields. In a relational database, data record is synonymous with *row*.

data redundancy In database management, the repetition of the same data in two or more data records.

data retrieval In database management programs, an operation that retrieves information from the database according to the criteria specified in a query.

data type In a database management program, a definition that governs the kind of data that you can enter in a data field.

database A collection of related information about a subject organized in a useful manner that provides a base or foundation for procedures such as retrieving information, drawing conclusions, and making decisions.

database design The choice and arrangement of data fields in a database so that fundamental errors (such as data redundancy and repeating fields) are avoided or minimized.

database management Tasks related to creating, maintaining, organizing, and retrieving information from a database.

database management program An application program that provides the tools for data retrieval, modification, deletion, and insertion. Such programs also can create a database and produce meaningful output on the printer or on-screen. In personal computing, three kinds of database management programs exist: flat-file, relational, and text-oriented.

database management system (DBMS) 1. In mainframe computing, a computer system organized for the systematic management of a large collection of information. 2. In personal computing, a program such as dBASE with similar information storage, organization, and retrieval capacities, sometimes including simultaneous access to multiple databases through a shared field (relational database management).

database structure In database management, a definition of the data records in which information is stored, including: the number of data fields; a set of field definitions that for each field specify the type of information, the length, and other characteristics; and a list of field names.

default extension The three-letter extension an application program uses to save and retrieve files, unless you override the default by specifying another file name.

default font The font that the printer uses unless you instruct otherwise.

desktop publishing (DTP) The use of a personal computer as an inexpensive production system for generating typeset-quality text and graphics. Desktop publishers often merge text and graphics on the same page and print pages on a high-resolution laser printer or typesetting machine.

disk capacity The storage capacity of a floppy disk or hard disk, measured in kilobytes (K) or megabytes (M).

disk drive A secondary storage medium such as a floppy disk drive or a hard disk. This term usually refers to floppy disk drives.

display type A typeface, usually 14 points or larger and differing in style from the body type, that is used for headings and subheadings.

dot-matrix printer An impact printer that forms text and graphics images by pressing the ends of pins against a ribbon.

dot pitch The size of the smallest dot that a monitor can display on-screen. Dot pitch determines a monitor's maximum resolution.

dots per inch (dpi) A measure of screen and printer resolution that counts the dots that the device can produce per linear inch.

double-click To click the mouse button twice in rapid succession. In many programs, double-clicking extends the action that results from single-clicking; double-clicking on a word, for example, selects the whole word rather than just one character. Double-clicking is also used not only to select an item, but to initiate an action. In a file list, for example, double-clicking a file name selects and opens the file.

double density A widely used recording technique that packs twice as much data on a floppy or hard disk as the earlier single-density standard.

downloadable font A printer font that must be transferred from the computer's (or the printer's) hard disk drive to the printer's random-access memory before the font can be used.

downloading The reception and storage of a program or data file from a distant computer through data communications links.

downloading utility A utility program that transfers downloadable fonts from your computer's (or printer's) hard disk to the printer's random-access memory (RAM).

draw program A computer graphics program that uses object-oriented graphics to produce line art.

e

electronic mail The use of electronic communications media to send textual messages (such as letters, memos, and reports).

emphasis The use of a non-Roman type style, such as underlining, italic, bold typefaces, and small caps, to highlight a word or phrase.

entry line In a spreadsheet program, the line in which the characters you type appear. The program does not insert the characters into the current cell until you press Enter.

expanded memory In IBM PC-compatible computers, a method of getting beyond the 640K DOS memory barrier by swapping programs and data in and out of the main memory at high speeds.

expanded memory board An adapter that adds expanded memory to an IBM-compatible computer.

expanded memory emulator A utility program for '386 and '486 IBM-compatible computers that uses extended memory to simulate expanded memory.

expanded memory manager A utility program that manages expanded memory in an IBM-compatible computer equipped with an expanded memory board.

expansion bus An extension of the computer's data bus and address bus that includes a number of receptacles (slots) for adapter boards.

expansion slot A receptacle connected to the computer's expansion bus, designed to accept adapters.

extended memory In '286 or later IBM-compatible computers, the random-access memory (RAM), if any, above 1M.

extended memory manager A utility program that allows DOS programs written to conform to the XMS standard to access extended memory.

eXtended Memory Specification (XMS) A set of rules for programmers to follow so that DOS programs can access extended memory in an orderly way. The device driver HIMEM.SYS, or an equivalent memory management program, must be present in your computer's CONFIG.SYS file before XMS memory can be accessed. The specification was jointly developed by Lotus Development Corporation, Intel Corporation, Microsoft Corporation, and AST.

extension A three-letter suffix to a DOS file name that describes the file's contents.

external command In DOS and OS/2, a command that cannot be used unless the program file is present in the current drive or directory.

extremely low-frequency (ELF) emission The magnetic field generated by commonly-used electrical appliances such as electric blankets, hair dryers, food mixers, and computer display monitors, and extending one to two meters from the source. ELF fields are known to cause tissue changes and fetal abnormalities in laboratory test animals, and may be related to reproductive anomalies and cancers among frequent users of computer displays.

f

fax board An adapter that fits into the expansion slot of a personal computer, providing much of the functionality of a fax machine at a significantly lower cost.

FCC certification An attestation, formerly made by the U.S. Federal Communications Commission, that a given brand and model of a computer meets the FCC's limits for radio frequency emissions.

field definition In a database management program, a list of the attributes that define the type of information that the user can enter into a data field. The field definition also determines how the field's contents appear on-screen.

field name In a database management program, a name given to a data field that helps you identify the field's contents.

file A named collection of information stored as an apparent unit on a secondary storage medium such as a disk drive.

file allocation table (FAT) A hidden table on a floppy disk or hard disk that stores information about how files are stored in distinct (and not necessarily contiguous) sectors.

file format The patterns and standards a program uses to store data on disk.

file name A name assigned to a file so that the operating system can find the file. You assign file names when the files are created. Every file on a disk must have a unique name.

flat-file database management program A database management program that stores, organizes, and retrieves information from one file at a time. Such programs lack relational database management features.

floppy disk A removable and widely used secondary storage medium that uses a magnetically sensitive flexible disk enclosed in a plastic envelope or case.

font One complete collection of letters, punctuation marks, numbers, and special characters with a consistent and identifiable typeface, weight (Roman or bold), posture (upright or italic), and font size.

footer In a word processing or page layout program, a short version of a document's title or other text positioned at the bottom of every page of the document.

format Any method of arranging information for storage, printing, or displaying.

g

global format In a spreadsheet program, a numeric format or label alignment choice that applies to all cells in the worksheet. With most programs, you can override the global format by defining a range format for certain cells.

graphical user interface (GUI) A design for the part of the program that interacts with the user, which takes full advantage of the bit-mapped graphics displays of personal computers.

h

hard disk A secondary storage medium that uses several nonflexible disks coated with a magnetically sensitive material and housed, together with the recording heads, in a hermetically sealed mechanism. Typical storage capacities range from 10M to 140M.

hardware platform A computer hardware standard, such as IBM PC-compatible or Macintosh personal computers, in which a comprehensive approach to the computer solution of a problem can be based.

header Repeated text (such as a page number and a short version of a document's title) that appears at the top of each page in a document.

high density A storage technique for secondary storage media such as floppy disks. This technique requires the use of extremely fine-grained magnetic particles. High-density disks are more expensive to manufacture than double-density disks. High-density disks, however, can store 1M or more of information on one 5 1/4- or 3 1/2-inch disk.

high memory area (HMA) In a DOS computer, the first 64K of extended memory above 1M. Programs that conform to the eXtended Memory Specification (XMS) can use HMA as a direct extension of conventional memory.

high resolution In computer monitors and printers, a visual definition that is sufficient to produce well-defined characters even at large type sizes, as well as smoothly-defined curves in graphic images. A high-resolution video adapter and monitor is capable of displaying 1,024 pixels horizontally by 768 pixels vertically, such as a Super VGA monitors; a high-resolution printer is capable of printing at least 300 dots per inch (dpi).

highlight A character, word, text block, or command displayed in reverse video on-screen. This term sometimes is used synonymously with *cursor*.

i

IBM Personal Computer A personal computer based on the Intel 8088 microprocessor.

IBM Personal Computer AT A personal computer, based on the Intel 80286 microprocessor, that was introduced in 1984.

IBM Personal Computer XT A personal computer, based on the Intel 8088 microprocessor and including a hard disk, that was introduced in 1983.

IBM Personal System/2 A series of personal computers introduced in 1987 based on the Intel 8086, 80286, and 80386 microprocessors. Most PS/2s contain a proprietary expansion bus format.

industry-standard user interface A set of *de facto*, unregulated standards that programmers can follow as they design the parts of a program that interact with the computer user.

integrated accounting package An accounting program that includes all the major accounting functions: general ledger, accounts payable, accounts receivable, payroll, and inventory.

integrated circuit A semiconductor circuit that contains more than one transistor and other electronic components.

integrated program A program that combines two or more software functions, such as word processing and database management.

Intel 8086 A microprocessor introduced in 1978 with a full 16-bit data bus structure.

Intel 8088 A microprocessor introduced in 1978 with an 8-bit external data bus and an internal 16-bit data bus structure used in the original IBM Personal Computer.

Intel 80286 A microprocessor introduced in 1984 with a 16-bit data bus structure and the capability to address up to 16M of random-access memory (RAM).

Intel 80287/Intel 80387 Numeric coprocessors designed to work (respectively) with the Intel 80286 and 80386.

Intel 80386 A microprocessor introduced in 1986 with a 32-bit data bus structure and the capability to address up to 4 gigabytes of main memory directly.

Intel 80386SX A microprocessor introduced in 1988 with all the electronic characteristics of the Intel 80386, except that the chip has a 16-bit external data bus structure that enables it to use the inexpensive peripherals developed for the Intel 80286.

Intel 80486 A microprocessor introduced in 1989 with a full 32-bit data bus structure and the capability to address 64 gigabytes of main memory directly.

interface An electronic circuit that governs the connection between two hardware devices and helps them exchange data reliably. Synonymous with *port*.

interface standard In hard disk drives, a set of specifications for the connection between the drive controller and the drive electronics. Common interface standards in personal computing include ST606/ST412, ESDI, and SCSI.

internal command In DOS and OS/2, a command such as DIR or COPY that remains in memory and is always available when the DOS or OS/2 prompt is visible on-screen.

j

justification The alignment of multiple lines of text along the left margin, the right margin, or both margins.

k

kilobyte (K) The basic unit of measurement for computer memory, equal to 1,024 bytes.

The prefix *kilo* suggests 1,000, but this world contains twos, not tens: $2^{10} =$ 1,024. Because one byte is the same as one character in personal computing, a memory of 1K can contain 1,024 characters (letters, numbers, or punctuation marks).

Early personal computers (mid-1970s) offered as little as 16K or 32K of random-access memory (RAM); memory chips were expensive. In IBM PC-compatible computing, 640K is considered a standard figure (the maximum under DOS); today, Macintosh computers are equipped with at least 1M of RAM.

l

laptop computer A lightweight, battery-powered, portable computer that uses a lightweight display device such as a liquid crystal display.

True laptops that weigh less than 12 pounds are different from *luggables*, portable computers that are too heavy to be carried around like a briefcase. The better laptops use backlit or gas-plasma screens that are easier to read, but these brighter screens consume more electricity, and require more frequent recharges.

laser printer A high-resolution printer that uses a version of the electrostatic reproduction technology of copying machines to fuse text and graphic images to the page.

LaserJet A series of laser printers manufactured by Hewlett-Packard and widely used in IBM PC-compatible computing.

LaserWriter A series of PostScript laser printers manufactured by Apple Computer and used with Macintosh and IBM PC-compatible computers.

line graph In presentation and analytical graphics, a graph that uses lines to show the variations of data over time or to show the relationship between two numeric variables. In general, the x-axis (categories axis) is aligned horizontally, and the y-axis (values axis) is aligned vertically. A line graph, however, may have two y-axes.

local area network (LAN) The linkage of personal and other computers within a limited area by high-performance cables so that users can exchange information, share expensive peripherals, and draw on the resources of a massive secondary storage unit (called a file server).

low resolution In computer monitors and printers, a visual definition that is not sufficient to produce well-defined characters or smoothly defined curves in graphic images, resulting in characters and graphics with jagged edges.

m

Macintosh A family of personal computers introduced by Apple Computer in 1984 that features a graphical user interface.

Macintosh II An open-bus, high-performance personal computer introduced by Apple Computer in 1987.

Macintosh Classic The successor to the popular Macintosh Plus and Macintosh SE, an entry-level Macintosh that employs the 68000 microprocessor running at 8MHz.

macro A stored list of two or more application program commands that, when retrieved, replays the commands to accomplish a task. Macros automate tedious and often-repeated tasks (such as saving and backing up a file up to a floppy) that would otherwise require the user to press several command keys or choose several options from menus.

magnetic disk In secondary storage, a random-access storage medium that is the most popular method for storing and retrieving computer programs and data files. In personal computing, common magnetic disks include 5 1/4-inch floppy disks, 3 1/2-inch floppy disks, and hard disks of various sizes.

magnetic media In secondary storage, the use of magnetic techniques to store and retrieve data on disks or tapes coated with magnetically sensitive materials.

magnetic tape In secondary storage, a high-capacity mass storage and backup medium.

mail merge A utility common in full-featured word processing programs that draws information from a database—usually a mailing list—to print multiple copies of a document. Each copy contains one or part of one of the database records and text that does not vary from copy to copy.

maintenance release A program revision that corrects a minor bug or makes a minor new feature available, such as a new printer driver. Maintenance releases are usually numbered in tenths (3.2) or hundreds (2.01), to distinguish them from major program revisions. Synonymous with *incremental update*.

megabyte (M) A unit of memory measurement equal to approximately one million bytes (1,048,576 bytes).

megahertz (MHz) A unit of measurement equal to one million electrical vibrations or cycles per second. Commonly used to compare the clock speeds of computers.

memory The computer's primary storage (random-access memory, or RAM, for example), as distinguished from its secondary storage (disk drives, for example).

memory-management program A utility program that increases the apparent size of random-access memory (RAM) by making expanded memory, extended memory, or virtual memory available for the execution of programs.

microcomputer Any computer with its arithmetic-logic unit (ALU) and control unit contained on one integrated circuit called a microprocessor.

microprocessor An integrated circuit that contains the arithmetic/logic unit (ALU) and control unit of a computer's central processing unit (CPU).

Microsoft Mouse A mouse and associated software for IBM and IBM-compatible personal computers, including IBM's PS/1 and PS/2 computers.

Microsoft Windows A windowing environment and application user interface (API) for DOS that brings to IBM-format computing some of the graphical user interface features of the Macintosh, such as pull-down menus, multiple typefaces, desk accessories (a clock, calculator, calendar, and notepad, for example), and the capability of moving text and graphics from one program to another via a clipboard.

millisecond (ms) A unit of measurement, equal to one-thousandth of a second, commonly used to specify the access time of hard disk drives.

minimize In Microsoft Windows, to shrink a window so that it collapses to an icon on the desktop. You minimize a window by clicking the minimize button (the down arrow in the right corner) or by choosing Minimize from the Control menu.

mode The operating state in which you place a program by choosing among a set of exclusive operating options. Within a given mode, certain commands and operations are available, but you may need to change modes to use other commands or operations.

modem A device that converts the digital signals generated by the computer's serial port to the modulated, analog signals required for transmission over a telephone line and transforms incoming analog signals to their digital equivalents. In personal computing, people frequently use modems to exchange programs and data with other computers, and to access on-line information services such as the Dow Jones News/Retrieval Service.

monochrome monitor A monitor that displays one color against a black or white background.

monospace A typeface such as Courier in which the width of all characters is the same, producing output that looks like typed characters.

motherboard A large, printed, computer circuit board that contains the computer's central processing unit (CPU), microprocessor support chips, random-access memory, and expansion slots. Synonymous with *logic board*.

mousable interface A program's user interface that responds to mouse input for such functions as selecting text, choosing commands from menus, and scrolling the screen.

mouse An input device, equipped with one or more control buttons, housed in a palm-sized case and designed to roll about on the table next to the keyboard. As the mouse moves, its circuits relay signals that move a pointer on-screen.

MS-DOS The standard, single-user operating system of IBM and IBM-compatible computers.

MultiColor Graphics Array (MCGA) A video display standard of IBM's Personal System/2. MCGA adds 64 gray-scale shades to the CGA standard and provides the EGA standard resolution of 640 x 350 pixels with 16 possible colors.

multiple program loading An operating system that enables you to start more than one program at a time; only one of the programs is active at any one time, however. You switch from one program to another by pressing a key.

multitasking The execution of more than one program at a time on a computer system. Multitasking should not be confused with multiple program loading, in which two or more programs are present in RAM, but only one program executes at a time.

multiuser system A computer system that enables more than one person to access programs and data at the same time.

n

nanosecond (ns) A unit of time equal to one billionth of a second.

network drive In a local area network, a disk drive that's made available to you through the network, as distinguished from a drive that's directly connected to the workstation you're using.

newspaper columns A page format in which two or more columns of text are printed vertically on the page so that the text flows down one column and continues at the top of the next.

Sometimes called snaking columns to suggest the flow of text, newspaper columns differ from side-by-side columns in which paragraphs are printed in linked pairs—one to the left and one to the right.

non-Windows application A DOS application program that wasn't designed to take full advantage of Microsoft Window's application program interface, including on-screen display of fonts and the Windows user interface conventions. Microsoft Windows can run non-Windows applications just as they would run under DOS. In Windows' standard or '386 enhanced modes, you can switch from one non-Windows application to another without quitting a program. In '386 Enhanced mode, you can multitask two or more DOS applications, each in its own window. Industry experts believe that many copies of Microsoft Windows have been purchased to run DOS applications in this way.

O

object-oriented graphic A graphic image composed of discrete objects, such as lines, circles, ellipses, and boxes, that you can move independently.

off-screen formatting In a word processing program, a formatting technique in which formatting commands are embedded in the text so that they affect printing, but the formatting is not visible on-screen.

open architecture A computer system in which all the system specifications are made public so that other companies will develop add-on products such as adapters for the system.

operating system A master control program for a computer that manages the computer's internal functions and provides you with a means to control the computer's operations.

outline font A printer or screen font in which a mathematical formula generates each character, producing a graceful and undistorted outline of the character, which the printer then fills in at its maximum resolution.

output The process of displaying or printing the results of processing operations.

Overtype mode An editing mode in word processing programs and other software that enables you to enter and edit text; the characters you type erase existing characters.

In WordPerfect, the Overtype mode is called the Typeover mode, which you can toggle on and off by pressing the Ins key.

overwrite To write data on a magnetic disk in the same area where other data is stored (destroying the original data).

p

page description language (PDL) A programming language that describes printer output in device-independent commands.

page layout program In desktop publishing, an application program that assembles text and graphics from a variety of files, with which you can determine the precise placement, sizing, scaling, and cropping of material in accordance with the page design represented on-screen.

paint program A program that enables users to paint the screen by switching on or off the individual dots or pixels that make up a bit-mapped screen display.

parallel port A port that supports the synchronous, high-speed flow of data along parallel lines to peripheral devices, especially parallel printers.

personal computer A stand-alone computer equipped with all the system, utility, and application software, and the input/output devices and other peripherals that an individual needs to perform one or more tasks.

pie graph In presentation graphics, a graph that displays a data series as a circle to emphasize the relative contribution of each data item to the whole.

point 1. To move the mouse pointer on the screen without clicking the button. 2. In typography, the fundamental unit of measure. 72 points equal an inch.

pointer An on-screen symbol, usually an arrow, that shows the current position of the mouse. In database management programs, a record number in an index that stores the actual physical location of the data record.

point-of-sale software A program that transforms a personal computer into a cash register, invoicing, and inventory-tracking system for retail businesses.

port 1. An entry/exit boundary mechanism that governs and synchronizes the flow of data into and out of the central processing unit (CPU) to external devices such as printers and modems. Synonymous with *interface*. 2. Reprogramming an application so that it runs on another type of computer.

PostScript A sophisticated page description language for medium- to high-resolution printing devices.

PostScript laser printer A laser printer that includes the processing circuitry needed to decode and interpret printing instructions phrased in PostScript—a page description language (PDL) widely used in desktop publishing.

power line filter An electrical device that smooths out the peaks and valleys of the voltage delivered at the wall socket.

power surge A brief and often very large increase in line voltage that is caused by appliances turning off, by lightning strikes, or by the reestablishment of power after a power outage.

precedence The order in which a spreadsheet program performs the operations in a formula. Typically, the program performs exponentiation (such as squaring a number) before multiplication and division; the program then performs addition and subtraction.

presentation graphics Text charts, column graphs, bar graphs, pie graphs, and other charts and graphs, which you enhance so that they are visually appealing and easily understood by your audience.

presentation graphics program An application program designed to create and enhance charts and graphs so that they are visually appealing and easily understood by an audience.

primary storage The computer's main memory directly accessible to the central processing unit (CPU), unlike secondary storage, such as disk drives.

In personal computers, primary storage consists of the random-access memory (RAM) and the read-only memory (ROM).

printer control language The command set used to control a printer of a given brand. Common printer control languages include the Epson command set for dot-matrix printers, the Hewlett-Packard Printer Control Language (HPPCL) for IBM-compatible laser printers, and the Diablo command set for letter-quality printers.

printer driver A file that contains information a program needs to print your work with a given brand and model of printer.

printer font A font available for printing, unlike screen fonts available for displaying text on-screen.

program A list of instructions in a computer-programming language that tells the computer what to do.

prompt A symbol or phrase that appears on-screen informing you that the computer is ready to accept input.

proportional spacing The allocation of character widths proportional to the character shape, so that a narrow character such as i receives less space than a wide character such as m.

pull-down menu A method of providing a command menu that appears on-screen only after you click the menu's name.

q

query In database management, a search question that tells the program what kind of data should be retrieved from the database.

query by example (QBE) In database management programs, a query technique that prompts you to type the search criteria into a template resembling the data record.

r

radio button In a graphical user interface, the round option buttons that appear in dialog boxes. Unlike check boxes, radio buttons are mutually exclusive; you can pick only one of the radio button options.

random access An information storage and retrieval technique in which the information can be accessed directly without having to go through a sequence of locations.

random-access memory (RAM) The computer's primary working memory in which program instructions and data are stored so that they are accessible directly to the central processing unit (CPU).

range In a spreadsheet program, a cell or a rectangular group of cells.

range format In a spreadsheet program, a numeric format or label alignment format that applies to only a range and overrides the global format.

range name In a spreadsheet program, a range of cells to which you attach a distinctive name.

read-only In DOS, a file whose read-only file attribute has been set so that the file can be viewed but not deleted or modified.

read-only memory (ROM) Pronounced "rahm." The portion of a computer's primary storage that does not lose its contents when the current is switched off and contains essential system programs, which neither you nor the computer can erase.

read/write The capability of an internal memory or secondary storage device to record data (write) and to play back data previously recorded or saved (read).

record-oriented database management program A database management program that displays data records as the result of query operations, unlike a table-oriented program in which the result of all data query operations is a table. Purists argue that a true relational database management program always treats data in tabular form, and any program that displays records as the result of queries, such as dBASE, does not deserve to call itself relational even if the program can work with two or more databases at a time.

relational database management An approach to database management in which data is stored in two-dimensional data tables. The program can work with two data tables at the same time, relating the information through links established by a common column or field.

relational database management system (RDBMS) A relational database management program, especially one that comes with all the necessary support programs and documentation needed to create, install, and maintain custom database applications.

relational operator A symbol used to specify the relationship between two numeric values.

relative cell reference In a spreadsheet program, a formula's cell reference adjusted when you copy the formula to another cell or a range of cells.

release number The number, usually a decimal number, that identifies an incrementally improved version of a program, rather than a major revision, which is numbered using an integer.

reliability The capability of computer hardware or software to perform as the user expects and to do so consistently, without failures or erratic behavior.

removable storage media A secondary storage device in which the actual storage medium, such as a magnetic disk, can be removed from the drive for safekeeping.

repetitive strain injury (RSI) A serious and potentially debilitating occupational illness caused by prolonged repetitive hand and arm movements, which may damage, inflame, or kill nerves in the hands, arms, shoulder, or neck.

resolution A measurement—usually expressed in linear dots per inch (dpi), horizontally and vertically—of the sharpness of an image generated by an output device such as a monitor or printer.

reverse video In monochrome monitors, a means of highlighting text on the display screen so that normally dark characters are displayed as bright characters on a dark background, or normally bright characters are displayed as dark characters on a bright background.

RGB monitor A color digital monitor that accepts separate inputs for red, green, and blue, and produces a much sharper image than composite color monitors.

root directory The top-level directory on a disk, the one DOS creates when you format the disk.

row In a spreadsheet program, a horizontal block of cells running across the breadth of the spreadsheet. In most programs, rows are numbered sequentially from the top. In a database, a row is the same as a record or data record.

S

sans serif Pronounced "san serr´-if." A typeface that lacks serifs, the fine cross strokes across the ends of the main strokes of a character.

scaling In presentation graphics, the adjustment of the y-axis (values axis) chosen by the program so that differences in the data are highlighted.

scanned image A bit-mapped, or TIFF, image generated by an optical scanner.

scanner A peripheral device that digitizes artwork or photographs and stores the image as a file that can be merged with text in many word processing and page layout programs.

scatter diagram An analytical graphic in which data items are plotted as points on two numeric axes.

screen font A bit-mapped font designed to mimic the appearance of printer fonts when displayed on medium-resolution monitors. Modern laser printers can print text with a resolution of 300 dpi or more, but video displays, except for the most expensive professional units, lack such high resolution and cannot display typefaces with such precision and beauty. What you see isn't necessarily what you get.

scroll To move the window horizontally or vertically so that its position over a document or worksheet changes.

scroll bar/scroll box A method of providing the user with horizontal and vertical scrolling capabilities by placing rectangular scrolling areas on the right and bottom borders of the window. You scroll the document horizontally or vertically by clicking the scroll box or scroll arrows, or by dragging the scroll box.

secondary storage A nonvolatile storage medium such as a disk drive that stores program instructions and data even when the power is switched off. Synonymous with *auxiliary storage* and *external storage*.

secondary storage medium The specific secondary storage technology used to store and retrieve data, such as magnetic disks, magnetic tapes, or optical disks.

select To highlight text so that the program can identify the text on which you want the next operation to be performed.

selection 1. A unit of text, ranging from one character to many pages, highlighted in reverse video for formatting or editing purposes. 2. In programming, a branch or conditional control structure. 3. In database management, the retrieval of records by using a query.

serial mouse A mouse designed to be connected directly to one of the computer's serial ports.

serial port A port that synchronizes and makes asynchronous communication between the computer and devices such as serial printers, modems, and other computers easier.

serial printer A printer designed to be connected to the computer's serial port.

serif The fine cross strokes across the ends of the main strokes of a character.

service bureau A firm that provides a variety of publication services such as graphics file format conversion, optical scanning of graphics, and typesetting on high-resolution printers such as Linotronics and Varitypers.

shareware Copyrighted computer programs made available on a trial basis; if you like and decide to use the program, you are expected to pay a fee to the program's author.

single density The earliest magnetic recording scheme for digital data used a technique called frequency modulation (FM) that resulted in low information densities (such as 90K per disk).

Disk drives designed for FM recording, therefore, could use disks (single-density disks) with relatively large-grained magnetic particles. Single-density recording disks have been superseded by double-density storage devices that use modified frequency modulation (MFM) storage techniques, double-density disks with finer grained particles, and high-density disks with even finer particles.

single-sided disk A floppy disk designed so that only one side of the disk can be used for read/write operations. Single-sided disks have low storage capacities and are used infrequently in today's personal computer systems.

single in-line memory module (SIMM) A plug-in memory module containing all the chips needed to add 256K or 1M of random-access memory to your computer.

slide show In presentation graphics, a predetermined list of on-screen charts and graphs displayed one after the other.

Small Computer System Interface (SCSI) Pronounced "scuzzy." An interface standard for peripheral devices such as hard disk drives and laser printers.

soft hyphen A hyphen formatted so that the program does not use it unless the hyphen is needed to improve the spacing on a line. Synonymous with *optional hyphen*.

soft page break In a word processing program, a page break inserted by the program based on the current state of the text; the page break may move up or down if insertions, deletions, margin changes, or page size changes occur.

software piracy The unauthorized and illegal duplication of copyrighted software without the permission of the software publisher.

sort An operation that reorders data in alphabetical or numerical order.

sort key In database management, the data field used to determine the order in which data records are arranged.

sort order The order in which a program arranges data when performing a sort. Most programs sort data in the standard order of ASCII characters. Synonymous with *collating sequence*.

spell checker A program often incorporated in word processing programs that checks for the correct spelling of words in a document. Each word is compared against a file of correctly spelled words.

split screen A display technique in which the screen is divided into two windows. In word processing programs that have split screen capabilities, independently displaying two parts of the same document is usually possible, as is displaying two different documents.

spreadsheet program A program that simulates an accountant's worksheet on-screen and enables you to embed hidden formulas that perform calculations on the visible data.

stand-alone computer A computer system dedicated to meeting the computing needs of a person working in isolation.

status line A line of an application program's display screen that describes the state of the program.

streaming tape drive A secondary storage device that uses continous tape, contained in a cartridge, for backup purposes.

strikeout An attribute, such as type, struck through with a hyphen to mark text.

style sheet In some word processing and page layout programs, a stored collection of user-created text-formatting definitions containing information such as typestyle, alignment, and line spacing specifications.

subdirectory In DOS, OS/2, and UNIX, a directory listed within a directory that, when opened, reveals another directory containing files and additional subdirectories.

submenu A set of lower level commands available when you choose a top-level command.

surge A momentary and sometimes destructive increase in the amount of voltage delivered through a power line.

surge protector An inexpensive electrical device that prevents high-voltage surges from reaching a computer and damaging its circuitry.

system disk A disk containing the operating system and all files necessary to start the computer.

system prompt In a command-line operating system, the prompt that indicates the operating system's availability for system maintenance tasks such as copying files, formatting disks, and loading programs. In DOS, the system prompt (a letter designating the disk drive, followed by a greater-than symbol) shows the current drive. When you see the prompt C>, for example, drive C is the current drive, and DOS is ready to accept instructions. You can customize the system prompt by using the PROMPT command.

system unit The case that houses the computer's internal processing circuitry, including the power supply, motherboard, disk drives, plug-in boards, and a speaker. Some personal computer system units also contain a monitor.

t

template In an application program, a document or worksheet that includes the text or formulas needed for some generic applications and is available repeatedly for customization.

terabyte A unit of memory measurement approximately equal to one trillion bytes (actually 1,099,511,627,776 bytes).

terminate-and-stay-resident (TSR) program An accessory or utility program designed to remain in the computer's random-access memory (RAM) at all times so that the user can activate it with a keystroke, even if another program also is in memory.

toner The electrically charged ink used in laser printers.

toner cartridge In laser printers, a cartridge containing the electrically charged ink that the printer fuses to the page.

tractor feed A printer paper-feed mechanism in which continuous (fanfold) paper is pulled (or pushed) into and through the printer using a sprocket wheel. The sprockets fit into prepunched holes on the left and right edges of the paper.

Trojan Horse A computer program that appears to perform a valid function but contains, hidden in its code, instructions that cause damage (sometimes severe) to the systems on which it runs.

troubleshooting The process of determining why a computer system or specific hardware device is malfunctioning.

turnkey system A computer system developed for a specific application, such as a point-of-sale terminal, and delivered ready-to-run, with all necessary application programs and peripherals.

typeface The distinctive design of a set of type, distinguished from its weight (such as bold or italic) and size.

typesetting The production of camera-ready copy on a high-end typesetting machine such as a Linotronic or Varityper.

type size The size of a font, measured in points (approximately 1/72 inch) from the top of the tallest ascender to the bottom of the lowest descender.

u

undelete utility A utility program that can restore a file accidentally erased from disk if no other data has been written to the disk since the erasure occurred.

unformat utility A utility program that is capable of restoring the data on a disk that has been inadvertently formatted. If the disk has been formatted using a safe format technique, the data is restored quickly. If the disk has been not been safe formatted, it is still possible to recover the data if you have been using the MIRROR utility provided with DOS 5.0 or certain utility programs, such as PC Tools.

uninterruptable power supply (UPS) A battery capable of supplying continuous power to a computer system in the event of a power failure.

user default A user-defined program operating preference, such as the default margins to be used in every new document that a word processing program creates.

user-friendly A program or computer system designed so that persons who lack extensive computer experience or training can use the system without becoming confused or frustrated.

user group A voluntary association of users of a specific computer or program who meet regularly to exchange tips and techniques, hear presentations by computer experts, and obtain public domain software and shareware.

user interface All the features of a program or computer that govern the way people interact with the computer.

utility program A program that assists you in maintaining and improving the efficiency of a computer system.

v

vaccine A computer program designed to detect the presence of a computer virus in a system.

value-added reseller (VAR) An organization that repackages and improves hardware manufactured by an original-equipment manufacturer (OEM).

vaporware A program still under development that is heavily marketed even though no one knows for sure whether the development problems will be solved.

vector graphics A graphics display technology in which images are formed on-screen by directly controlling the motions of the electron gun to form a specific image, such as a line or a circle, rather than requiring the gun to travel across the whole screen line-by-line (as in raster displays). Vector graphics are not used for personal computer displays but are occasionally used for professional workstations in such fields as architectural or engineering design.

version A specific release of a software or hardware product.

vertical application An application program created for a narrowly defined market, such as the members of a profession or a specific type of retail store.

video adapter The adapter that generates the output required to display computer text (and, with some adapters, graphics) on a monitor.

Video Graphics Array (VGA) A color bit-mapped graphics display standard, introduced by IBM in 1987 with its PS/2 computers. VGA adapters and analog monitors display as many as 256 continuously variable colors simultaneously with a resolution of 640 pixels horizontally by 480 vertically.

video RAM The random-access memory (RAM) needed by a video adapter to construct and retain a full-screen image of a high-resolution video display. As much as 512K of video RAM may be needed by VGA video adapters.

view In database management programs, an on-screen display of only part of the information in a database—the part that meets the criteria specified in a query.

virus A computer program, designed as a prank or sabotage, that replicates itself by attaching to other programs and carrying out unwanted and sometimes damaging operations.

W

warm boot A system restart performed after the system has been powered and operating; a restart is the electronic equivalent of turning on the system because it clears the memory and reloads the operating system.

weight The overall lightness or darkness of a typeface design, or the gradations of lightness to darkness within a font family.

what-if analysis In spreadsheet programs, an important form of data exploration in which key variables are changed to see the effect on the results of the computation.

what-you-see-is-what-you-get (WYSIWYG) Pronounced "wizzy wig." A design philosophy for word processing programs in which formatting commands directly affect the text displayed on-screen, so that the screen shows the appearance of the printed text.

wild cards Characters, such as asterisks and question marks, that stand for any other character that may appear in the same place.

window A rectangular, on-screen frame through which you can view a document, worksheet, database, or other application.

windowing environment An applications program interface (API) that provides the features commonly associated with a graphical user interface (such as windows, pull-down menus, on-screen fonts, and scroll bars or scroll boxes) and makes these features available to programmers of application packages.

Windows application An application specifically designed to run in the Microsoft Windows windowing environment, taking full advantage of Windows' application program interface (API), its ability to display fonts and graphics on-screen, and its ability to exchange data dynamically between applications.

word One unit of memory storage, measured in bits.

word processing program An application program specifically designed to make the creation, editing, formatting, and printing of text easier.

word wrap A feature of word processing programs (and other programs that include text-editing features) that wraps words down to the beginning of the next line if they go beyond the right margin.

worksheet In spreadsheet programs, the two-dimensional matrix of rows and columns within which you enter headings, numbers, and formulas. The worksheet resembles the ledger sheet used in accounting. Synonymous with *spreadsheet*.

write A fundamental processing operation in which the central processing unit (CPU) records information in the computer's random-access memory (RAM) or the computer's secondary storage media, such as disk drives.

write-protect A procedure for preventing a disk or tape from being written to.

write-protect notch On a 5 1/4-inch floppy disk, a small notch cut out of the disk's protective jacket that, when covered by a piece of tape, prevents the disk drive from performing erasures or write operations to the disk.

X

x-axis In a business graph, the x-axis is the categories axis, which usually is the horizontal axis.

XMS memory In a '286, '386, or '486 computer, memory that has been configured as extended memory by a memory management program. Some DOS programs can use XMI memory to break the 640K RAM barrier.

y

y-axis In a business graph, the y-axis is the values (vertical) axis.

z

z-axis In a three-dimensional graphics image, the third dimension of depth.

zero-slot LAN A local area network designed to use a computer's serial port instead of requiring the user to purchase a network interface card that occupies one of the computer's expansion slots.

zoom box In a graphical user interface, a box (usually positioned on the window border) that you use to zoom the window to full size or restore the window to normal size by clicking the mouse.

Index

Computer Books From Que Mean PC Performance!

Spreadsheets

1-2-3 Database Techniques	$29.95
1-2-3 Graphics Techniques	$24.95
1-2-3 Macro Library, 3rd Edition	$39.95
1-2-3 Release 2.2 Business Applications	$39.95
1-2-3 Release 2.2 PC Tutor	$39.95
1-2-3 Release 2.2 QueCards	$19.95
1-2-3 Release 2.2 Quick Reference	$ 8.95
1-2-3 Release 2.2 QuickStart, 2nd Edition	$19.95
1-2-3 Release 2.2 Workbook and Disk	$29.95
1-2-3 Release 3 Business Applications	$39.95
1-2-3 Release 3 Workbook and Disk	$29.95
1-2-3 Release 3.1 Quick Reference	$ 8.95
1-2-3 Release 3.1 QuickStart, 2nd Edition	$19.95
1-2-3 Tips, Tricks, and Traps, 3rd Edition	$24.95
Excel Business Applications: IBM Version	$39.95
Excel Quick Reference	$ 8.95
Excel QuickStart	$19.95
Excel Tips, Tricks, and Traps	$22.95
Using 1-2-3/G	$29.95
Using 1-2-3, Special Edition	$27.95
Using 1-2-3 Release 2.2, Special Edition	$27.95
Using 1-2-3 Release 3.1, 2nd Edition	$29.95
Using Excel: IBM Version	$29.95
Using Lotus Spreadsheet for DeskMate	$22.95
Using Quattro Pro	$24.95
Using SuperCalc5, 2nd Edition	$29.95

Databases

dBASE III Plus Handbook, 2nd Edition	$24.95
dBASE III Plus Tips, Tricks, and Traps	$24.95
dBASE III Plus Workbook and Disk	$29.95
dBASE IV Applications Library, 2nd Edition	$39.95
dBASE IV Programming Techniques	$24.95
dBASE IV Quick Reference	$ 8.95
dBASE IV QuickStart	$19.95
dBASE IV Tips, Tricks,and Traps, 2nd Edition.	$24.95
dBASE IV Workbook and Disk	$29.95
Using Clipper	$24.95
Using DataEase	$24.95
Using dBASE IV	$27.95
Using Paradox 3	$24.95
Using R:BASE	$29.95
Using Reflex, 2nd Edition	$24.95
Using SQL	$29.95

Business Applications

Allways Quick Reference	$ 8.95
Introduction to Business Software	$14.95
Introduction to Personal Computers	$19.95
Lotus Add-in Toolkit Guide	$29.95
Norton Utilities Quick Reference	$ 8.95
PC Tools Quick Reference, 2nd Edition	$ 8.95
Q&A Quick Reference	$ 8.95
Que's Computer User's Dictionary	$ 9.95
Que's Wizard Book	$ 9.95
Quicken Quick Reference	$ 8.95
SmartWare Tips, Tricks, and Traps 2nd Edition	$24.95
Using Computers in Business	$22.95
Using DacEasy, 2nd Edition	$24.95
Using Enable/OA	$29.95
Using Harvard Project Manager	$24.95
Using Managing Your Money, 2nd Edition	$19.95
Using Microsoft Works: IBM Version	$22.95
Using Norton Utilities	$24.95

Using PC Tools Deluxe	$24.95
Using Peachtree	$27.95
Using PFS: First Choice	$22.95
Using PROCOMM PLUS	$19.95
Using Q&A, 2nd Edition	$23.95
Using Quicken: IBM Version, 2nd Edition	$19.95
Using Smart	$22.95
Using SmartWare II	$29.95
Using Symphony, Special Edition	$29.95
Using Time Line	$24.95
Using TimeSlips	$24.95

CAD

AutoCAD Quick Reference	$ 8.95
AutoCAD Sourcebook 1991	$27.95
Using AutoCAD, 3rd Edition	$29.95
Using Generic CADD	$24.95

Word Processing

Microsoft Word 5 Quick Reference	$ 8.95
Using DisplayWrite 4, 2nd Edition	$24.95
Using LetterPerfect	$22.95
Using Microsoft Word 5.5: IBM Version, 2nd Edition	$24.95
Using MultiMate	$24.95
Using Professional Write	$22.95
Using Word for Windows	$24.95
Using WordPerfect 5	$27.95
Using WordPerfect 5.1, Special Edition	$27.95
Using WordStar, 3rd Edition	$27.95
WordPerfect PC Tutor	$39.95
WordPerfect Power Pack	$39.95
WordPerfect Quick Reference	$ 8.95
WordPerfect QuickStart	$19.95
WordPerfect 5 Workbook and Disk	$29.95
WordPerfect 5.1 Quick Reference	$ 8.95
WordPerfect 5.1 QuickStart	$19.95
WordPerfect 5.1 Tips, Tricks, and Traps	$24.95
WordPerfect 5.1 Workbook and Disk	$29.95

Hardware/Systems

DOS Tips, Tricks, and Traps	$24.95
DOS Workbook and Disk, 2nd Edition	$29.95
Fastback Quick Reference	$ 8.95
Hard Disk Quick Reference	$ 8.95
MS-DOS PC Tutor	$39.95
MS-DOS Power Pack	$39.95
MS-DOS Quick Reference	$ 8.95
MS-DOS QuickStart, 2nd Edition	$19.95
MS-DOS User's Guide, Special Edition	$29.95
Networking Personal Computers, 3rd Edition	$24.95
The Printer Bible	$29.95
Que's PC Buyer's Guide	$12.95
Understanding UNIX: A Conceptual Guide, 2nd Edition	$21.95
Upgrading and Repairing PCs	$29.95
Using DOS	$22.95
Using Microsoft Windows 3, 2nd Edition	$24.95
Using Novell NetWare	$29.95
Using OS/2	$29.95
Using PC DOS, 3rd Edition	$24.95
Using Prodigy	$19.95

Using UNIX	$29.9
Using Your Hard Disk	$29.9
Windows 3 Quick Reference	$ 8.9

Desktop Publishing/Graphics

CorelDRAW Quick Reference	$ 8.9
Harvard Graphics Quick Reference	$ 8.9
Using Animator	$24.9
Using DrawPerfect	$24.9
Using Harvard Graphics, 2nd Edition	$24.9
Using Freelance Plus	$24.9
Using PageMaker: IBM Version, 2nd Edition	$24.9
Using PFS: First Publisher, 2nd Edition	$24.9
Using Ventura Publisher, 2nd Edition	$24.9

Macintosh/Apple II

AppleWorks QuickStart	$19.9
The Big Mac Book, 2nd Edition	$29.9
Excel QuickStart	$19.9
The Little Mac Book	$ 9.9
Que's Macintosh Multimedia Handbook	$24.9
Using AppleWorks, 3rd Edition	$24.9
Using Excel: Macintosh Version	$24.9
Using FileMaker	$24.9
Using MacDraw	$24.9
Using MacroMind Director	$29.9
Using MacWrite	$24.9
Using Microsoft Word 4: Macintosh Version	$24.9
Using Microsoft Works: Macintosh Version, 2nd Edition	$24.9
Using PageMaker: Macinsoth Version, 2nd Edition	$24.9

Programming/Technical

Assembly Language Quick Reference	$ 8.9
C Programmer' sToolkit	$39.9
C Quick Reference	$ 8.9
DOS and BIOS Functions Quick Reference	$ 8.9
DOS Programmer's Reference, 2nd Edition	$29.9
Network Programming in C	$49.9
Oracle Programmer's Guide	$29.9
QuickBASIC Advanced Techniques	$24.9
Quick C Programmer's Guide	$29.9
Turbo Pascal Advanced Techniques	$24.9
Turbo Pascal Quick Reference	$ 8.9
UNIX Programmer's Quick Reference	$ 8.9
UNIX Programmer's Reference	$29.9
UNIX Shell Commands Quick Reference	$ 8.9
Using Assembly Language, 2nd Edition	$29.9
Using BASIC	$24.9
Using C	$29.9
Using QuickBASIC 4	$24.9
Using Turbo Pascal	$29.9

For More Information, Call Toll Free!

1-800-428-5331

All prices and titles subject to change without notice
Non-U.S. prices may be higher. Printed in the U.S.A

Complete Coverage From A To Z!

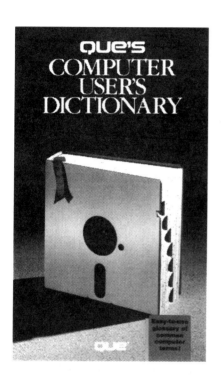

Que's Computer User's Dictionary

Que Development Group

This compact, practical reference contains hundreds of definitions, explanations, examples, and illustrations on topics from programming to desktop publishing. You can master the "language" of computers and learn how to make your personal computers more efficient and more powerful. Filled with tips and cautions, *Que's Computer User's Dictionary* is the perfect resource for anyone who uses a computer.

IBM, Macintosh, Apple, & Programming

Order #1086   **$10.95 USA**

0-88022-540-8, 500 pp., 4 3/4 x 8

The Ultimate Glossary Of Computer Terms— Over 200,000 In Print!

"Dictionary indeed. This whammer is a mini-encyclopedia...an absolute joy to use...a must for your computer library...."

Southwest Computer & Business Equipment Review

**To Order, Call:
(800) 428-5331 OR (317) 573-2510**

Enhance Your Personal Computer System With Hardware And Networking Titles From Que!

Upgrading and Repairing PCs

Scott Mueller

This book is the ultimate resource for personal computer upgrade, maintenance, and troubleshooting information! It provides solutions to common PC problems and purchasing descisions and includes a glossary of terms, ASCII code charts, and expert recommendations.

IBM Computers & Compatibles

Order #882   **$29.95 USA**

0-88022-395-2, 724 pp., 7 3/8 x 9 1/4

Introduction To Personal Computers

Katherine Murray

IBM, Macintosh, & Apple II

Order #1085 $19.95 USA

0-88022-539-4, 400 pp., 7 3/8 Xx9 1/4

The Printer Bible

Scott Foerster

IBM & Macintosh

Order #1056 $29.95 USA

0-88022-512-2, 550 pp., 7 3/8 x 9 1/4

Networking Personal Computers, 3rd Edition

Michael Durr & Mark Gibbs

IBM & Macintosh

Order #955 $24.95 USA

0-88022-417-7, 400 pp., 7 3/8 x 9 1/4

Using Novell NetWare

Bill Lawrence

Version 3.1

Order #1013 $29.95 USA

0-88022-466-5, 400 pp., 7 3/8 x 9 1/4

To Order, Call:
(800) 428-5331 OR (317) 573-2510

Free Catalog!

Mail us this registration form today, and we'll send you a free catalog featuring Que's complete line of best-selling books.

Name of Book _____

Name _____

Title _____

Phone (___) _____

Company _____

Address _____

City _____

State _____ ZIP _____

Please check the appropriate answers:

1. Where did you buy your Que book?
   - ☐ Bookstore (name: _____)
   - ☐ Computer store (name: _____)
   - ☐ Catalog (name: _____)
   - ☐ Direct from Que
   - ☐ Other: _____

2. How many computer books do you buy a year?
   - ☐ 1 or less
   - ☐ 2-5
   - ☐ 6-10
   - ☐ More than 10

3. How many Que books do you own?
   - ☐ 1
   - ☐ 2-5
   - ☐ 6-10
   - ☐ More than 10

4. How long have you been using this software?
   - ☐ Less than 6 months
   - ☐ 6 months to 1 year
   - ☐ 1-3 years
   - ☐ More than 3 years

5. What influenced your purchase of this Que book?
   - ☐ Personal recommendation
   - ☐ Advertisement
   - ☐ In-store display
   - ☐ Price
   - ☐ Que catalog
   - ☐ Que mailing
   - ☐ Que's reputation
   - ☐ Other: _____

6. How would you rate the overall content of the book?
   - ☐ Very good
   - ☐ Good
   - ☐ Satisfactory
   - ☐ Poor

7. What do you like *best* about this Que book?
   _____
   _____

8. What do you like *least* about this Que book?
   _____
   _____

9. Did you buy this book with your personal funds?
   - ☐ Yes   ☐ No

10. Please feel free to list any other comments you may have about this Que book.
    _____
    _____
    _____

que

Order Your Que Books Today!

Name _____

Title _____

Company _____

City _____

State _____ ZIP _____

Phone No. (___) _____

Method of Payment:

Check ☐ (Please enclose in envelope.)

Charge My: VISA ☐   MasterCard ☐

American Express ☐

Charge # _____

Expiration Date _____

Order No.	Title	Qty.	Price	Total

You can **FAX** your order to **1-317-573-2583**. Or call **1-800-428-5331, ext. ORDR** to order direct.
Please add $2.50 per title for shipping and handling.

Subtotal _____

Shipping & Handling _____

Total _____

que

NO POSTAGE
NECESSARY
IF MAILED
IN THE
UNITED STATES

BUSINESS REPLY MAIL
First Class Permit No. 9918   Indianapolis, IN

Postage will be paid by addressee

11711 N. College
Carmel, IN 46032

NO POSTAGE
NECESSARY
IF MAILED
IN THE
UNITED STATES

BUSINESS REPLY MAIL
First Class Permit No. 9918   Indianapolis, IN

Postage will be paid by addressee

11711 N. College
Carmel, IN 46032